AN INTRODUCTION TO ELEMENT THEORY

An Introduction to Element Theory

Phillip Backley

Edinburgh University Press

© Phillip Backley, 2011

Edinburgh University Press Ltd
22 George Square, Edinburgh

www.euppublishing.com

Typeset in Adobe Sabon by
Servis Filmsetting Ltd, Stockport, Cheshire

A CIP record for this book is available from the British Library

ISBN 978 0 7486 3742 3 (hardback)
ISBN 978 0 7486 3743 0 (paperback)

The right of Phillip Backley
to be identified as author of this work
has been asserted in accordance with
the Copyright, Designs and Patents Act 1988.

CONTENTS

List of Figures	viii
List of Tables	x
Preface	xi

Chapter 1 A Theory of Elements — 1
1.1 Segments Have Internal Structure — 1
1.2 Articulation and Perception — 2
1.3 The Speech Signal — 5
1.4 Monovalency — 7
1.5 Elements and the Grammar — 11
1.6 Summary — 14
     Further Reading — 15
     References — 15

Chapter 2 Elements for Vowels — 17
2.1 Introduction — 17
2.2 What Makes |I U A| Special? — 18
2.3 Simplex Expressions — 22
2.4 Element Compounds — 24
     2.4.1 Phonetic Evidence for Element Compounds — 24
     2.4.2 Phonological Evidence for Element Compounds — 26
2.5 Central Vowels — 31
     2.5.1 Phonetic Evidence for Empty Vowels — 31
     2.5.2 Phonological Evidence for Empty Vowels — 34
2.6 Front Rounded Vowels — 38
2.7 Element Dependency — 40
2.8 Vowels in English — 43
     2.8.1 Introduction — 43
     2.8.2 Short Vowels — 43
     2.8.3 Long Vowels — 46
     2.8.4 Weak Vowels — 50
     2.8.5 Diphthongs — 54

2.9	Summary	59
	Further Reading	59
	References	60

Chapter 3   Place Elements in Consonants — 62

3.1	Consonant–Vowel Unity	62
	3.1.1 Shared Features	62
	3.1.2 Shared Elements	64
3.2	Glides	65
	3.2.1 Phonetic Properties	65
	3.2.2 Vowel/Glide Alternations	66
	3.2.3 Glide Formation in English	68
3.3	|I U A| as Place Elements	69
3.4	The |I| Element	71
	3.4.1 Palatals	71
	3.4.2 Coronals with |I|	72
3.5	The |U| Element	77
	3.5.1 Labials	77
	3.5.2 Velars	79
3.6	The |A| Element	84
	3.6.1 Gutturals	84
	3.6.2 Coronals with |A|	87
	3.6.3 Retroflexes	91
	3.6.4 Summary	96
3.7	Complex Resonance	98
	3.7.1 Labiodentals	98
	3.7.2 Uvulars	98
	3.7.3 Palatovelars	101
	3.7.4 Palatals Again	105
3.8	A Note on Affricates	108
	Further Reading	110
	References	111

Chapter 4   Manner Elements in Consonants — 114

4.1	Introduction	114
4.2	The |?| Element	115
	4.2.1 Stops	115
	4.2.2 Ejectives	118
	4.2.3 Implosives	120
	4.2.4 Laryngealised Vowels	122
4.3	The |H| Element	124

		4.3.1	Frication	124

	4.3.1	Frication	124
	4.3.2	Consonant Weakening	126
	4.3.3	Voicelessness	134
	4.3.4	High Tone	143
4.4	The |L| Element		145
	4.4.1	Nasality	145
	4.4.2	Obstruent Voicing	151
	4.4.3	Low Tone	157
4.5	Combining the Manner Elements		159
	Further Reading		162
	References		162
Chapter 5	Liquids, Licensing and Antagonistic Elements		165
5.1	Liquids		165
	5.1.1	Liquids as a Natural Class	165
	5.1.2	Rhotics	168
	5.1.3	Linking and Intrusive *r* in English	172
	5.1.4	Laterals	175
	5.1.5	Summary	183
5.2	Elements and Prosodic Structure		184
	5.2.1	Introduction	184
	5.2.2	The Syllable Domain	185
	5.2.3	The Foot Domain	186
	5.2.4	The Word Domain	188
	5.2.5	Summary	193
5.3	Relations between Elements		194
	5.3.1	Antagonistic Pairs	194
	5.3.2	Resonance: |A| versus |ʔ|	195
	5.3.3	Frequency: |L| versus |H|	197
	5.3.4	Colour: |U| versus |I|	198
	5.3.5	Dark versus Light	200
	Further Reading		203
	References		204

Language Index — 207
Subject Index — 209

LIST OF FIGURES

1.1	Stages of acquisition	4
1.2	The communication process (hearers)	5
1.3	The communication process (speakers)	6
2.1	|I| (*dIp* pattern)	22
	(a) Spectral pattern of [i]	
	(b) Spectrogram of [i]	
2.2	|U| (*rUmp* pattern)	23
	(a) Spectral pattern of [u]	
	(b) Spectrogram of [u]	
2.3	|A| (*mAss* pattern)	24
	(a) Spectral pattern of [a]	
	(b) Spectrogram of [a]	
2.4	|I A| (*dIp* + *mAss* pattern)	26
	(a) Spectral pattern of [e]	
	(b) Spectral pattern of [i] (|I|)	
	(c) Spectral pattern of [a] (|A|)	
2.5	|U A| (*rUmp* + *mAss* pattern)	27
	(a) Spectral pattern of [o]	
	(b) Spectral pattern of [u] (|U|)	
	(c) Spectral pattern of [a] (|A|)	
2.6	The energy pattern for schwa	32
	(a) Spectral pattern of [ə]	
	(b) Spectrogram of [ə]	
2.7	Central vowels in the acoustic vowel space	33
2.8	|I U| (*dIp* + *rUmp* pattern) and |I U A| (*dIp* + *rUmp* + *mAss* pattern)	39
	(a) Spectral pattern of [y] (|I U|)	
	(b) Spectral pattern of [ø] (|I U A|)	
2.9	The energy patterns for [e] and [ɛ]	42
	(a) Spectral pattern of [e] (|I̱ A|)	
	(b) Spectral pattern of [ɛ] (|I A|)	
2.10	The energy patterns for [ʌ] and [ɑː]	44

	(a) Spectral pattern of [ʌ] (|A̲|)	
	(b) Spectral pattern of [ɑː] (|A̲|)	
2.11	The energy patterns for [e] and [æ]	45
	(a) Spectral pattern of [e] (|I̲ A|)	
	(b) Spectral pattern of [æ] (|I A̲|)	
3.1	*dIp* in [i] and [j]	66
	(a) Spectrogram of *see* [siː]	
	(b) Spectrogram of *yet* [jet]	
3.2	*rUmp* in [u] and [w]	67
	(a) Spectrogram of *you* [juː]	
	(b) Spectrogram of *way* [weɪ]	
3.3	Formant patterns for [d], [b] and [g]	75
	(a) Spectrogram of [ada]	
	(b) Spectrogram of [aba]	
	(c) Spectrogram of [aga]	
3.4	Formant patterns for [z], [ʒ] and [j̠]	76
	(a) Spectrogram of [aza]	
	(b) Spectrogram of [aʒa]	
	(b) Spectrogram of [aj̠a]	
3.5	Spectral profiles of [k] and [p]	82
	(a) Spectral pattern of [k]	
	(b) Spectral pattern of [p]	
4.1	Energy pattern of |ʔ|	115
	(a) Spectrogram of [apa]	
	(b) Spectrogram of [ada]	
	(c) Spectrogram of [aʔa]	
4.2	Energy pattern of nasals and laterals	116
	(a) Spectrogram of [ana]	
	(b) Spectrogram of [ala]	
4.3	Glottal pulses in creaky and modal voice	122
	(a) Spectrogram of [ma̰] (creaky voice)	
	(b) Spectrogram of [ma] (modal voice)	
4.4	Spectrogram of *missed* [ˈmɪst]	125
4.5	Typology of two-way laryngeal distinctions	136
4.6	Energy patterns of nasal murmur	146
	(a) Spectrogram of [ana]	
	(b) Spectrogram of [ama]	
5.1	Spectrogram of [əɹ]	170

LIST OF TABLES

2.1	Vowel reduction in English simplex vowels	52
2.2	Vowel reduction in English compound vowels	53
3.1	Consonants in Ngiyambaa	90
3.2	Resonance properties of |I U A|	97
3.3	Consonant categories with simplex resonance	98
3.4	Consonants in Yanyuwa	102
3.5	Simplex and compound consonant categories	104
3.6	Consonant place categories	108
3.7	Plosive–affricate complementarity	109
4.1	Spirantisation	128
4.2	Non-release	128
4.3	Glottaling	129
4.4	Debuccalisation	129
4.5	Vocalisation	130
4.6	Tapping	130
4.7	Interpreting single elements	132
4.8	The |H| element in English stops	142
4.9	The |H| element in English fricatives	142
5.1	Representations for glides	184

PREFACE

Phonology is the branch of linguistics that describes what humans know about the sound structure of their native language. This knowledge is fairly diverse, but in this book we will focus on just one aspect of it – our knowledge of segments, their internal structure and their behaviour in languages. The book is aimed at students of linguistics who are already familiar with basic concepts in phonology. However, it is also accessible to those who are new to the subject, and equally, to those with a background in phonology who wish to explore recent developments in the field.

Most phonology textbooks present the subject from a traditional angle, using ideas and terminology that have not changed very much in several decades. The advantage of this standard approach is that it offers an ideal context for introducing basic theoretical concepts such as contrast, alternation and derivation. But there are also some disadvantages: it does not reflect how our understanding of phonology is changing, and also, it overlooks the possibility that some aspects of the standard approach may be flawed. This book questions one particular aspect of the standard approach – namely, the use of binary features such as [±cont], [±ant], [±high] and so on. Features provide a rich and powerful means of representing segmental structure, which is why they have shown such a remarkable endurance. Indeed, the features in use today are not radically different from those employed by early generative phonologists during the 1960s and 1970s. But despite their widespread appeal, features turn out to be problematic in at least two respects. First, they are mostly based on articulation, even though there is no particular reason why segments should be described from the speaker's point of view. And second, they have two values, [+f] and [–f], even though using [–f] to mark the absence of a property leads to incorrect predictions about the behaviour of segments.

This book addresses these problems by introducing elements as an alternative to traditional features. The version of Element Theory described here uses a set of six elements which make up the internal structure of segments. But although elements take the place of features, the two are different in kind. Unlike features, elements are monovalent; that is, they are single-valued and represent only positive (marked) segmental properties. And unlike features, elements do not refer to articulation; in fact, Element Theory does not consider speaker knowledge to be central to the grammar. Instead, elements are associated with acoustic properties of the speech signal, which helps us to account for certain segmental patterns that appear fairly arbitrary when they are described in feature terms. Replacing features with elements also has implications for the way we view the phonological component. Unlike a single feature such as [+cont], which cannot be pronounced on its own, a single element can be phonetically realised without support from other elements. This means that the grammar has no need for a separate level of phonetic representation, so phonology is free to operate on a single level. So although elements perform a similar function to features, they require us to rethink our overall approach to phonology and its role in the grammar.

Element Theory has been around for some time, and even before it became established as an autonomous theory, the elements themselves were being used to represent segments in a framework that came to be known as Government Phonology. In essence, Government Phonology is a theory of representations which advocates a restrictive approach to phonological structures based on general principles and parameters rather than on specific rules. However, there is no necessary connection between Government Phonology and elements. In fact, elements can be traced back to similar units that were being used in other theories including Dependency Phonology and Particle Phonology, both of which predate Government Phonology. In this book we will assume that elements exist independently of any particular theory of phonology, and wherever possible they will be described in a theory-neutral way. Despite their historical connection with Government Phonology, elements are, in principle, flexible enough to be used in any phonological theory.

Although this book is intended mainly as an introduction to elements, it also serves as a general introduction to segmental phonology. In order to describe elements fully, we need to describe how they behave in different languages. This means studying the kinds of contrasts they produce, the kinds of consonant and vowel systems they create, and the kinds of phonological processes they participate in. Put together, this provides us with a clear picture of what a phonological system should look like. For example, by studying elements we can learn how to distinguish between contrasts that are widely used in languages, contrasts that are generally avoided, and contrasts that are impossible. We also gain an understanding of what makes a possible or an impossible inventory of segments, and what counts as a possible or an impossible phonological process. To learn about language typology we have to study phonological data from a broad range of languages. So although this book includes many examples from different dialects of English, it is not a study of English phonology. Rather, it is a study of phonological knowledge in general – elements represent what humans know about the sound system of their native language, whichever language that may be.

The book is organised as follows. Chapter 1 sets the theoretical scene by answering the following questions: First, what are the problems associated with traditional features? Second, why do elements provide a good alternative to features? And third, why are elements the way they are? This chapter is therefore concerned with conceptual issues – it is about phonological concepts and not about analysing phonological data. The next four chapters introduce the elements themselves and show how they are active in the sound systems of different languages. These chapters should be studied in order. Chapter 2 deals with elements for vowels. It shows how the three resonance elements |I U A| combine to create vowel systems ranging from the simplest to the most marked. This chapter also includes a detailed analysis of the vowel systems of English. In Chapter 3 we turn to consonants, focusing on how the same resonance elements |I U A| are also used to represent consonant place. Then Chapter 4 describes other aspects of consonant structure by introducing the remaining elements |ʔ H L|. These elements represent what are traditionally described as manner and laryngeal properties. Finally, Chapter 5 explores a number of topics including the structure of liquids and the relation between elements and prosodic structure.

This book owes its existence to all those scholars who have contributed to the development of Element Theory over the years. Most of them will find things in here that they disagree with, which is part and parcel of working with a theory that is still evolving. Singled out for special thanks are three people whose contributions have been particularly valuable. I am indebted to John Harris, whose insights into phonology in general and Element Theory in particular have had a profound influence on this book's content. I am also very grateful to Kuniya Nasukawa, with whom I have collaborated on a number of element-based projects. Our joint work has helped to shape many of the ideas that are presented here. My sincere thanks also go to Andrew Nevins, who read an earlier draft of this book and provided me with numerous comments and additional examples that have greatly improved the book's overall appearance.

Chapter 1

A THEORY OF ELEMENTS

❦

1.1 SEGMENTS HAVE INTERNAL STRUCTURE

Language sounds are usually described in terms of segments. For example, the English spelling system uses alphabetic segments (letters) to symbolise sounds, while dictionaries use phonemic segments such as /fəˈnɒlədʒi/ to describe a word's pronunciation. And in linguistics we use segments to represent speech sounds, either as phonetic objects in the physical world or as phonological objects in the grammar. But actually, segments are not the most basic units of sound structure. By observing how sounds behave in languages, we uncover a set of even smaller units that combine to create individual segments. Determining what these basic units look like is what drives the study of segmental phonology.

Segments that have basic units in common should behave in a similar way, whereas segments with no shared units should behave independently of one another. Successfully identifying these units is therefore an important part of explaining segmental patterns. For example, knowing which basic units are present in the grammar helps us to understand why segments cluster and interact in certain ways. In this book we will frequently refer to whole segments, because this is a convenient way of talking about language sounds. But our main focus will be the set of basic units which make up individual segments. In standard phonology these units are called features: bundles of features represent segments while single features represent phonological classes. Segments are said to belong to the same class if they have a particular feature – and therefore, a particular phonological property – in common. For example, the feature [–son] brings together stops, fricatives and affricates as a single class of obstruents. And we see obstruents behaving as a single group in many languages; in Russian and German, for example, all [–son] segments are voiceless word-finally.

1.2 Articulation and Perception

We know that segments are made up of smaller units, because in all languages we find evidence for phonological classes. But there is disagreement over what these units look like and which properties they represent. As already mentioned, standard phonology uses features as the basic units of segmental structure, most of these having been inherited or adapted from *The Sound Pattern of English* (Chomsky and Halle 1968), hereafter *SPE*.

Traditionally, features are seen as having two functions: their linguistic function is to represent natural classes, segmental contrasts and phonological processes, while their phonetic function is to characterise the physical properties of individual segments. With names such as [±high], [±voice], [±lateral], [±anterior] and [±round], it is clear that these features have their origins in phonetics – and specifically, in speech production, since most of them refer to articulatory properties like tongue position, lip position and glottal state. In other words, features describe segments from the speaker's point of view.

And yet there is no necessary link between features and articulation. In fact before the time of *SPE*, phonological features were mostly defined in auditory–acoustic terms – that is, from the hearer's point of view. For example, the set of features proposed in *Fundamentals of Language* (Jakobson and Halle 1956) includes [compact] and [diffuse], which describe how acoustic energy is distributed across the spectrum: in compact sounds (low vowels, back consonants) energy is concentrated in the centre of the spectrum, while in diffuse sounds (high vowels, front consonants) it is more widely distributed. However, the use of auditory–acoustic features like [compact] and [diffuse] came to an abrupt end following the publication of *SPE*, which replaced them with the set of articulatory features we have already mentioned. *SPE*'s articulatory features quickly caught on, despite its authors having given no particular reasons for rejecting auditory–acoustic features in the first place. And *SPE*-type features still dominate segmental phonology today, although some researchers now doubt whether they really offer the most appropriate way of representing phonological knowledge. After all, if we wish to maintain the original goal of generative grammar, which was to model the linguistic knowledge of an ideal speaker–hearer, then it seems odd that we should follow *SPE* in employing features that refer mostly to articulation or speaker knowledge. Of course, it would be equally odd to use auditory–acoustic features of the kind developed by Jakobson and Halle, which focus on the linguistic knowledge of the hearer.

Unlike the feature theories just described, Element Theory (hereafter ET) represents segments in a way which favours neither the speaker nor the hearer; instead, it captures the linguistic knowledge that is shared by speakers and hearers. It does this by associating features or 'elements' directly with the speech signal, as this is the only aspect of the communication process which involves both parties: speakers use their vocal organs to create sound patterns in the speech signal, while hearers recover the same patterns from the speech signal and decode them into meaningful language. Because elements are based on the speech signal rather than on articulatory or auditory properties, ET is able to focus on the linguistic knowledge shared by all language users, speakers and hearers alike. This brings the grammar a little closer to that somewhat neglected notion of the ideal speaker–hearer.

Capturing the knowledge of an ideal speaker–hearer is not a priority for most feature theories. In fact, because features are based on speech production, and therefore on speaker knowledge, they have little to say about what hearers know about segments. In general it is assumed that, because speakers are also hearers, it is possible for them to understand utterances by matching what they hear with the articulatory movements needed to produce those utterances. There are several ways in which this might work. In Direct Realist Theory it is claimed that the hearer is able to perceive the movements of the articulators directly. This seems unlikely, however, given that the speech organs are not visible during speech production. On the other hand, the Motor Theory of Speech Perception proposes that the hearer first perceives spoken language as an acoustic event, and then translates it into the correct articulatory movements for reproducing it as a speaker. Unfortunately this scenario is equally unlikely, given that infants are able to perceive speech much earlier than they can produce it themselves.

Broadly speaking, the acquisition process involves at least the three stages shown in Figure 1.1. Importantly, stage 1 is necessary for successful language acquisition whereas stage 3 is not. Those who cannot speak because of physical abnormalities (of the vocal tract, for example) are still able to acquire a normal grammar; in other words, the inability to articulate speech is not a barrier to perceiving speech. By contrast, those who encounter problems at stage 1, such as the profoundly deaf, who do not perceive language

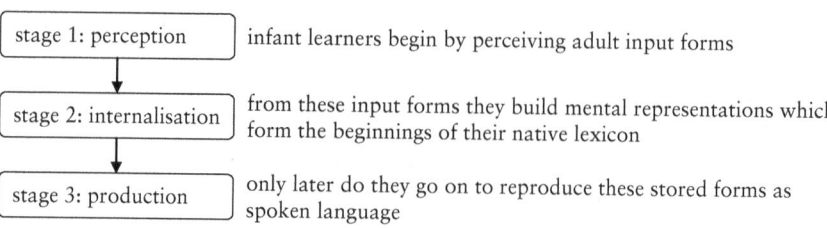

Figure 1.1 *Stages of acquisition*

via an auditory–acoustic input, rarely go on to develop native-like spoken language. All this suggests that speech perception may be more fundamental to the grammar than speech production, which supports Jakobson's idea that features should be based on acoustic properties. And as we examine the nature of elements in the following chapters, we will see that elements have more in common with Jakobson's acoustic features than with *SPE*'s articulatory features. However, ET's aim is to represent segments in a way which favours neither the speaker nor the hearer, but rather, captures the linguistic knowledge common to both. This means focusing on the speech signal, which acts as an intermediary between the origin of a sound (the vocal organs of the speaker) and its target (the auditory system of the hearer).

The speech signal is physical – it can be described in concrete terms; so for example, we can measure its acoustic properties by referring to amplitude, formant structure, and so on. But actually, precise measurements like these are mostly irrelevant to the grammar, and as such, do not need to be represented by features or elements. Music works in a similar way. Although the notes of a melody can be described in terms of physical properties such as frequency and duration, we do not need information of this kind in order to perceive them, memorise them or sing them aloud. Rather, we identify a musical note by its overall acoustic shape and by its relation to other notes, not by its raw acoustic values. Like musical notes, speech sounds are not classified according to their acoustic properties. It is true that phoneticians may use phonetic data such as formant frequency to describe speech sounds or to compare different languages, but these data do not count as linguistic knowledge, and for this reason, have nothing to do with segmental structure.

So which properties of the speech signal *are* relevant to the grammar and to communication? According to ET, humans are able to pick out certain acoustic patterns from the speech signal which carry linguistic information; and because these patterns contain linguistic information, they are represented by elements. An element is the smallest unit of segmental structure to appear in phonological representations.

1.3 THE SPEECH SIGNAL

ET makes two basic assumptions. First, it assumes that when hearers perceive speech they instinctively pay attention to the linguistic information it contains and filter out everything else. That is, language users have the ability to extract from running speech the acoustic patterns that are relevant to language. Second, it assumes there is a direct mapping between these acoustic patterns and phonological categories in the grammar. In later chapters we will examine these phonological categories in detail; for the moment let us just say that they mostly coincide with familiar segment classes such as stops, nasals, labials, front vowels, ejectives, and so on. And because phonological categories are represented by elements, it means that elements have a double association: they are associated with physical patterns in the acoustic signal and also with segmental representations in the mental grammar. In other words, elements function both as mental objects and as physical objects: they are mental objects in the sense that they represent abstract phonological information, and also physical objects in the sense that they connect to the physical world through their link with acoustic patterns in the speech signal.

From a hearer's point of view, communication proceeds as in Figure 1.2. Hearers perceive the speech signal and extract from it certain acoustic patterns that convey linguistic information. They then match those patterns with elements in the phonological structure of morphemes. But because the speech signal is a shared medium, it must serve the needs of speakers too. The same

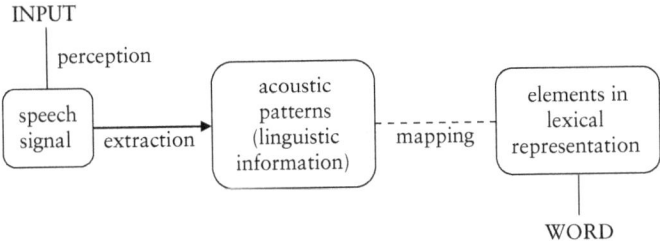

Figure 1.2 *The communication process (hearers)*

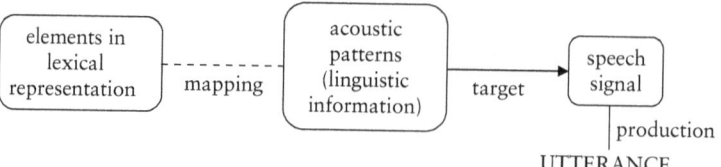

Figure 1.3 The communication process (speakers)

information-bearing acoustic patterns are also relevant to speakers in which case they serve as speech production targets rather than as perceptual cues. To pronounce a word, speakers must retrieve that word from the lexicon and associate the elements in its phonological structure with their corresponding acoustic patterns. These patterns then act as targets which speakers must try to reproduce using their vocal organs. The process is sketched in Figure 1.3. This way, the grammar need not contain any information about articulation. When speakers produce utterances, they know which production targets to aim for, and are free to use their lips, tongue, glottis and other vocal organs in whichever way they think will help them realise those targets. So the grammar does not stipulate how a segment should be articulated. In fact this is not always realistic, as there is often more than one way of using the articulators to produce a particular acoustic pattern. For instance, retroflex consonants are characterised by a low third formant, which speakers can reproduce in several different ways: they can round the lips, or retract the tongue body, or form an obstruction in the post-alveolar region, or do any combination of these things.

Let us summarise what we have said so far. Elements are mental objects which are present in phonological representations; their linguistic function is to encode lexical contrasts. But they also relate to the physical world by mapping onto acoustic patterns in the speech signal which carry linguistic information. Although the elements in a representation tell speakers which patterns they must try to reproduce, they do not specify how to reproduce them: it is through experience and experimentation during acquisition that infants learn how to articulate the sounds of their native language. In other words, speech production is not controlled by the grammar – tongue position, glottal state, lip position and the like are not part of linguistic knowledge. Instead, they function as a vehicle for delivering the speech signal and for carrying the linguistic message. Consider the communication process once again. When a hearer perceives linguistic patterns in the speech signal, these patterns act as cues to the elements in a representation – it makes no difference whether the signal was articulated by a human voice or produced by a synthesised voice from a computer. In both cases the linguistic message is the same, whether the vocal organs are involved or not. This is because articulation is not a component of the grammar.

So although there is a tradition in standard phonology of employing articulatory features to represent segments, it is doubtful whether information about articulation should really be included in the grammar. Elements provide an alternative to features in the sense that they are linked to the acoustic signal rather than to articulation. However, they are not just acoustic features, since they also function as abstract units of phonological structure which carry linguistic information about segments. In fact most versions of ET consider the role of elements to be primarily linguistic and only secondarily acoustic.

1.4 Monovalency

The use of features is questionable not only because they are biased towards articulation, but also because they are mostly bivalent – that is, they can have either a plus value or a minus value. And this is a problem for standard phonology because it forces the grammar to make incorrect predictions about the way segments behave in languages. We will look at an example of this in a moment. The alternative is a system that uses monovalent features, which are inherently positive – they can refer to the presence of a property but not to its absence. *SPE* uses bivalent features, where the positive value of a feature marks the presence of a phonological property while the negative value marks its absence. For example, *l* sounds are marked [+lateral] while all other segments are [–lateral]. This describes the distinction we want, but it also has the effect of giving [+lateral] and [–lateral] equal status, allowing the grammar to refer to [–lateral] just as easily as it does to [+lateral]. Yet this does not reflect the way languages work.

On the other hand, in monovalent systems the presence or absence of a feature indicates the presence or absence of a certain phonological property. Take the contrast [ɒ]–[ɑ], for example. In a monovalent system this is represented as [round] vs. Ø (where Ø stands for an unspecified property), whereas in a bivalent system it is represented as [+round] vs. [–round]. Initially, the difference between Ø and

[−round] looks trivial because both describe the same value, non-round. But on closer examination we see that the two systems actually make different predictions about how segments are grouped into natural classes and how they participate in phonological processes.

A natural class is a group of segments which display similar phonological behaviour and which may also have phonetic properties in common. For example, nasal segments such as [n ŋ ã] form a natural class: in some languages they all trigger nasal harmony, and more generally, they are all pronounced with nasal resonance. We may therefore assume that each contains nasality in its structure, which can be represented as [+nasal] in a bivalent system or as [nasal] in a monovalent system. Let us see how the predictions of the two systems differ. Warao has a contrast between oral and nasal vowels, as shown in (1a). In a monovalent system [ã] is marked [nasal] while [a] is unspecified for nasality and is therefore pronounced as an oral vowel. In a bivalent system [ã] is [+nasal] while [a] is [−nasal].

(1) a. [ja] 'sun'   b. [inãw̃ãh̃ã] 'summer'
       [jã] 'walking'   [õĩh̃õro] 'kind of tree'

This language also has a process of nasal harmony, as illustrated in (1b). Harmony is triggered by any segment containing [nasal]/[+nasal], producing nasalisation on target segments (vowels, laryngeals, glides) to its right. Predictably, oral segments in Warao do not trigger harmony because they do not contain [nasal]/[+nasal]. And furthermore they do not form a natural class, because they are not phonologically active as a group – the fact that oral segments collectively do *not* do something is not a reason to treat them as a class. And yet this is exactly what the bivalent feature system does. Allowing [−nasal] to appear in representations gives it a grammatical status equal to that of [+nasal], making it possible for phonological processes to employ [−nasal] as an active property in the same way that they might employ [+nasal]. But unfortunately, there is no evidence that [−nasal] is phonologically active. If it were, then we would expect to find languages with oral harmony in which [−nasal] is the active property, just as we find languages with nasal harmony in which [+nasal] is active. In fact, nasal harmony is relatively common whereas oral harmony is unattested – there are no examples of processes in which [−nasal] turns nasal segments into oral segments. This simple illustration shows how easy it is for bivalent features to make incorrect predictions about segmental behaviour: bivalency predicts that [−nasal] and [+nasal] should both function as active phonological properties and that each should define a distinct natural class. Both predictions turn out to be false.

The specific problem with bivalent features is their ability to refer to negative values – that is, to properties which are absent from a segment's structure; for example, oral vowels in Warao are [–nasal] because they lack nasality. The problem is not limited to nasality, however. Oral vowels have other negative features too, such as [–lateral]. And again, non-lateral does not define a natural class – it applies to a range of unrelated segments (obstruents, nasals, rhotics, vowels) which have no phonological characteristics in common and no shared phonetic properties. Compare this with a genuine natural class such as the class of nasals. In languages such as Warao it is only the nasal segments which act as harmonic triggers because it is only these sounds that contain the active feature [+nasal].

In a monovalent feature system it is easy to express the fact that nasals form a grammatical set whereas oral segments do not. Like [+nasal], the monovalent feature [nasal] is positive and identifies nasals as a natural class. Importantly, however, there is nothing equivalent to [–nasal], which means that the grammar cannot refer to oral segments as a group. This reflects the fact that oral segments do not have any shared phonological properties – they form an arbitrary collection of sounds comprising oral vowels and non-nasal consonants. And without a feature to unite them as a class, they have no status as a formal linguistic category. Clearly, monovalency leads to a more restrictive grammar than bivalency, because bivalency involves the use of negative properties which have the potential to participate actively in phonological processes. In essence, the problem is one of overgeneration: bivalency predicts the possibility of many phonological processes, and therefore many grammars, that we simply do not observe.

The overgeneration problem was even acknowledged by the authors of *SPE*, who admitted that the two values of a feature are unequal in a way that cannot be captured simply by using plus and minus. To remedy the situation, they proposed a theory of markedness which assigned each feature a marked value and an unmarked value; marked values could be phonologically active whereas unmarked values were inactive, and therefore redundant. The process of choosing which feature values should be marked was based on observations of the way each feature behaves in different languages. Markedness theory was developed in order to tackle the overgeneration problem head on, but viewed from a less sympathetic angle we might also take it to be an admission that bivalent features are not an ideal way of representing segmental structure.

Distinguishing between marked and unmarked feature values eventually led to the development of Underspecification Theory, which attempted to exclude unmarked feature values from lexical representations. And once these unmarked values were removed, there remained only the marked feature values needed for representing contrasts. The result was something close to monovalency, since the phonology could only refer to one value of a bivalent feature. However, because Underspecification Theory had its roots in the *SPE* tradition, it was still biased towards articulation. And representations containing only marked features were considered too abstract for speakers to pronounce in their underspecified form. In order to be pronounceable a segment had to be fully specified, which meant supplying all the missing feature values via redundancy rules. Inevitably, the effect of adding unmarked feature values was to reintroduce bivalency and its associated problems into the grammar. For example, it meant that a phonological process could target an unmarked feature value that had been introduced by an earlier rule. Overgeneration was therefore still an issue in derived representations.

In view of the problems with bivalency, it makes sense to eliminate bivalent features from the grammar altogether. In ET, all elements are monovalent – they represent only positive phonological properties and describe only genuine natural classes. There is one thing, however, which appears as though it could prevent us from recasting a bivalent representation system in monovalent terms: some bivalent features, such as [±anterior] and [±distributed], have plus and minus values that behave as though they are both marked. It has been argued, for example, that [+ant] and [−ant] are both phonologically active in the grammar, and as such, identify separate natural classes in their own right. So, unlike the case of nasality we discussed earlier, which can be represented in either bivalent or monovalent terms (2a), there is no easy way of doing the same with anterior in (2b).

(2) a. *Nasal* b. *Anterior*
bivalency: [+nasal] vs. [−nasal] [+ant] vs. [−ant]
monovalency: [nasal] vs. Ø [ant] vs. ?

Nasality has an unmarked value, non-nasal, which can be unspecified (shown as Ø) or represented as [−nasal]. But anterior has no unmarked value; both of its values are marked and must each be represented by a positive feature. This makes it difficult to redefine

[±anterior] as a monovalent feature. The only feasible option is to view anterior as two features in one, with its plus and minus values functioning as two separate positive properties. In a monovalent system these would have to be represented by two independent features; for example, we could redefine [+ant] vs. [−ant] as an opposition between [anterior] and [posterior]. More generally, if we wish to abandon bivalency altogether in favour of a system which uses only monovalent units, then some phonological properties – even well-established ones such as [±anterior] – will need to be reclassified.

1.5 Elements and the Grammar

Features emerged at a time when phonological patterns were mostly described using rules. Since then, there have been major changes to the way the phonological component is organised. For many, the rewrite rules of early generative phonology are now a thing of the past, having been replaced by more general statements such as structural principles and grammaticality constraints. Yet despite these changes to the overall shape of the grammar, features have remained remarkably stable. For example, the features being used in current versions of Optimality Theory are mostly the same as the features that were being used several decades ago in *SPE*. In other words, features can be transferred successfully from one theoretical approach to another without the need for much modification. The same is not true of elements. In this section we will see that using elements to represent segmental structure commits us to a particular view of how phonology is organised. We have already seen that elements should be linked to the acoustic signal rather than to articulation (§1.3), and that they should be monovalent rather than bivalent (§1.4). Now we consider how these two things shape our view of the phonology as a whole. In particular we see how they affect the role of derivation, and by extension, the notion of abstractness.

In the standard model a segment needs a full specification of features before it can be articulated or perceived. This means that every feature must have a positive or negative value. This goes for Underspecification Theory too, where missing feature values are filled in by rule in order to create something pronounceable at the phonetic level. By contrast, elements are monovalent, which prevents ET from referring to unmarked values at any level of representation. From a feature-based perspective, this makes representations in ET look incomplete, and therefore, unpronounceable. This is not the case, however, because even a single element, unlike a single feature, can be phonetically realised. In standard phonology the smallest pronounceable unit is a feature matrix, which represents a fully specified segment; individual features do not contain sufficient phonological information to allow them to be pronounced on their own – you cannot hear [+anterior], for instance, nor can you pronounce [–lateral]. For a feature to be interpretable it must belong to a full set of features which collectively describe a segment. As the ET literature puts it, 'each prime [feature] is small enough to fit inside a segment, and not big enough to be phonetically realised without support from other primes [features]' (Harris and Lindsey 1995: 34).

ET takes a quite different approach to the way segmental structure is phonetically interpreted. Each element has its own acoustic identity, allowing it to be pronounced without support from other elements. A segment may therefore have just one element in its representation, though in practice most segments contain more than one element. Importantly, if an element can be pronounced by itself, then the grammar does not have to add any unmarked properties – the representation is already complete and pronounceable as it is. (In fact, given that elements are monovalent, it is not clear how an unmarked value could be specified, because it is not possible to refer to the absence of a marked property.) The phonetic interpretability of elements will be described fully in later chapters, but let us briefly consider some examples here. The element called |I| (pronounced [i]) has an acoustic pattern in which a high F2 converges with F3; and when |I| stands alone it is phonetically interpreted as [i] or [j]. That is, we associate this element with front vowels and palatal consonants. [i] and [j] are represented by just one element because they have only one marked property. Of course, these segments have other phonetic qualities besides frontness and palatality; for example, they are both high and non-round. But these properties are unmarked and therefore not phonologically active: the reason why [i] and [j] are phonetically high is that they lack a 'low' element, where low is a marked property; similarly, they are non-round because they contain no 'round' element. To take another example, the element called |H| is associated with high-frequency aperiodic energy. On its own |H| is pronounced as [h] – a placeless fricative characterised by bare frication; this is the only way speakers can reproduce aperiodic energy without also introducing other marked properties such as place of articulation.

As already mentioned, the possibility of pronouncing single elements has implications that go beyond segmental structure:

specifically, if a phonological representation can be phonetically realised as it stands, then the grammar needs no separate level of phonetic representation. Elements are therefore naturally suited to a monostratal grammar in which phonological information is organised on a single level. This departs from the traditional arrangement shown in (3), where two (or more) levels of representation are required, each performing a different grammatical function.

(3)   underlying representation   function: lexical storage
                              ↓   units: abstract, contrastive

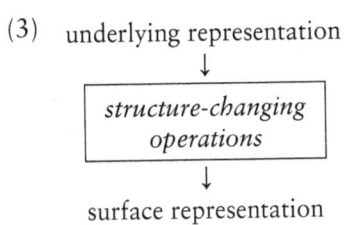

                              ↓
   surface representation   function: input to articulation/perception
                                          units: concrete, phonetic

According to (3), phonology acts as a device for generating phonetic forms. That is, it takes abstract phonological representations and turns them into concrete phonetic ones, which then become the input to external language processes such as articulation and perception. This gives phonology the appearance of a performance system, since it generates phonetic representations and monitors grammaticality in spoken utterances. Strictly speaking, it also takes phonology beyond the scope of linguistic competence – which directly contradicts our understanding of what phonological knowledge is about. So, the traditional model in (3) gives phonology an ambiguous role, associating it with both the competence and performance grammars: it relates to competence by describing the segmental patterns and phonological processes of a language, and it also relates to performance in the sense that it prepares lexical forms for articulation and perception. This is at odds with the general view that phonology belongs in the core grammar.

ET avoids this ambiguity by keeping phonology entirely within linguistic competence. Phonological processes in ET are not designed to generate pronounceable forms, in fact, they are not even directly connected with spoken language. Their role is not to convert an abstract representation into a physical one, but rather, to impose phonological regularities on abstract lexical representations so that they conform to the grammar of a given language. For example, they may require adjacent consonants to agree in voicing, or they may shorten vowels in closed syllables. And these are conditions which control phonological representations, not pronunciation. In other words, phonological processes ensure grammaticality by generating the set of grammatical representations in a language. Importantly, these processes produce output forms that are just as abstract as their input forms: processes in ET only change a phonological object into another phonological object. But even though the ET grammar does not generate phonetic forms, it still connects to the physical world through the elements themselves, which are phonetically interpretable; and we have already described how elements are mapped onto acoustic patterns in the speech signal. This applies whether the elements are in a lexical representation or in a representation that has been shaped by the phonology – in fact there is little difference between the two, since both employ the same structural units and both represent abstract phonological information. So in principle, speakers may pronounce a lexical form as it is, although in practice this may produce an ill-formed utterance if it has not been modified by the phonology.

1.6 SUMMARY

Traditionally, standard phonology modifies lexical forms in order to generate phonetic forms; it therefore acts as a bridge between the cognitive and the physical worlds. By contrast, ET takes a more abstract view of phonology in the sense that it deals exclusively with abstract or cognitive objects. Its function is to describe what language users know about the internal structure of segments and, by extension, morphemes. From an ET perspective, phonology slots into the competence grammar as follows:

Component	*Controls . . .*	*Determining . . .*
syntax	sentence structure	how words behave in sentences
morphology	word structure	how morphemes behave in words
phonology	morpheme structure	how elements behave in morphemes

Because ET sees phonology as a component of the mental grammar, it has little to say about raw phonetics. There is little doubt that phonetic factors such as perceptibility and ease of articulation can influence phonological behaviour; but unlike standard phonology, ET does not include phonetic information in phonological representations. This places speech production outside the grammar: its role is to transmit language, which gives articulation a status similar to that of writing – both serve as media for delivering linguistic information but neither constitutes the information itself. After all, the inability to write does not prevent a person from acquiring a normal grammar, and neither does the inability to speak.

This chapter has outlined the nature of phonological knowledge from an ET perspective. However, at the heart of ET are the elements themselves, and these will be introduced in the following chapters. We have seen that elements are monovalent units, and that they form the building blocks of segmental structure. Primarily, they are mental categories that carry linguistic information about segments and morphemes, but for communication purposes they also connect to the physical world by mapping onto information-bearing patterns in the speech signal. This bias towards the cognitive properties of elements has a bearing on the way we analyse segments in ET: to determine which elements a segment contains, we focus primarily on its phonological behaviour and only secondarily on its acoustic properties. In other words, elements are mainly identified by analysing phonological data rather than by listening.

FURTHER READING

A detailed analysis of the theoretical issues relating to the ET approach can be found in Harris (1994), while the nature of elements is discussed in Cyran (2010), Harris and Lindsey (2000) and Nasukawa and Backley (2008). For differing views on the question of monovalency, see Durand (1995), Kaye (1989) and Roca (1994). Direct Realist Theory is described in Fowler (1986) and the Motor Theory of Speech Perception in Liberman and Mattingly (1985). Descriptions of Underspecification Theory can be found in Archangeli (1988) and Steriade (1995). The Warao data are from Botma (2005).

REFERENCES

Archangeli, Diana (1988), 'Aspects of underspecification theory', *Phonology* 5, 183–207.

Botma, Bert (2005), 'Nasal harmony in Yuhup: a typological anomaly?' in N. Kula and J. van de Weijer (eds), *Papers in Government Phonology*: special issue of *Leiden Papers in Linguistics* 2.4, University of Leiden, pp. 1–21.

Chomsky, Noam and Morris Halle (1968), *The Sound Pattern of English*, New York: Harper and Row.

Cyran, Eugeniusz (2010), *Complexity Scales and Licensing in Phonology*, Berlin and New York: Mouton de Gruyter.

Durand, Jacques (1995), 'Universalism in phonology: atoms, structures and derivations', in J. Durand and F. Katamba (eds), *Frontiers of Phonology: Atoms, Structures, Derivations*, Harlow: Longman, pp. 267–88.

Fowler, Carol (1986), 'An event approach to the study of speech perception from a direct-realist perspective', *Journal of Phonetics* 14, 3–28.

Harris, John (1994), *English Sound Structure*, Oxford: Blackwell.

Harris, John and Geoff Lindsey (1995), 'The elements of phonological representation', in J. Durand and F. Katamba (eds), *Frontiers of Phonology: Atoms, Structures, Derivations*, Harlow: Longman, pp. 34–79.

Harris, John and Geoff Lindsey (2000), 'Vowel patterns in mind and sound', in N. Burton-Roberts, P. Carr and G. Docherty (eds), *Phonological Knowledge: Conceptual and Empirical Issues*, Oxford: Oxford University Press, pp. 185–205.

Jakobson, Roman and Morris Halle (1956), *Fundamentals of Language*, The Hague: Mouton.

Kaye, Jonathan M. (1989), *Phonology: A Cognitive View*, Hillsdale, NJ: Lawrence Erlbaum.

Liberman, Alvin M. and Ignatius G. Mattingly (1985), 'The motor theory of speech perception revised', *Cognition* 21, 1–36.

Nasukawa, Kuniya and Phillip Backley (2008), 'Affrication as a performance device', *Phonological Studies* 11, 35–46.

Roca, Iggy (1994), *Generative Phonology*, London: Routledge.

Steriade, Donca (1995), 'Underspecification and markedness', in J. A. Goldsmith (ed.), *The Handbook of Phonological Theory*, Cambridge, MA and Oxford: Blackwell, pp. 114–74.

Chapter 2

ELEMENTS FOR VOWELS

2.1 INTRODUCTION

In Chapter 1 we outlined some of the problems associated with traditional features, but said that these problems could be reduced by eliminating bivalency and allowing only monovalent (single-valued) features to represent phonological categories. In ET these features are called elements. They describe the lexical shape of morphemes and also map onto linguistically significant patterns in the acoustic signal.

The version of ET described in this book uses six elements to represent the segmental properties of languages. (There are other versions of ET, some of which employ more or fewer than six elements, and we will refer to these where relevant.) The six elements naturally divide into the two groups shown in (1). The elements |I U A| (pronounced [i u a]) are primarily associated with vowel structure, while |ʔ H L| mostly describe consonant structure. Note that elements are written inside verticals.

(1) vowel elements: |I|, |U|, |A|
     consonant elements: |H|, |L|, |ʔ|

In reality, dividing the elements in this way is an oversimplification, since vowel elements regularly appear in consonants and consonant elements can also appear in vowels. However, for convenience we will continue to refer to the vowel elements and the consonant elements as separate groups. This chapter introduces the vowel elements |I U A|, describes their acoustic properties and examines their phonological behaviour in different languages. It ends with a study of the vowel system(s) of English.

We begin by comparing the vowel elements with the vowel features typically used in standard theories.

(2) vowel elements: |I|, |U|, |A|
     vowel features: [±high], [±low], [±back], [±round], [±ATR]

The first thing to notice is that there are more vowel features than there are vowel elements. In the past this was thought to be significant, because it meant that a feature-based grammar could generate a much larger number of feature combinations than was possible in an element-based grammar – particularly as each feature is bivalent and therefore has two chances of combining with other features, whereas monovalent elements have only one. And this led to the criticism that feature theories tend to overgenerate; that is, the number of possible segments they can produce exceeds the number that we observe in any one language. But actually, ET has the potential to overgenerate too. Initially, the problem with ET was one of undergeneration – simple combinations of |I|, |U| and |A| could not describe all of the vowel contrasts that we find in natural languages, which forced ET to find ways of increasing its generative power. It did this by allowing elements to combine in unequal proportions. As we will see later, this had the effect of boosting ET's ability to express phonological patterns and natural classes, but at the same time it also increased the theory's generative capacity to a level not far below that of some feature theories. So when it comes to comparing ET and feature-based models, generative capacity is not a particularly useful measure. However, there are ways in which we can compare ET with standard feature theories, and in this chapter we will focus on the predictions that the two approaches make regarding the phonological behaviour of vowels.

2.2 What Makes |I U A| Special?

Feature theories classify vowels mainly on the basis of properties such as tongue position and lip rounding. So it is easy to see why articulatory features such as [±high] and [±round] are used to represent them. But in the case of ET it is less obvious why the basic units in vowels should be |I U A|. In fact, the reasons have more to do with phonological behaviour and language typology than with phonetics.

Surveys of segment inventories tell us that the vowel system in (3) is universally unmarked – it is cross-linguistically the most commonly occurring vowel system.

(3) i   u

   e   o

      a

It is therefore reasonable to assume that the vowels [i u e o a] are more basic than other vowels, and that they are represented by basic or unmarked phonological structures. For instance, we might suppose that each one corresponds to a vowel element, giving [i u e o a] the structures |I|, |U|, |E|, |O| and |A| respectively. But actually the phonological evidence does not support this. Instead, what we find is that [i u a] behave as basic vowels whereas [e o] do not. Here, the term 'basic' means 'cannot be broken down into smaller units', so it follows that the vowels [i u a] are indivisible units which may each be represented by a single element: in ET they have the structures |I|, |U| and |A| respectively. Note that, because of the triangular shape of the vowel system in (3), [i u a] are sometimes known as the corner vowels. Unlike the corner vowels, the mid vowels [e o] are not structurally basic: they consist of more than one element and can be broken down into their constituent elements. Phonology therefore makes a distinction between [i u a], which are structurally simplex, and [e o], which have compound structures.

The basic vowels [i u a] display a number of special properties. Most notably, they are extremely common cross-linguistically, appearing in almost all known languages. And in languages with very small vowel systems, they are invariably the only vowels. Some examples are listed in (4).

(4) Tamazight   [i u a]
     Quechua   [ɪ ʊ ɐ]
     Moroccan Arabic   [i u a]
     Greenlandic   [i u ɐ]
     Gadsup   [i u ɜ]
     Amuesha   [e o ɐ]

You will notice that the vowel systems in (4) show small differences in phonetic quality. For example, [a] in Tamazight has the centralised equivalents [ɐ] in Greenlandic and [ɜ] in Gadsup. Similarly, [e o] in Amuesha are equivalent to [i u] in the other languages. Despite these phonetic differences, however, the vowels concerned are phonologically the same. Among these three-vowel systems, for instance, [a ɐ ɜ] all have the representation |A|, while [i ɪ e] are all represented as |I| and [u ʊ o] all have |U|. Actually, phonetic variation of this kind is to be expected because the vowels in (4) are tokens of abstract phonological categories, and languages differ in the way they choose to phonetically interpret these categories. The same applies to five-vowel systems such as Spanish [a i u e o] and Zulu [a i u ɛ ɔ]; although Spanish [e] and Zulu [ɛ] are phonetically different, these vowels display similar phonological behaviour within their respective vowel systems. What counts in ET is the way a segment behaves, particularly in relation to natural classes and to other segments in the system. Its behaviour determines its phonological identity, and therefore, its element structure.

Several phonetic explanations have been given for why languages favour [i u a] over other vowel sounds. Quantal Theory claims that [i u a] occupy areas of the vowel space that have the clearest, most stable phonetic qualities. And in the next section we will see how each of the [i u a] regions is associated with a strong, easily identifiable acoustic pattern. This makes it possible for language users to tolerate a certain amount of phonetic variation and signal distortion when they hear or produce these vowels. But in the case of other vowels, the same is not true; in order for the mid vowels [e o] to be transmitted successfully, a higher degree of accuracy is required on the part of speakers and hearers. For example, if [e] is not pronounced accurately enough, it can be confused with acoustically similar vowels such as [ɪ] or [ɛ], which contrast with [e] in some languages. By contrast, [a i u] are rarely involved in errors of this kind. Dispersion Theory offers an alternative explanation for the universal appearance of corner vowels. It claims that languages prefer [i u a] because these vowels are maximally dispersed – they occupy the most extreme points in the acoustic vowel space by virtue of having maximally distinct acoustic properties. This sounds reasonable, given that the purpose of speech is to communicate linguistic information. We can expect languages to have evolved in a way that makes the communication process as efficient as possible, and one way of doing this is to favour sounds that are easily perceived, such as [i u a].

We therefore have typological evidence and phonetic evidence that [i u a] are basic vowels. And in ET the basic vowels have basic representations: [i u a] are represented by the single-element expressions |I|, |U| and |A| respectively. The elements |I U A| are basic in the sense that they cannot be broken down into anything smaller, and as such, they serve as the building blocks of vowel structure. And when |I U A| are phonetically interpreted, they map onto acoustic patterns in the speech signal which produce vowel sounds approximating to the corner vowels [i u a]. Obviously, most languages have vowel systems with more than three vowels, so ET also needs a way of expanding the set of element expressions it can generate. It does this by allowing elements to combine and be phonetically interpreted together: in §2.4 we will see that the mid vowels [e o] are each represented by combinations of two elements.

At this point let us briefly compare |I U A| with their equivalent features. By treating |I U A| as basic phonological units, ET emphasises the special status of [i u a] as basic vowels. But with traditional features it is not possible to single out the corner vowels in any natural way. As (5) shows, feature theories cannot differentiate between the basic vowels [i u a] and the non-basic vowels [e o], the same number of feature values being needed to describe both.

(5)
	i	u	a	e	o
[±high]	+	+	−	−	−
[±back]	−	+	+	−	+
[±round]	−	+	−	−	+

By using features, then, the special status of [i u a] is not recognised: the feature matrices for [i u a] in (5) appear to have nothing in common, and certainly they give no indication that these sounds form a natural grouping. As we noted in §1.4, to capture generalisations like this in feature theories it is necessary to look beyond the features themselves to some additional device such as markedness.

Another difference between elements and features concerns the predictions they make about the shape of vowel systems. Because |I U A| mark the extreme points of the vowel space, we derive a triangular vowel system by default. And indeed, triangular systems such as those in (6) are cross-linguistically the most common.

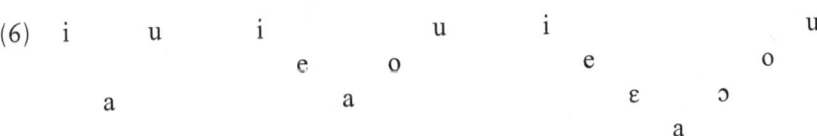

But in feature theories, the boundary of the vowel space is defined by [±high] and [±back]. And because these features are both bivalent, they create a quadrilateral vowel space such as the one shown in (7).

(7) [+hi] _____ [+hi]
     [−bk] i   u [+bk]
            \\ |
     [−hi] æ _____ ɑ [−hi]
     [−bk]   [+bk]

The arrangement in (7) is similar in shape to the vowel quadrilateral used by phoneticians to show the link between vowel quality and tongue position. In fact the similarity is not surprising, given that [±high] and [±back] both refer to tongue position too. But importantly, the quadrilateral in (7) fails to capture the special status of [i u a], and therefore misses a generalisation about the shape of vowel systems. If Dispersion Theory is correct in assuming that the unmarked vowels are those that are maximally distinct, then (7) predicts that the corner vowels [i u æ ɑ] are the unmarked ones. This is clearly not correct, since [æ] is cross-linguistically more marked than either [i] or [u].

2.3 SIMPLEX EXPRESSIONS

As we have already said, elements are abstract units of linguistic structure; they determine the lexical shape of morphemes and behave as active properties in phonological processes. We therefore determine the element structure of segments by studying phonological data – contrasts, distributional patterns, dynamic processes and the like. And in §2.4.2 we will examine how |I U A| behave as active phonological units. But elements are also linked to the physical world through their association with acoustic patterns in the speech signal. So let us first describe the acoustic properties of |I U A|.

To produce and perceive vowel sounds, language users focus on three acoustic patterns in the speech signal. These are patterns of energy distribution occurring within the frequency range 0–3kHz. Following Harris (1994: 139) we will refer to them by their informal names *dIp* (for the |I| pattern), *rUmp* (for the |U| pattern) and *mAss* (for the |A| pattern). The pattern for each element is shown here as a spectral cross-section (left) and as a spectrogram (right).

The pattern for |I| in Figure 2.1(a) shows two energy peaks with an intervening dip, hence the mnemonic label *dIp*. One peak occurs at a fairly low frequency, at around 500 Hz, and the other at around

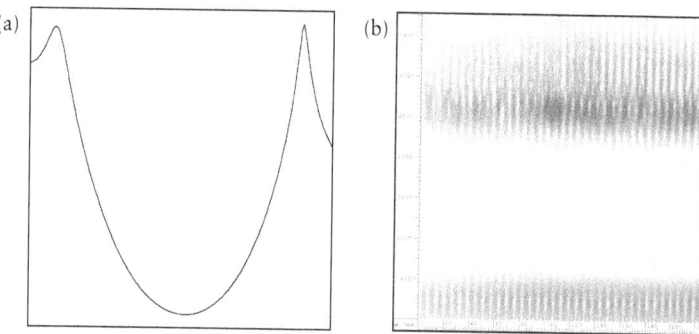

Figure 2.1 |I| (dIp *pattern). (a) Spectral pattern of [i]; (b) Spectrogram of [i]*

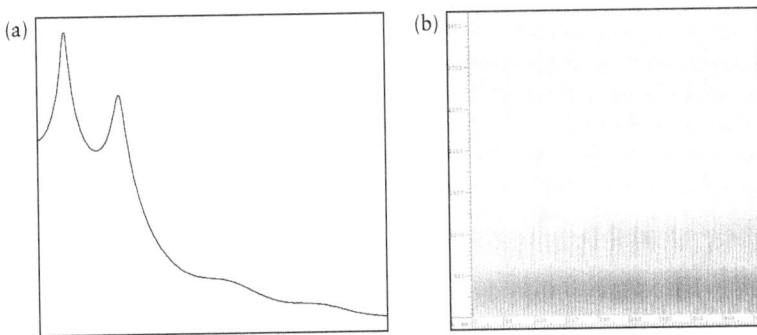

Figure 2.2 |U| *(rUmp pattern). (a) Spectral pattern of [u]; (b) Spectrogram of [u]*

2.5 kHz (frequency is read horizontally in Figures 2.1(a), 2.2(a) and 2.3(a)). The peaks themselves represent bands of intense energy, often resulting from the convergence of two formants. The same pattern can also be read off the spectrogram in Figure 2.1(b), which shows a low F1 (the first peak) and a high F2 which has merged with F3 at around 2.5 kHz (the second peak). The sharp dip in energy shown in Figure 2.1(a) corresponds to the unshaded area in the 1–2 kHz frequency range in Figure 2.1(b) (frequency is read vertically in Figures 2.1(b), 2.2(b) and 2.3(b)). This dip is the pattern that identifies |I|. Later we will see that the |I| element is present in front vowels.

The speech signal pattern for |U| is characterised by a concentration of energy at lower frequencies. In Figure 2.2(a), energy peaks within the range 0–1 kHz and then drops rapidly as frequency increases. This falling spectral shape is informally known as the *rUmp* pattern. Again, the spectral pattern in Figure 2.2(a) is mirrored by the spectrogram in Figure 2.2(b), where all formants are lowered: F1 occurs at around 500 Hz and F2 at around 1 kHz. One way of producing this falling pattern is to round the lips. The |U| element is therefore present in round vowels.

Finally, the signal pattern for |A| has the informal name *mAss* because its spectral shape in Figure 2.3(a) is dominated by a mass of energy in the lower central part of the spectrum. The peak occurs at around 1 kHz, with a drop in energy on either side. The same characteristic *mAss* pattern is also visible in the spectrogram in Figure 2.3(b); the energy peak is the result of a high F1 merging with F2 at around 1 kHz. The |A| element is present in most mid and low vowels.

The spectral shapes and formant patterns shown in these figures can vary between speakers. But as already mentioned, low-level

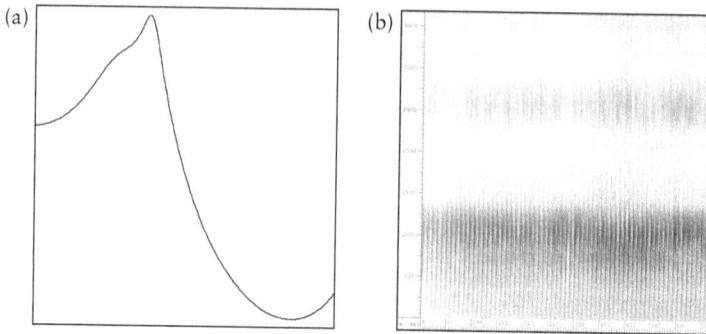

Figure 2.3 |A| (m*Ass pattern*). *(a) Spectral pattern of [a]; (b) Spectrogram of [a]*

phonetic variation does not affect the linguistic message: language users focus on the overall acoustic shape of segments – that is, on the patterns *dIp*, *rUmp* and *mAss* – and not on phonetic details. So although we have just described |I U A| using specific acoustic measurements such as frequency values, these details do not form part of our linguistic knowledge, and as such, have no place in the ET grammar.

We have now illustrated the acoustic patterns associated with |I U A| when each element is pronounced individually. Next we turn to compound expressions, in which elements are combined and phonetically interpreted together.

2.4 ELEMENT COMPOUNDS

2.4.1 Phonetic Evidence for Element Compounds

According to Quantal Theory (§2.2), each corner of the vowel triangle is associated with a unique and unambiguous acoustic pattern. And as we have just seen, this is exactly what characterises each of the vowel elements |I U A|. Language users identify |I U A| by their spectral shapes, to which we gave the impressionistic labels *dIp*, *rUmp* and *mAss*. In order to compare these patterns more easily, they can be restated in terms of the three broad frequency values high, central and low.

(8)

	|I|	|U|	|A|
position of peak(s):	low, high	low	central
position of trough(s):	central	central, high	low, high

Expressed in these terms, we can see how each vowel element has a pattern that is unique and highly distinctive, making the contrasts between [i], [u] and [a] easy to perceive and also difficult to confuse, just as Quantal Theory describes. But of course, most languages have vowel systems with more than three vowels, so elements must be allowed to combine and form compound expressions. In this section we see how element compounding affects the speech signal. Then in §2.4.2 we will consider the phonological properties of compounds.

Although the unmarked vowel system in (3) contains five vowels, it is only the corner vowels [i u a] that are phonologically basic. And for this reason, it is only these vowels that have basic (single-element) representations. By contrast, the mid vowels [e o] do not behave as basic vowels; for example, they are not present in all vowel systems, and their acoustic patterns are not as robust as the patterns for [i u a]. In addition, we have phonological evidence that [e o] each contain two elements in their structure: [e] is represented by the compound |I A| and [o] by the compound |U A|. Now, if single elements show simple acoustic patterns, then we can expect element compounds like |I A| and |U A| to show complex patterns, that is, patterns in which two simple patterns combine. The spectral pattern for [e] is given in Figure 2.4(a) and for [o] in Figure 2.5(a). For comparison, the patterns for their constituent elements are given on the right.

The vowel [e] in Figure 2.4(a) is a combination of |I| and |A|, both elements contributing to its overall spectral shape. In the centre we see the dip associated with |I|, though it is smaller here than in the pure *dIp* pattern in Figure 2.4(b). The pattern associated with |A| is also visible: to the right of the dip there is an energy mass with troughs on either side, similar in shape to the pure *mAss* pattern in Figure 2.4(c). So [e] has a composite spectral pattern that incorporates the acoustic characteristics of both |I| and |A|. If we were to restate this in articulatory terms, we would say that [e] combines the frontness of |I| with the openness of |A| to produce a non-high front vowel. It is a similar story with [o], which is a combination of |U| and |A|. In Figure 2.5(a) we see a concentration of energy at the lower end of the spectrum, indicating |U|; this is similar to the pure *rUmp* pattern in Figure 2.5(b). But unlike [u], there is also a *mAss* pattern in [o] with a drop in energy on either side, indicating |A| (Figure 2.5(c)). In other words, [o] has a composite spectral pattern that incorporates the acoustic characteristics of both |U| and |A|. Restated in terms of

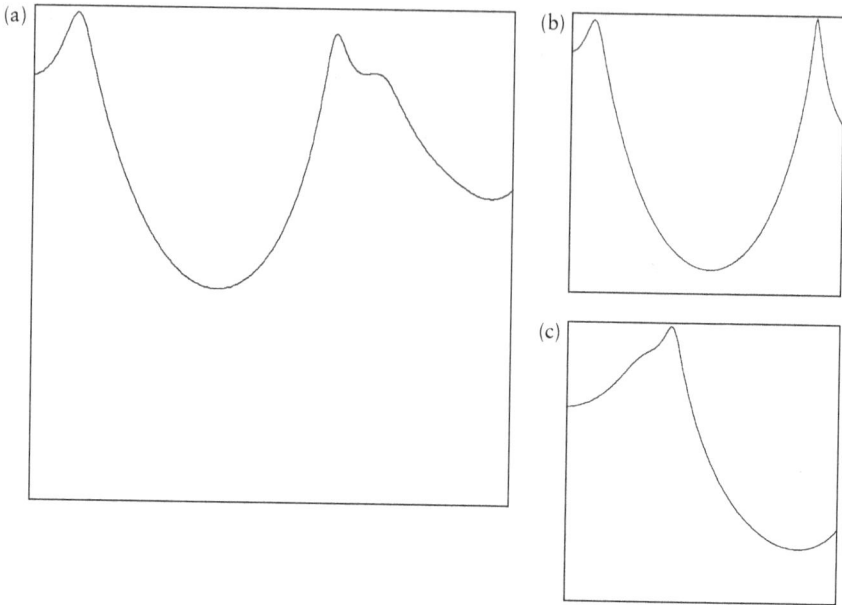

Figure 2.4 |I A| *(dIp + mAss pattern). (a) Spectral pattern of [e]; (b) Spectral pattern of [i] (|I|); (c) Spectral pattern of [a] (|A|)*

articulation, [o] combines the rounding of |U| with the openness of |A| to produce a non-high round vowel. The absence of |I| (for frontness) means that this vowel must be a back vowel.

2.4.2 Phonological Evidence for Element Compounds

Having reviewed the acoustic evidence that mid vowels are structurally complex, let us now consider the phonological facts. Conveniently, the individual elements in a compound sometimes become visible when they are targeted by phonological processes; in other words, the phonology allows us to see inside element compounds. In fact the following examples have a dual purpose: not only do they support the existence of element compounds, but they also verify that |I U A| are basic phonological units by showing that these elements are regularly active in phonological systems. For the moment we will only deal with processes that involve the five vowels we have already discussed, namely [i u a e o]. Most of these processes cause the elements in a vowel's representation to be reorganised in some way; the processes we will focus on are monophthongisation, diphthongisation and vowel coalescence. Other processes that reveal the internal

ELEMENT COMPOUNDS 27

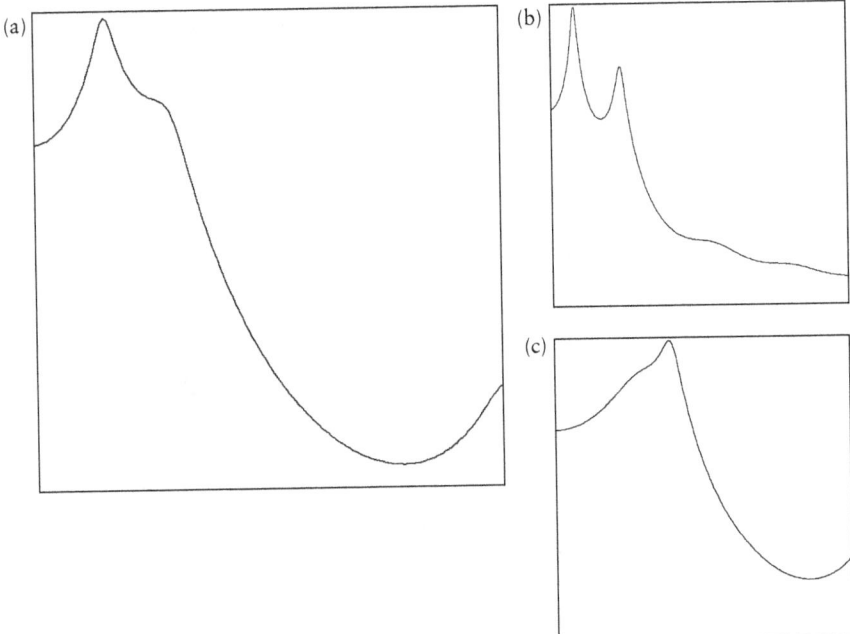

Figure 2.5 |U A| *(rUmp + mAss pattern). (a) Spectral pattern of [o]; (b) Spectral pattern of [u] (|U|); (c) Spectral pattern of [a] (|A|)*

structure of vowels include vowel harmony and vowel weakening, which will also be mentioned below.

The history of English provides useful examples of monophthong and diphthong formation. For instance, some dialects of late Middle English had the diphthongs [ai]~[æi] and [au] in the following words:

(9)   *Middle English* [ai]~[æi]   *Middle English* [au]
    [dai]   *day* 'day'   [lau]   *law* 'law'
    [aiçt]   *eight* 'eight'   [dauxtər]   *dauhter* 'daughter'
    [vain]   *vain* 'vain'   [nauxt]   *naught* 'not'
    [pai]   *pay* 'pay'   [baul]   *baul* 'ball'

During the sixteenth and seventeenth centuries, these diphthongs developed the monophthong realisations [ɛː] and [ɔː] respectively, which have survived in British English (*law* [lɔː], *caught* [kɔːt]) and more specifically in some northern British dialects (*eight* [ɛːt], *pay* [pɛː]). In ET, monophthongisation involves a simple reorganisation of the original elements, as illustrated in (10).

(10) a. [ai] → [ɛː]   b. [au] → [ɔː]

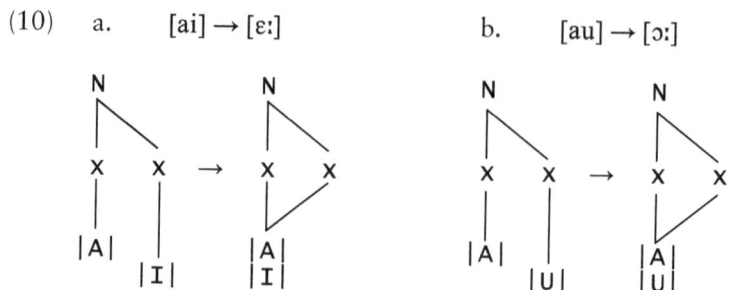

(10a) shows how the phonetic interpretation of |I A| has changed over time. In late Middle English |A| and |I| were interpreted separately, producing the diphthong [ai]. Then later, language users began to merge the two, resulting in the long mid vowel [ɛː]. (For the moment we make no distinction between [ɛː] and [eː], since both are compounds of |I| and |A|. However, in languages where these vowels contrast, they will need to have different representations.) Like [ai], the back diphthong [au] also became a monophthong. This is shown in (10b).

You will notice from (10) that monophthongisation involves minimal changes to the representation itself. The prosodic structure is unchanged – there is a long nucleus in the original diphthong and also in the monophthong. Furthermore, no elements have been added to, or removed from, the representation. What we have, then, is a process in which language users have simply reinterpreted the existing phonological structure. So it should come as no surprise to find that there are other ways of reinterpreting the same structures too. For example, most dialects of English have since reverted to a diphthong realisation of |I A|: Estuary English spoken in south-east England has *day* [daɪ], *eight* [aɪt] (11a) while RP and many other dialects have *day* [deɪ], *eight* [eɪt] (11b).

(11) a. *Estuary English: day* [daɪ]   b. *RP English: day* [deɪ]

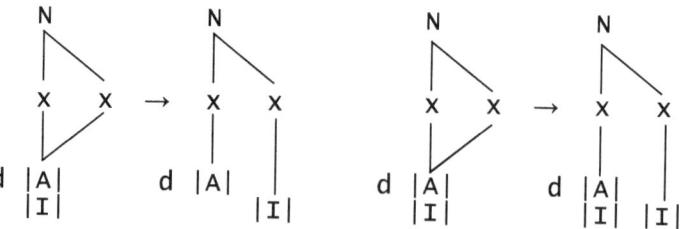

Dialect differences are often a useful source of information about segmental structure, and in this case they highlight the compound structure of mid vowels. Further support for the compounds |I A| and

|U A| comes from varieties of African English, in which the segments produced as diphthongs in most dialects are realised as in (12), where vowel shortening is accompanied by monophthongisation.

(12) [aɪ]→[ɛ]:   [lɛk]   *like*   Sierra Leone, Liberia
                 [ˈfɛndɪŋ]   *finding*   Zambia
                 [ˈprɛməri]   *primary*   Kenya
                 [trɛb]   *tribe*   Uganda

      [aʊ]→[ɔ]:   [rɔn(d)]   *round*   Kenya
                 [mɔt]~[mɔp]   *mouth*   West African Pidgin
                 [tɔn]   *town*   Liberia
                 [ɔs]   *house*   Krio

Here, monophthongisation is a natural result of vowel shortening: if a long nucleus is reduced to a single position then everything must be phonetically interpreted in that single position. For instance, in *town* [tɔn] the vowel cannot be realised as [aʊ] in a short nucleus so its constituent elements |A| and |U| are interpreted simultaneously as [ɔ] instead (for now we will treat [ɛ ɔ] as phonetic variants of [e o]). Again, these patterns reinforce the idea that |I U A| are basic units of segmental structure, and additionally, that mid vowels are represented by the compounds |I A| and |U A|.

Looking beyond English, we find more evidence for the structures |I A| and |U A| in languages as diverse as Japanese and Maga Rukai. In Japanese there are two processes of monophthongisation, one historical and the other synchronic. Towards the end of the Middle Japanese period, [au] was reinterpreted as [o:] in Sino-Japanese words, as shown in (13). This process operated along the lines of (10b).

(13) [au] → [o:]   'cherry tree'
      [kau] → [ko:]   'high', 'fidelity'
      [kjau] → [kjo:]   'capital', 'home town'

Meanwhile, in Modern Japanese the reinterpretation process represented by (10a) has become a feature of casual speech, in which [ai] is monophthongised to [e:]. Because the diphthong [ai] is retained in formal speech, we get alternations such as those in (14).

(14) [taigai] ~ [te:ge:]   'usually'
      [itai] ~ [ite:]   'painful'

Maga Rukai further illustrates the internal structure of mid vowels. This language has a process of vowel coalescence which produces mid vowels that were not present in the proto-language. In (15a) for example, the vowel sequence [a] . . . [u] in negative forms corresponds to [o] in positive forms. This [o] is the result of merging |A| and |U| from the original vowels, as we saw in (13). (15b) shows a parallel alternation between [a] . . . [i] and [e].

(15)   Negative   Positive
  a.   i-k-valu: vlo: 'bee'
         i-k-taldu: tlodo   'bridge'
         i-k-palŋu: ploŋo   'pan'

  b.   i-k-damli: dmele   'hemp'
         i-k-valsi: vlese   'tooth'
         i-k-caki: cke: 'excrement'

Vowel merger in Maga Rukai is triggered by vowel syncope, which is itself controlled by the language's iambic foot structure. As (16) demonstrates, when the leftmost nucleus is removed, the |A| element associated with it is retained. This stray |A| element then links to the adjacent nucleus and is interpreted together with any elements already there.

(16)   a.   (i-k-)caki: b.   cke:

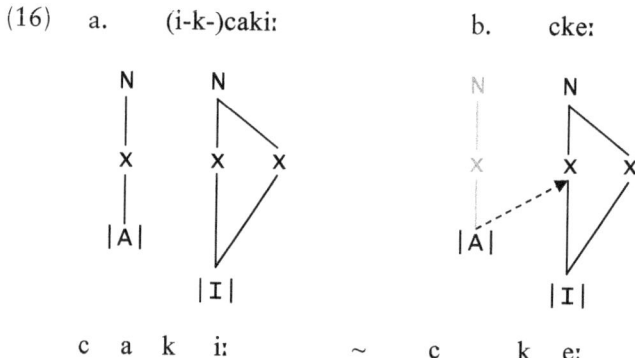

So once again we have a process which allows us to view the internal structure of mid vowels: the merger of |A| and |I| produces [e], as (16) shows, while a similar merger of |A| and |U| creates [o] in forms such as [ploŋo] 'pan'.

You may have noticed that the representations we are using follow the conventions of autosegmental phonology in allowing most elements to occupy separate tiers or levels in the segmental structure. For example, in (16) you can see that |A| and |I| reside on separate tiers. Being separated like this makes it possible for them to combine, and hence, to be interpreted together. This way of arranging the elements is not crucial, but it does provide a convenient way of distinguishing between elements which can combine (because they belong to different tiers) and elements which cannot (because they share the same tier). For example, in the unmarked vowel system [i u a e o], |I A| and |U A| are possible compounds whereas |I U| is not. And representations can show this by having |I| and |U| share the same tier. Because |A| occupies its own tier it is free to combine with either |I| or |U|.

We have now seen acoustic and phonological evidence to indicate that [i u a] are structurally basic while [e o] are compounds. In §2.6 we return to the topic of element compounds when we consider how to represent larger and more marked vowel systems. Before that, let us turn to another important property of many vowel systems, the presence of schwa.

2.5 CENTRAL VOWELS

2.5.1 Phonetic Evidence for Empty Vowels

Schwa looks like the definitive neutral vowel, as its presence or absence makes little difference to whether a vowel system is marked or unmarked. As the examples in (17) show, [ə] (or in some cases, [ɨ]) may appear in vowel systems of any size. Vowel length and nasality have been omitted.

(17)   [a i u] + [ə]   Wapishana
       [a i u ɛ ɔ] + [ə]   Chukchi
       [æ ɪ ʊ e ɒ ʌ] + [ə]   RP English (short vowels)
       [a i u e o ɛ ɔ] + [ə]   Wolof
       [a i u e o ü ö] + [ɨ]   Turkish
       [a i u e o ɛ ɔ ɪ ʊ] + [ə]   Bari

The ability of schwa to slot into any vowel system suggests that it does not participate in the usual segmental relationships with other vowels. For example, it is not obvious where schwa stands with regard to natural classes. It is as though schwa lies outside the |I U A| system altogether. And in fact, this is exactly what ET assumes. Here we will review the reasons for analysing schwa as an unspecified vowel.

We begin with the phonetic evidence. In §2.3 we saw that |I U A| have unique acoustic patterns which are used as acoustic cues by listeners and as pronunciation targets by speakers. These patterns are based on the way energy is distributed at different frequencies,

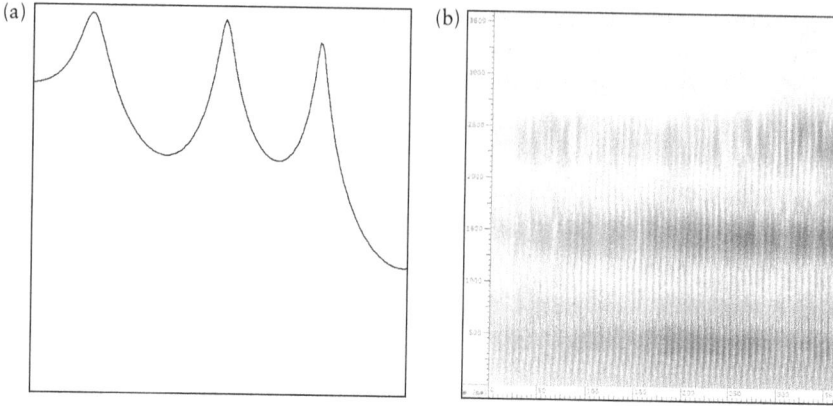

Figure 2.6 The energy pattern for schwa. (a) Spectral pattern of [ə]; (b) Spectrogram of [ə]

and in particular, on the location of energy peaks as described in (8). But as Figures 2.6(a) and 2.6(b) show, the energy pattern for schwa has nothing in common with the *dIp*, *rUmp* and *mAss* patterns for |I U A|. Unlike *dIp*, *rUmp* and *mAss*, the pattern for schwa in Figure 2.6(a) has regularly spaced peaks. The same information can also be read off the spectrogram in Figure 2.6(b), where the formants are equally spaced at around 500 Hz (F1), 1.5 kHz (F2) and 2.5 kHz (F3). In other words, the formants for schwa do not converge, which indicates that schwa lacks linguistic information (recall that the information-bearing patterns *dIp*, *rUmp* and *mAss* have energy peaks created by converging formants). To produce a schwa the articulators must be in a neutral or relaxed position, giving the vocal tract a fairly uniform shape. And by adopting this shape, speakers cannot control formant values in any linguistically meaningful way. The result is a schwa-like central vowel which, in many languages, has no positive properties, either acoustic or phonological.

Because schwa has an acoustic pattern which shows none of the characteristics of *dIp*, *rUmp* or *mAss*, we can assume that it does not contain |I|, |U| or |A| in its representation. This leaves a nucleus containing no elements – that is, an unspecified or 'empty' vowel. And as Harris and Lindsey (2000) note, a phonologically empty segment is an informationally empty segment, since linguistic information is represented by elements. Later we will examine what it means to be informationally empty; for the moment, let us just say that an empty vowel is usually non-contrastive. Now, the obvious question is this:

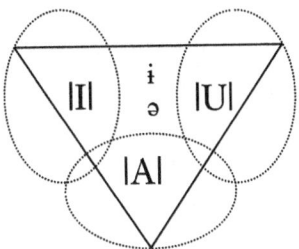

Figure 2.7 Central vowels in the acoustic vowel space

if schwa has no elements, then how do we hear it and pronounce it? According to Harris and Lindsey (1995), the spectral pattern in Figure 2.6(a) acts as an acoustic baseline which exists latently in all vowels. Usually this baseline resonance is not heard because it is masked by the more marked patterns *dIp*, *rUmp* and *mAss* that appear when |I U A| are present. But in the case of schwa, which has no elements, this baseline resonance is exposed. Language users associate baseline resonance with the central region of the acoustic space, because this is the only area of the vowel space not coloured by |I|, |U| or |A| (see Figure 2.7). To help us understand the nature of baseline resonance, Harris and Lindsey suggest that it may be likened to an artist's blank canvas. Like baseline resonance, a blank canvas provides a neutral background which becomes hidden when different colours (or elements) are added to it. And whether the canvas is white, or grey, or some other neutral colour, we perceive it as being colourless (or phonologically empty) as long as it remains blank.

As we have already noted, vowel systems of any shape or size may contain a neutral vowel, which can vary between [ə]~[ɨ]~[ɯ]. And from the stylised vowel space in Figure 2.7 we can see why this phonetic variation is possible, even expected. The only area unaffected by |I U A| is the central region, and this region accommodates a range of vowel qualities, giving languages a choice of how to phonetically interpret an empty nucleus. In most languages, then, it is a trivial matter as to whether speakers use [ə] or [ɨ], since both represent the same linguistic object – a phonologically empty vowel. Having said that, we should bear in mind that this does not apply to all languages, as there are some systems in which [ə] and [ɨ] are contrastive. And in such cases one vowel will be empty while the other will contain elements. Perhaps surprisingly, English is one such example, which we examine in §2.8.4.

2.5.2 Phonological Evidence for Empty Vowels

Because elements are phonological units, it should ideally be phonological evidence that we use to determine which elements a segment contains. So how do we verify the structure of schwa? After all, if it contains no elements then there is nothing to observe. Actually, it is still possible to view schwa as a phonological object because, like other vowels, it is linked to a syllable nucleus, which we can analyse phonologically. Another reason for treating empty vowels as genuine phonological objects is that they are sometimes produced by phonological processes. For example, some processes cause vowels to lose elements; and if a vowel happens to lose all of its elements, then the result is an empty nucleus – which can be interpreted as a schwa-like baseline resonance. This is what happens in Bulgarian and Turkish, which are both described below.

Like English, Bulgarian has a full set of vowel contrasts in stressed syllables but a reduced set in unstressed syllables. The two systems are shown in (18a), with examples given in (18b).

(18) a. stressed   i e u o ə a

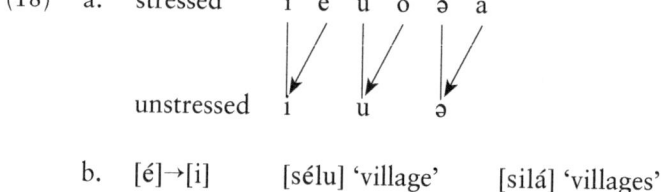

　　　　　unstressed   i   u   ə

　　b. [é]→[i]   [sélu] 'village'   [silá] 'villages'
　　　 [ó]→[u]   [róguf] 'of horn'   [rugát] 'horned'
　　　 [á]→[ə]   [rábutə] 'work'   [rəbótnik] 'worker'

Bulgarian demonstrates a fairly common pattern in which unstressed syllables support only a subset of the vowel contrasts that are possible in stressed syllables: in (18) we see that [i e] neutralise to [i], [u o] to [u] and [a ə] to [ə] in weak syllables. Using features it is not easy to express these changes as a single process: [–high] → [+high] describes [e] → [i] and [o] → [u], but because the feature [±high] is not relevant to [a] → [ə] (because both vowels are non-high) we have to use [+low] → [–low] instead. Yet it is clear that the changes in (18b) are all triggered by the same conditioning factor – namely, the inability of weak syllables to support certain vowel properties. In ET terms it is a straightforward matter to identify this rogue vowel property as |A|: the |A| element is suppressed in weak syllables, leaving any remaining elements still pronounceable.

(19) a. high vowels are unchanged (|A| not present)
   [i]→[i] |I|→|I|
   [u]→[u] |U|→|U|

b. mid vowels are raised (|A| suppressed)
   [e]→[i] |A I|→|A I|
   [o]→[u] |A U|→|A U|

c. central vowels become empty (|A| suppressed)
   [ə]→[ə] | |→| |
   [a]→[ə] |A|→|A|

This vowel weakening process targets |A|, so [i u] in (19a) are unaffected because they lack |A|. By contrast, [e o] both have |A| in their structure, which is interpreted in stressed positions but suppressed in weak positions. And when |A| is lost it leaves |I| and |U| remaining, which are interpreted as [i] and [u] respectively. Meanwhile, (19c) provides evidence that schwa is an unspecified vowel. Because it contains no |A|, schwa is not affected by vowel weakening. But on the other hand [a] does contain |A|, and when |A| is lost in unstressed syllables the result is an empty nucleus, since [a] has no elements other than |A|. This empty nucleus is interpreted as baseline resonance, hence [a] → [ə]. In this way ET manages to express Bulgarian vowel weakening as a unified process by assuming that the grammar permits empty nuclei. Russian displays a similar weakening process, but with one notable variation: [o] reduces to [a] in the weak syllable before a stress and to [ə] elsewhere, hence *gorod-ók* [gərad-ók] 'cities'. So together, Russian and Bulgarian provide us with the full set of possibilities as far as the weakening of |U A| ([o]) is concerned: in Bulgarian [o] loses |A| to leave |A U| ([u]), while in Russian it loses |U| to leave |A U| ([a]) or loses both elements to leave an empty nucleus [ə].

Turkish is another language in which empty nuclei are visible. Like some other Altaic languages, Turkish has a vowel harmony process which causes suffix vowels to agree in backness with root vowels. The active property is therefore usually assumed to be [±back], which has no direct equivalent in ET. However, the |I| element has a phonological function which partly overlaps with that of [±back] – recall from §2.3 that |I| is present in front vowels. In other words, |I| roughly corresponds to [−back]. In Turkish vowel harmony, |I| in a root vowel extends to the suffix vowel. So for example, the vowel of the genitive singular suffix [ɨn] is phonologically empty (realised as [ɨ], rather than the more usual [ə]), but under harmony conditions it copies |I| from the root vowel and is reinterpreted as [i], as in (20b). The process is illustrated in (21b).

(20)   Nominative   Genitive   Nominative
       singular   singular   plural
   a. kɨz   kɨz-in   kɨz-lar   'girl'
       sap   sap-ɨn   sap-lar   'stalk'

   b. ip   ip-in   ip-ler   'rope'
       ev   ev-in   ev-ler   'house'

The nominative plural suffix [lar] also harmonises. In harmonising contexts it is reinterpreted as [ler], a compound of active |I| and its original |A| element. This is shown in (21c).

(21)   a. kɨz-ɨn   b. ip-in   c. ev-ler

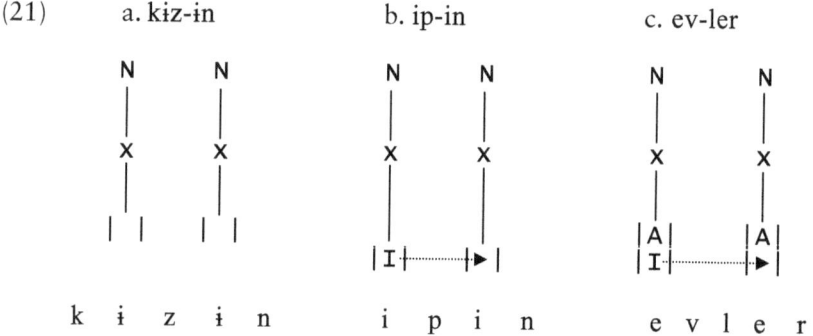

Although these examples describe only one aspect of vowel harmony in Turkish, they demonstrate how certain generalisations are possible if we treat the central vowel [ə]~[ɨ] as a phonologically empty structure. At this point, however, another question arises: if schwa is really empty, then why is it not interpreted as silence? We have already mentioned that a baseline acoustic pattern is latently present in vowels, and that this is audible when no elements are present. But why should we hear it at all, if it carries no linguistic information? The answer is that it does carry information, but not the kind of information that relates to segments. All vowels, even empty ones, are tied to nuclear positions; and these empty nuclei combine to form higher prosodic units such as feet and words – units which turn out to be essential for speech perception and efficient lexical access (§5.2). For example, there is evidence that listeners pay particular attention to the beginnings of foot and word domains when they process running speech. So, if an empty nucleus is interpreted as silence rather than as [ə] or [ɨ], then information about prosodic units can be lost.

This is not to say that empty nuclei can never be silent, however. In fact silent empty nuclei are possible in many languages including English, for example [ˈfæmØli] *family*, [ʌnØˈbrəʊkən] *unbroken* (where Ø marks a silent nucleus). But if a nucleus is silent, then how can we be sure it is there? English provides an answer to this question by showing how the same nucleus can be silent in certain contexts and audible in others. According to one innovative approach to syllable structure described in Kaye (1990), all well-formed lexical representations end in a nucleus. And in some languages such as Italian this final nucleus must be phonetically realised. Predictably, then, all native Italian words are vowel-final, hence *casa* 'house' but *cas. Additionally, many loanwords in Italian have become vowel-final through adaptation: *gallon* (English) → *gallone* (Italian). By contrast, other languages allow a final empty nucleus to be silent, which means that words may end phonetically in a consonant, for example *peach* [piːtʃ] (English), *schlimm* [ʃlɪm] 'bad' (German), *rhad* [r̥ad] 'cheap' (Welsh).

Using Kaye's model of syllabification, the English word *peach* is represented as in (22a) with a silent word-final empty nucleus. The plural suffix in (22b) also has a silent nucleus, as it constitutes a separate morpheme; note that the English plural suffix is lexically [z] and not [s] (§4.3.3). And when (22a) and (22b) combine to form the plural *peaches*, the result is (22c).

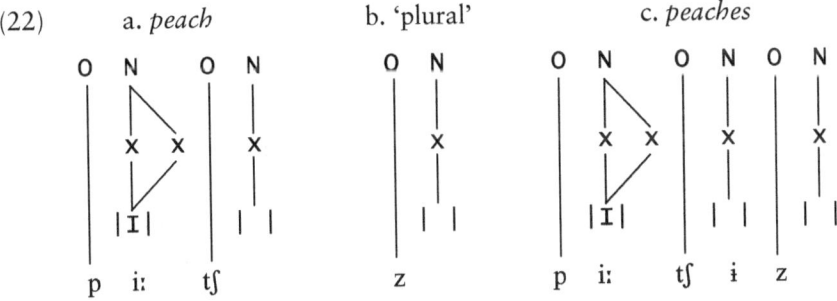

(22)   a. *peach*   b. 'plural'   c. *peaches*

(22c) has two empty nuclei, one from *peach* and the other from *-s*. It also has the two sibilants [tʃ] and [z], which are problematic in the sense that they are difficult to distinguish when they are adjacent. However, it is possible to perceive them both if we phonetically interpret the intervening empty nucleus as baseline resonance, hence [piːtʃɨz]. (Note that baseline resonance in English is pronounced [ɨ] rather than [ə]. The status of English [ə] will be discussed in §2.8.4.) In this way we need not rely on arbitrary processes such as vowel insertion in order to explain the presence of [ɨ]. This way of analysing the [ɨz] form of *-s* departs from standard accounts of English phonology in two respects. First, it assumes that [ɨ] is the phonetic realisation of an empty nucleus belonging to the original representation; it is not something inserted by the phonology. This is presumably a gain for restrictiveness, given the potentially random nature of vowel insertion rules. And second, it has a clear linguistic motivation: interpreting the empty nucleus as [ɨ] enhances the perceptibility of surrounding consonants, and therefore, improves the recoverability of linguistic information. By contrast, the traditional analysis involving vowel epenthesis tends to be driven by notions such as ease of articulation, which we have already described as being non-linguistic in nature.

2.6 FRONT ROUNDED VOWELS

So far we have seen how |I U A| can be used to represent the unmarked triangular vowel systems [a i u] and [a i u e o]. And because some grammars allow empty nuclei, we can also add a neutral vowel [ə] or [ɨ] to these, creating vowel systems of up to six vowels. Together, these systems account for around 60 per cent of grammars. But ET should be able to describe larger and more marked vowel systems too, which means that we need to increase the generative capacity of the |I U A| system further. Introducing another element is not an option here: we know there are three basic units of vowel structure, represented by |I U A|, but we have no evidence of any other vowel properties that are similarly unmarked. However, there are two things we can do to increase the capacity of the vowel elements. One involves changing the way elements are allowed to combine. By allowing them to combine in more complex ways – for example, in unequal proportions – ET can describe more contrasts without losing its ability to capture natural classes. This will be explored in §2.7. There is also a much simpler way of increasing the number of contrasts |I U A| can generate. We have already discussed the two element combinations |I A| and |U A|, but logically there are two more possibilities, both of which turn out to be relatively marked. The first is |I U|, a combination of *dIp* and *rUmp* that is interpreted as a high front rounded [y]. In terms of articulation, |I U| represents a front vowel [i] which has been rounded to [y] through the addition of |U|. The spectral pattern for this vowel is given in Figure 2.8(a), which shows a *dIp* within the falling *rUmp* pattern. In perceptual terms [y] is not very distinctive because its formant structure contains a conflict: |I|

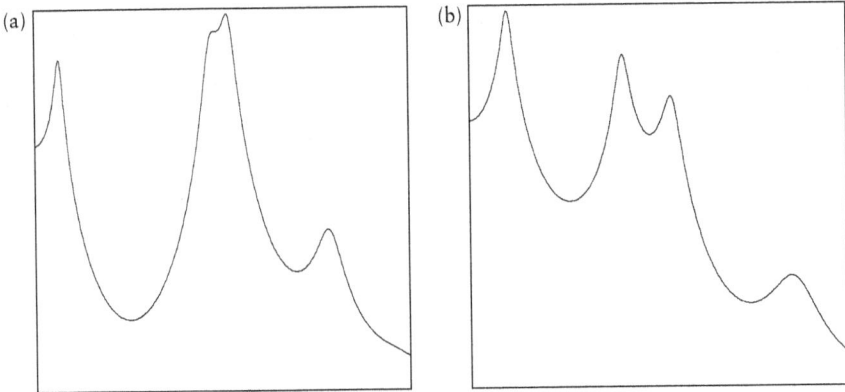

Figure 2.8 |I U| (dIp + rUmp *pattern*) and |I U A| (dIp + rUmp + mAss *pattern*). (a) Spectral pattern of [y] (|I U|); (b) Spectral pattern of [ø] (|I U A|)

causes F2 to increase while |U| has the opposite effect of decreasing F2 (and other formants too). By lowering F2, |U| masks the acoustic characteristics of |I| and suppresses the linguistic information associated with it. It is not surprising, therefore, that expressions which combine |I| and |U| are universally marked. After all, communication succeeds by transmitting linguistic information, not by concealing it.

The remaining combination is |I U A|, which is interpreted as a mid front rounded [ø]. Because it combines |I| and |U|, this is also a marked sound – it is reported that front rounded vowels such as [y ø] are found in less than 7 per cent of the world's languages. The spectral pattern for [ø] is given in Figure 2.8(b), where it is just possible to identify traces of the individual *dIp*, *rUmp* and *mAss* patterns. As we can see from its representation, [ø] combines |I U| with the |A| element; in terms of articulation, then, it is a lowered version of [y]. The representation of [ø] as |I U A| is confirmed by the pattern of vowel harmony we find in Altaic languages such as Mongolian.

(23)   *Nominative*   *Instrumental*
    a.   gal   gal-aːr   'fire'
    b.   deːl   deːl-eːr   'coat'
    c.   doroː   doroː-goːr   'stirrup'
    d.   nøxør   nøxør-øːr   'comrade'

The vowel of the instrumental suffix [aːr] contains only |A|. But like Turkish (§2.5.2), Mongolian has an |I| element which is harmonically active, so when |I| appears in a stem vowel it extends to the suffix. For example, [aːr] is reinterpreted as [eːr] in (23b) after it gains |I| from the stem vowel [eː]. In addition, |U| is harmonically active in this language, so when |U| appears in the stem vowel it extends to the suffix too. In (23c) therefore, the suffix vowel [aː] |A| is reinterpreted as [oː] |U A| after copying |U| from the stem *doroː* 'stirrup'. Finally, (23d) shows how |I| and |U| harmony operate together: because |I| and |U| are both present in the stem vowel [ø], both are copied to the suffix, hence [aːr]→[øːr]. The process is shown in (24b).

(24) a. *Instrumental* [aːr]   b. [nøxør-øːr]

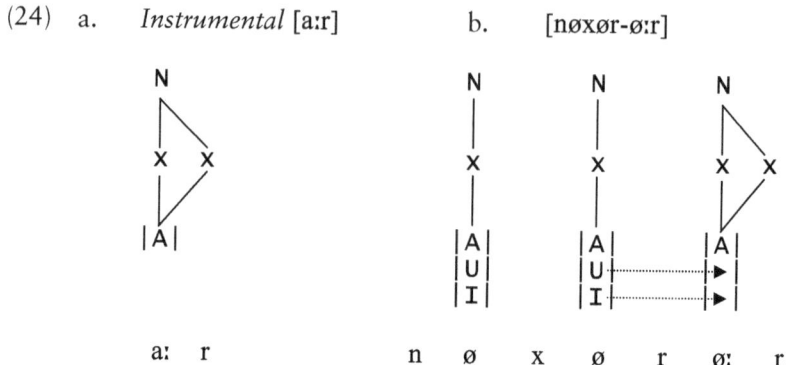

Despite the prevalence of front rounded vowels in Altaic (and also Uralic) languages, these sounds are cross-linguistically uncommon. As we have noted, this can be explained by the fact that |I| and |U| make a marked combination owing to their conflicting acoustic properties.

Let us now look at a second way of increasing ET's expressive power. The following section describes how elements may combine in unequal proportions to form asymmetric compounds.

2.7 ELEMENT DEPENDENCY

In linguistics it is often assumed that if two objects in a structure are formally linked, they must be unequal. In other words, structural relations are thought to be asymmetric. This asymmetry is usually expressed in terms of head-dependency, where a head sanctions or licenses its dependent; for example, in morphology there is said to be an asymmetric relation between roots and affixes. Typically, head-dependency manifests itself as a difference between strong and weak, which can take various forms depending on which part of the grammar is involved. In the case of morphology, a dependent affix may be weak in the sense that it supports a smaller set of lexical contrasts than its head, or it may function as a harmonic target but not as a trigger. Head-dependency also applies to phonology, most obviously to prosodic structure. When two syllables form a metrical foot, for example, the relation between them is always unequal: in some languages a foot is right-dominant and in others left-dominant. Either way, the head syllable will display strong characteristics of some kind. For instance, in some languages only strong syllables can bear stress, while in other languages they can support segmental properties that may not be possible in weak syllables. A clear example is aspiration in English, which is tied to the strong syllable in a foot. More generally, we tend to find a wider range of contrasts in head syllables than in dependent syllables.

So clearly, head-dependency is an established feature in formal linguistics. The question is whether it should apply to segmental structure in the same way that it does to prosodic and morphological structure. Following Dependency Phonology, ET assumes that it should, and this section shows how head-dependency or 'headedness' has an important function in ET representations. To see this, consider how ET represents the vowel system of Tunica in (25). Headed elements are underlined.

(25)   i   u |I| |U|
        e   o |I̲ A| |U̲ A|
         ɛ   ɔ |I A| |U A|
           a |A|

This system has two pairs of mid vowels, [e o] and [ɛ ɔ], so the symmetrical compounds |I A| and |U A| are no longer sufficient – we need a way of expressing the difference between [e o] and the more open [ɛ ɔ]. Let us focus on the [e]–[ɛ] contrast. If we compare the acoustic properties of these vowels, as shown in Figures 2.9(a) and 2.9(b), we find that the |I| element is more prominent in [e] than in [ɛ]; in impressionistic terms, it has a more palatal quality. In Figure 2.9(a) the *dIp* pattern dominates the expression; *mAss* is also visible at the upper end of the frequency range, but it is *dIp* which occupies the central region and gives [e] its palatal or |I|-like character. We express this asymmetry between |I| and |A| by making |I| the head of the compound, hence |I̲ A|. In general, heads make a greater contribution than dependents to the overall acoustic shape of a segment.

Now compare this with [ɛ] in Figure 2.9(b). In [ɛ] the *dIp* pattern is still visible but it does not dominate the expression, suggesting that it is not a head. On the other hand, the *mAss* pattern for |A| appears to be more prominent in [ɛ] than in [e]. We could take this to mean that |A| is headed, giving [ɛ] the structure |I A̲|. And indeed, some

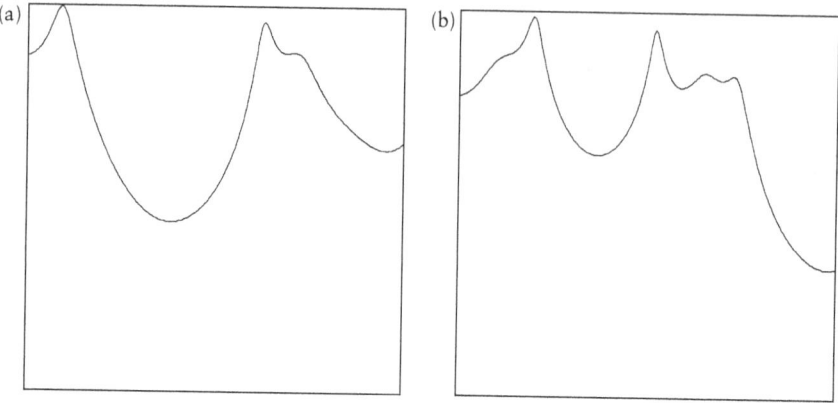

Figure 2.9 The energy patterns for [e] and [ɛ]. (a) Spectral pattern of [e] (|I̲ A|); (b) Spectral pattern of [ɛ] (|I A̲|)

versions of ET do represent [ɛ] as |I A̲| – not necessarily because |A| is prominent, but because they require all expressions to have a head, and if |I| is non-headed then |A| must be headed. However, there are other versions of ET that follow Dependency Phonology in allowing the grammar to contain non-headed expressions too, in which case [ɛ] may be represented as |I A|. Clearly the difference is not crucial here, because the [e]–[ɛ] contrast is already captured by headed versus non-headed |I|. For the moment we will take the first approach and assume that all expressions have a head (although this will have to be revised when we analyse the English vowel system in §2.8). On this basis, the vowel system of Tunica can now be represented as in (26). Notice that, because this is a symmetrical vowel system, the back vowels can be treated in parallel with the front vowels. This means that [o] has headed |U̲| and that [ɔ] has headed |A̲|.

(26) i   u |I̲| |U̲|
        e   o |I̲ A| |U̲ A|
         ɛ   ɔ |I A̲| |U A̲|
            a |A̲|

All the expressions in (26) have a head, even simplex ones. Thus, [i u a] are represented as |I̲|, |U̲| and |A̲| respectively. This makes sense, because if headedness gives an element acoustic prominence, then a single element should always be headed because its acoustic pattern entirely dominates the expression.

So, headedness offers a convenient way of representing certain vowel contrasts that cannot be captured through simple element

VOWELS IN ENGLISH

combinations. And in addition, headedness relates to strength in the sense that a head element displays a stronger and more prominent acoustic pattern than a dependent element. In the next section we analyse the vowel system of English, where the connection between headedness and strength takes a slightly different form: headed expressions are interpreted as full vowels while non-headed expressions are realised as weak vowels.

2.8 VOWELS IN ENGLISH

2.8.1 Introduction

English has a large and relatively complex vowel system which varies between dialects. Here we will focus mainly on RP, which has the vowels in (27).

(27)   short: [ɪ ʊ ʌ e æ ɒ]
       long: [iː uː ɑː ɔː ɜː]
       diphthong: [aɪ eɪ ɔɪ aʊ əʊ iə eə (ʊə)]
       reduced: [ə ʊ ɪ]

In analysing the RP system, we will make two assumptions. The first assumption has already been mentioned, namely, that headed expressions represent full vowels and non-headed expressions represent weak vowels. Vowels are weak if they appear in weak positions, that is, in an unstressed syllable or in the dependent (right-hand) slot of a diphthong. The second assumption we will make is that vowel length is the property that distinguishes [uː] from [ʊ], [iː] from [ɪ] and so on. The reasoning behind these assumptions will become clear as we proceed.

2.8.2 Short Vowels

RP has the six short vowels [ɪ ʊ ʌ e æ ɒ]. These are full vowels, as opposed to weak or reduced vowels, in the sense that they can contrast in stressed syllables. In ET they are represented as in (28).

(28)   [ɪ] |I̲| m*i*ss, b*ui*lding
       [ʊ] |U̲| p*u*t, c*oo*king
       [ʌ] |A̲| l*o*ve, s*u*btle
       [e] |I̲ A| s*e*nd, def*e*nd
       [æ] |I A̲| g*a*s, *a*ction
       [ɒ] |U A̲| wr*o*ng, t*o*nic

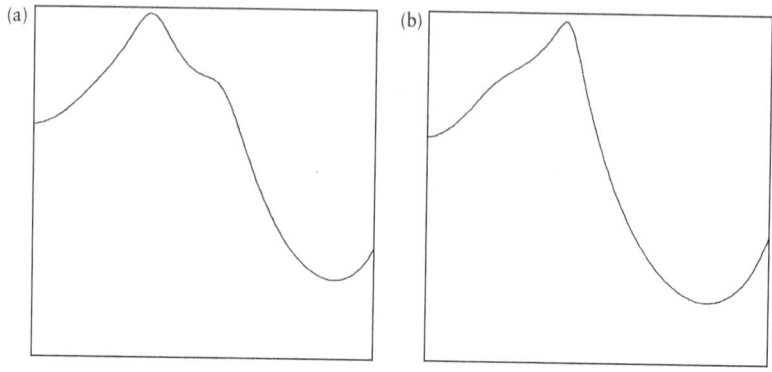

Figure 2.10 The energy patterns for [ʌ] and [ɑː]. (a) Spectral pattern of [ʌ] (|A|); (b) Spectral pattern of [ɑː] (|A|)

Let us examine these representations more closely, beginning with |I| and |U|. In fact |I| and |U| require little explanation, as they are cued by the simple acoustic patterns *dIp* and *rUmp* and interpreted as short [ɪ] and [ʊ]. As Figure 2.10(a) shows, [ʌ] also involves a simple acoustic pattern, namely, the *mAss* pattern corresponding to |A|. Note that *mAss* is also the pattern for the long vowel [ɑː], which is shown in Figure 2.10(b) for comparison. You can see that the patterns are almost identical, suggesting that [ʌ] and [ɑː] have the same element structure |A|. The contrast between [ʌ] and [ɑː] therefore comes down to length: [ʌ] is the interpretation of |A| in a short nucleus while [ɑː] comes from interpreting |A| in a branching nucleus (§2.8.3). The vowels [e] and [æ] are both compounds of |I| and |A|, but they differ in headedness. In [e] the *dIp* pattern dominates the central region of the spectrum, indicating that |I| is headed. This gives [e] the representation |I̲ A|. But in [æ] it is *mAss* which dominates, making |A| the head and giving [æ] the representation |I A̲|. Figures 2.11(a) and 2.11(b) show the spectral patterns for [e] and [æ].

Now, to verify these representations we would ideally like to have phonological evidence describing how [e] and [æ] behave in English. But unfortunately, the short vowels in English are mostly inert and rarely participate in phonological processes of the kind that could reveal anything about their internal structure. However, we can still learn something about them by observing how they behave in loanwords. Consider the examples of English loanwords in Japanese listed in (29). What these forms illustrate is the way Japanese adapts loanwords so that they conform to its own phonological system. Japanese has the five-vowel system [i e a o ɯ].

VOWELS IN ENGLISH 45

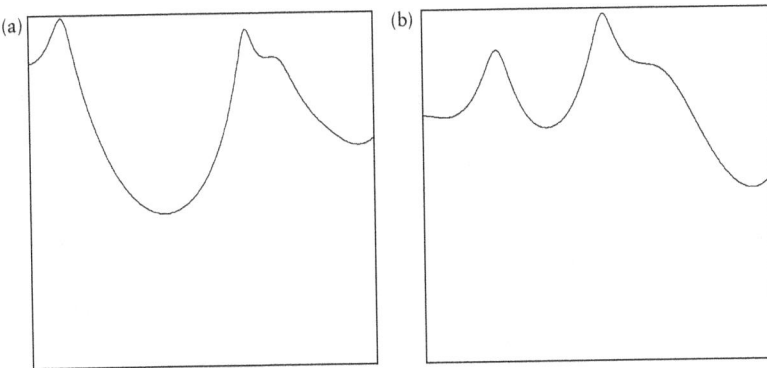

Figure 2.11 The energy patterns for [e] and [æ]. (a) Spectral pattern of [e] (|I A|); (b) Spectral pattern of [æ] (|I A|)

(29)
                                    RP   *Japanese*

    a.   [e] → [e]   k<u>e</u>tchup   [kettʃappɯ]
                           g<u>ue</u>st   [gesto]

    b.   [ʌ] → [a]   c<u>ou</u>ple   [kappɯrɯ]
                           g<u>u</u>ts   [gatsɯ]

    c.   [æ] → [i͡a]   c<u>a</u>mpus [ki͡ampasɯ]
                           g<u>a</u>ng   [gi͡aŋgɯ]

(29a) shows that when Japanese borrows an English word containing [e], the vowel remains unchanged, as in [kettʃappɯ] *ketchup*. This is because English and Japanese both have the vowel [e], and in both languages this vowel is represented as |I A|. In (29b), however, English [ʌ] is reinterpreted as [a] in Japanese, as in [kappɯrɯ] *couple*. This is what we expect, given that English [ʌ] and Japanese [a] are both realisations of the same representation |A|. And in (29c), English [æ] is reinterpreted as the light diphthong [i͡a] in Japanese. In segmental terms, [i͡a] consists of [a] with an [i] on-glide – in element terms, |I| followed by |A|. This suggests that Japanese listeners perceive [æ] as a compound of |I| and |A|, but one which is distinct from |I A| (= [e]). In other words, they analyse [æ] as |I A|. But because the Japanese vowel system does not have a vowel with the structure |I A|, speakers have no option but to interpret it as a sequence of native sounds, [i] (|I|) followed by [a] (|A|), hence [i͡a]. In this way, |I A| adheres to the phonology of Japanese, and at the same time, it reflects the structure of the original English vowel. What we learn from this brief diversion into loanword phonology is that RP [e ʌ æ] must have the representations |I A|, |A| and |I A| respectively.

Finally we turn to [ɒ]. As a low rounded vowel it is presumably a compound of |U| (rounding) and |A| (openness), though its headedness is not immediately clear. Historical evidence suggests that [ɒ] is basically an |A| vowel to which |U| has been added (via lip rounding), giving the representation |A U|. Consider, for example, words in which RP [ɒ] has the spelling <a> (*watch, quantity*). As the spelling indicates, [ɒ] had the earlier pronunciation [a], which underwent rounding to [ɒ] in Middle English following a labial [w]. This may be viewed as an assimilation in which the *rUmp* pattern in [w] came to be interpreted on the adjacent vowel, hence |A| + |U| → |A U|. Another source of RP [ɒ] is the Old English short vowel [ɔ], which corresponds to the spelling <o> (*song, long*). Again, the relatively open quality of [ɔ] (as opposed to [o]) suggests that the original vowel was represented by an expression in which |A| was dominant.

In one sense, identifying the headedness of [ɒ] is not crucial because no contrasts rely on it. Nevertheless, language learners presumably assign headedness to the |A|–|U| compound anyway, since head-dependency relations are an integral part of element structure. So how do they determine which element is headed? Clearly, the historical facts we have just described are of no help, because infants do not have access to historical information when building their phonological grammars – they cannot refer to spelling or to earlier sound changes, for example. Rather, infants build their lexicons only on the basis of what they perceive. And by focusing their attention on the acoustic properties of the input language, learners are likely to identify a predominant *mAss* pattern in [ɒ], which would lead them to construct the |A|-headed representation |A U|. In this way, children end up acquiring a grammar that describes only the synchronic properties of their native phonology. As McMahon (2000) points out, historical facts can sometimes help us to understand how grammars have come to be the way they are, but these facts do not form part of a language user's phonological knowledge.

2.8.3 Long Vowels

In this book we will assume that contrasts such as [iː]–[ɪ] are based on length rather than on vowel quality. This means that it is possible for two vowels to differ in length but still have the same element structure; for example, long [uː] and short [ʊ] both contain |U|. In this section we focus on the long monophthongs in RP, which are represented as in (30).

(30) [iː] |I| p*ie*ce, gr*ee*n
      [uː] |U| ch*oo*se, am*u*se
      [ɑː] |A| f*a*ther, *A*rctic
      [ɔː] |U A| c*augh*t, c*our*t
      [ɜː] |A| s*er*ve, th*ir*ty

Owing to their length difference, long [uː] and short [ʊ] display distinct phonological behaviour. For example, like other long vowels [uː] cannot precede [ŋ] (*[suːŋ], cf. [suːn]); and like other short vowels [ʊ] cannot appear word-finally in a stressed syllable (*[bʊ], cf. [bʊk]). Furthermore, in most dialects of English the length difference between [uː] and [ʊ] is accompanied by a difference in vowel quality, often described in terms of tenseness. According to one tradition, this quality difference is the main distinguishing property that separates tense vowels such as [iː uː] from lax vowels such as [ɪ ʊ]. In this book, however, we will treat differences in tenseness as a matter for phonetic interpretation and not phonological structure. So, in the ET grammar the same phonological expression can be interpreted differently depending on whether it is linked to a short or long nucleus. As mentioned in §2.2, this kind of phonetic variation is a characteristic of ET.

It should be noted that some versions of ET do express differences in tenseness using element structure. For example, Harris (1994) distinguishes tense and lax vowels using both length and segmental structure: tense vowels are represented by headed expressions in long nuclei, while lax vowels are non-headed and appear in short nuclei. This captures a useful generalisation, namely, that tense vowels in English show a natural tendency to occur in long nuclei. But as Harris notes, tenseness in Germanic languages like English works quite differently from tenseness in African languages such as Akan and Wolof, where it behaves unmistakably as a segmental property and is often referred to as advanced tongue root (ATR). In African languages, ATR can be harmonically active and can cause other vowels to agree in tenseness. Moreover, tenseness in these languages behaves independently of vowel length, so in Wolof the vowel of a tense verb root can be either long ([toːy] 'to be shy') or short ([tox] 'to smoke'), as can the vowel of a lax verb root. In cases like Wolof it makes sense to represent tense versus lax as a segmental distinction, and for this purpose Harris's approach works well. But in the case of Germanic languages like English, tenseness is tied to prosodic structure, and specifically, to the length of the nucleus. Furthermore, tenseness in these languages rarely displays any active phonological behaviour; so although English displays vowel tensing effects, we never observe processes such as tenseness assimilation. On balance, it seems appropriate to view tenseness in English as a prosodic property – specifically, one associated with vowel length – and not as a segmental property. We will therefore take long–short pairs such as [uː]–[ʊ] to have the same element structure. But in that case, how do we account for the quality difference between tense and lax? This may be just a way for speakers to emphasize the linguistic distinction between long and short nuclei. After all, physical duration is not a reliable cue to phonological length – compare the vowels of *peach* and *pitch*, for example, which are similar in duration but differ phonologically.

The long monophthongs [iː uː ɑː ɔː ɜː] in RP have the structures shown in (31). In effect, [iː uː ɑː ɔː] are the long counterparts of the short vowels [ɪ ʊ ʌ ɒ] respectively, since [iː] has the same element structure as [ɪ], and so on.

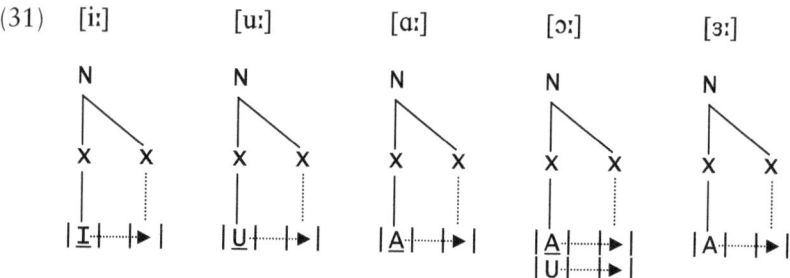

(31)   [iː]   [uː]   [ɑː]   [ɔː]   [ɜː]

Notice that each element expression is linked to the head (left-hand) position of the nucleus, from where it extends to the (right-hand) dependent position. Strictly speaking, then, the dependent position has no content of its own, since the elements it contains belong to the head. In fact it is very common to find element spreading taking place between positions that stand in a head-dependency relation – for instance, many cases of assimilation can be accounted for in this way. We may even think of a branching nucleus as a local assimilation domain; as (31) shows, assimilation is total in the case of long monophthongs.

In a moment we will review the evidence for the element structures in (31), which comes mainly from patterns of vowel weakening in which the long vowels are weakened in unstressed syllables. Before that, some comments are in order regarding the representation of [ɜː] as |A|. You will notice that [ɜː] is a full vowel but is represented by a non-headed expression, which contradicts the generalisation we made earlier that full vowels always have a headed element. In one sense it is unfortunate that [ɜː] is an exception to the general pattern, but nevertheless there are sound historical reasons for supposing that |A| is the correct structure for [ɜː]. Among the vowel elements, |A| appears to be particularly strong. When we come to look at the structure of diphthongs in §2.8.5 we will see that non-headed |A| is strong enough to pattern with headed expressions whereas non-headed |I| and |U| are not. And the same appears to be true here: non-headed |A| can be interpreted as a long vowel, despite this being a role that only headed expressions normally perform. The unique behaviour of |A| is well known within ET, and some scholars are now exploring ways of reworking ET in a way which can capture the special status of |A| in the grammar – see, for example, recent work by Markus Pöchtrager and Jonathan Kaye.

Returning to the question of [ɜː], let us consider why |A| should be pronounced in this way. In §2.8.4 we will see that, in English, non-headed |A| in a short nucleus is interpreted as [ə]. So logically, in a long nucleus |A| should sound something like [əː]. Now, phoneticians tell us that the central vowel [ɜː] is similar in vowel quality to [ə]: 'The quality of /ɜː/ often coincides with that of /ə/, the difference between the two being only one of length' (Cruttenden 2001: 125). In other words, [ɜː] and [əː] are different ways of transcribing what is phonetically the same vowel. So, if [ə] has the structure |A|, then perhaps [ɜː] has the same structure. And if so, the only difference between them is the length of the nucleus, long in [ɜː] and short in [ə]; the representation of English schwa as |A| will be discussed fully in the following section. In some descriptions of English, [ɜː] is called the rhotic vowel because it is restricted to words with historical *r* in the spelling. Indeed, the reason why [ə] lengthened to [ɜː] is linked directly to the loss of *r* in non-rhotic dialects during the 1700s. Most present-day instances of [ɜː] in RP derive from a Middle English sequence consisting of a short vowel plus *r*.

(32) [ɛ] + *r*   *earth, heard, fern*
      [ɪ] + *r*   *shirt, birth, myrrh*
      [ʊ] + *r*   *word, journey, spur*

By the end of the 1800s, [ɛ ɪ ʊ] had neutralised to [ə] before word-final or pre-consonantal *r*, so [ɛɹ ɪɹ ʊɹ] all became [əɹ]. This was followed by a process of *r* loss in non-rhotic dialects, which left a gap into which the neutralised [ə] could spread, thereby creating a long vowel [əː]/[ɜː]. Like other long–short pairs such as [iː]–[ɪ] and [uː]–[ʊ], the vowels [ɜː] and [ə] differ in length but not in element structure – both are represented as |A|. And as a result of these historical changes, we are left with an anomalous situation in which a long central vowel [ɜː] behaves as a full vowel and appears in stressed syllables, but is nevertheless non-headed. Historical *r* is also responsible for creating certain diphthongs in RP, which will be discussed in §2.8.5.

2.8.4 Weak Vowels

RP has a total of three weak vowels, [ɪ ʊ ə]. Some speakers have just [ɪ ə] while others have [ʊ] in addition. Recall from §2.5.2 that there is also [ɨ], the interpretation of an empty nucleus which is pronounced in words such as *dish*[ɨ]*s* and *wait*[ɨ]*d* in order to make the surrounding consonants easier to perceive. In this section we focus on [ɪ ʊ ə], the weak vowels that have element content. At the outset we claimed that weak vowels are represented by non-headed expressions, and here we will look at the phonological reasons for this. We will conclude that [ɪ ʊ ə] are the phonetic realisation of non-headed |I U A|, respectively.

(33)   [ə] |A| *ab̲out, bett̲er*
        [ɪ] |I| *de̲cide, be̲cause*
        [ʊ] |U| *influ̲ence, tu̲torial*
        [ɨ] | | *washe̲s, mende̲d*

Before analysing [ɪ ʊ ə], let us consider the general properties of weak vowels. Modern English shows a relation between stress and vowel distribution: stressed syllables contain full (non-reduced) vowels whereas unstressed syllables usually contain weak (reduced) vowels. This means that vowel contrasts mostly occur in stressed syllables, as shown in (34a). The weak vowels we get in weak syllables can sometimes contrast (*bátt*[ə] versus *bátt*[ɪ]), as in (34b), but more commonly they are non-contrastive (*r*[ə]*péat* ~ *r*[ɪ]*péat*).

(34)   a.   *b*[ɪ]*tter, b*[e]*tter, b*[ʌ]*tter, b*[æ]*tter, b*[iː]*ter, b*[ɑː]*ter, b*[əʊ]*ter*. . .
        b.   *bátt*[ə], *bátt*[ɪ]

Ultimately, this relation between stress and vowel distribution comes down to one of strength. Because full vowels are linguistically strong (contrastive) and acoustically strong (headed), they can appear in strong (stressed) syllables. On the other hand, weak vowels are linguistically weak (non-contrastive) and acoustically weak (non-headed), so they are limited to weak (unstressed) syllables. But what does it mean if we say that a vowel is weak? ET expresses segmental weakness in two ways: a weak vowel is non-headed, and in addition, it has only one element in its representation. ET assumes that weak vowels are non-headed because non-headed elements are associated with a lack of prominence (§2.7). And indeed, it is true that weak vowels are less prominent than full vowels. More generally, non-heads play a less important role than heads because they contain less linguistic information. And again this describes weak vowels, which usually appear in neutralising contexts where contrastive information has been lost. On this basis, we can be fairly certain that the weak vowels [ɪ ʊ ə] are represented by non-headed structures.

The second point about weak vowels is that they have just a single element in their representation. This is clear in the case of [ɪ] and [ʊ], which are cued by the single patterns dIp and rUmp respectively. But it is less obvious that [ə] should be represented by the single element |A|. To help us confirm the structure of [ə] we turn to vowel alternations conditioned by stress. The general pattern in English is that stressed positions allow speakers to pronounce a full vowel whereas unstressed positions force speakers to 'reduce' a full vowel to one of the weak vowels [ɪ ʊ ə]. Vowel reduction can be understood in two ways. First, in linguistic terms it refers to a decrease in a vowel's ability to contrast; in this sense the unstressed vowels in (34b) are reduced vowels. In ET terms, reduced vowels carry reduced amounts of linguistic information, as described in Harris and Urua (2001). And second, in representational terms it refers to a loss or suppression of material from a vowel's structure. Clearly there is some overlap between these two definitions of reduction, given that the units in a structure represent linguistic information. With regard to the second definition, the relevant question is this: what kind of material is suppressed when a vowel is reduced? Vowel representations in ET contain three kinds of information, all of which may be targeted by reduction processes:

Information	Reduction effect
length of nucleus	a long (branching) nucleus is shortened (non-branching)
headedness	a headed expression becomes non-headed
element structure	individual elements are suppressed

Table 2.1 Vowel reduction in English simplex vowels

Stressed				Unstressed		
Vowel	Structure	Example		Vowel	Structure	Example
[iː]	|I|	d*e*fect (n.)		[ɪ]	|I|	d*e*fective
[ɪ]		h*i*story				h*i*storical
[uː]	|U|	b*eau*ty	→	[ʊ]	|U|	b*eau*tician
[ʊ]		w*oo*d				Hollyw*oo*d
[ɑː]	|A|	dr*a*ma		[ə]	|A|	dr*a*matic
[ʌ]		s*u*lphur				s*u*lphuric

The examples in Table 2.1 illustrate how simplex expressions are affected by vowel reduction in unstressed syllables. Long nuclei are routinely shortened, causing long [iː uː ɑː] to be reinterpreted as short [ɪ ʊ ə]. In addition, these short vowels lose their headedness and become non-headed expressions: headed |I| reduces to non-headed |I|, headed |U| reduces to non-headed |U|, and importantly, headed |A| reduces to non-headed |A|. As the table shows, non-headed |A| is interpreted as [ə] when it is unstressed. This results in a situation where each vowel element can be interpreted in up to three different ways depending on whether it is long and stressed, as in [iː uː ɑː], short and stressed, as in [ɪ ʊ ʌ], or unstressed, as in [ɪ ʊ ə]. So, contrary to what is generally assumed, [ə] is not an unspecified vowel in English; rather, it has |A| in its structure. We can therefore distinguish [ə] from the truly unspecified vowel [ɨ]. For non-rhotic speakers these are contrastive in, for instance, the words *badgers* and *badges*.

(35) a. *badgers* [ˈbædʒəz]   b. *badges* [ˈbædʒɨz]

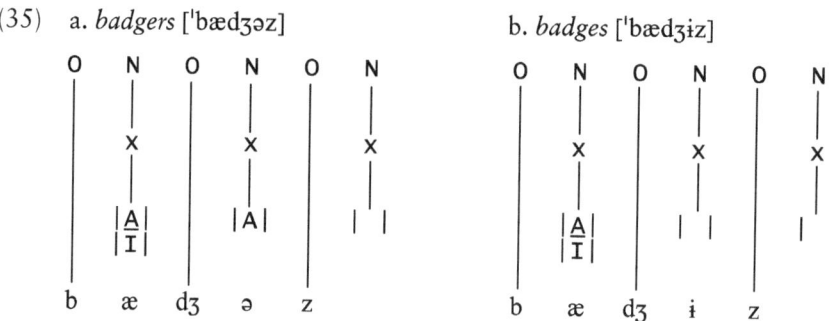

Table 2.2 Vowel reduction in English compound vowels

Stressed			Unstressed		
Vowel	Structure	Example	Vowel	Structure	Example
[æ]	|A I|	m*a*lice	[ə]	|A|	m*a*licious
[e]	|A I|	d*e*sperate →	[ɪ]	|I|	d*e*spair
[ɒ]	|A U|	c*o*ngress	[ə]	|A|	c*o*ngressional
[ɔː]		inst*a*ll			inst*a*llation

The singular form *badger* has a word-final [ə] represented lexically as |A|, and this is retained in the plural form shown in (35a). By contrast, *badge* has a silent empty nucleus word-finally. But when the plural suffix is added to make *badges*, this empty nucleus is interpreted with a default [ɨ], as shown in (35b), its purpose being to break up the newly created consonant sequence [dʒ] + [z] (§2.5.2). [ɨ] therefore differs phonologically from [ə], and for most speakers, it also has a different pronunciation.

Compound expressions undergo vowel reduction too. Again, long vowels become shortened and headed structures become non-headed. But in addition, there is a third effect: individual elements are suppressed to leave just a single element. Typically it is the original headed element that remains, though this varies from one dialect to another, for example *despair* [dɪsˈpeə] ~ [dəsˈpɛə]. As the examples in Table 2.2 show, language users interpret whatever segmental material is available, whether vowel weakening takes place or not. Stressed positions can support compound expressions, which speakers interpret in full. But in weak positions part of the element structure is suppressed, and language users can only interpret whatever remains following element suppression.

The ET approach to vowel reduction fares well against feature theory descriptions, in which the feature values for a full vowel are simply (and arbitrarily) replaced by a different set of values when that vowel is weakened. Compare the weakening effects [æ] → [ə] (*m*a*lice* ~ *m*a*licious*) and [ɒ] → [ə] (*c*o*ngress* ~ *c*o*ngressional*), for example. In the first [−back] becomes [+back], whereas in the second [+round] becomes [−round]. These changes appear to be unconnected because they employ different features, which misses the point that vowel weakening is actually a single process leading to a reduction or loss of lexical contrasts.

In this section we have seen that a reduced vowel is, in effect, a minimal vowel: reduction causes long to become short, compound to become simplex, and headed to become non-headed. Next, we turn our attention to diphthongs. We will see that the properties of weak vowels are the same properties that characterise vowels in the weak position of diphthongs.

2.8.5 Diphthongs

Traditional RP has the eight diphthongs [aɪ eɪ ɔɪ aʊ əʊ ɪə eə ʊə]. However, most speakers now lack [ʊə], which has merged with [ɔː] in words such as *poor*, *tour*. [eə] is also becoming rare; for many speakers it has monophthongised to [ɛː] in *chair*, *hairy*. Diphthongs have a similar distribution to long monophthongs; for example, both can be word-final in a stressed syllable, as in *tree* [triː], *try* [traɪ] (cf. *[trɪ]). This is expected, given that both are linked to long nuclei. The main difference between the two can be seen in (36).

(36) a.   [ɑː]   b.   [aɪ]

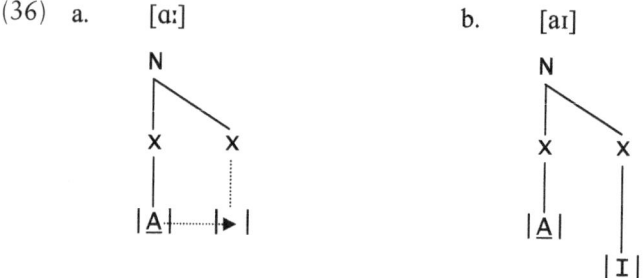

In long monophthongs a single element expression is anchored to the head (left-hand) position of the nucleus, from where it extends to the dependent position; the expression itself is phonetically interpreted in both slots, producing a long vowel. By contrast, diphthongs have separate expressions in each position, which are phonetically interpreted in sequence. And as we are about to see, English imposes certain restrictions on the way elements are distributed between the two positions.

Like other prosodic units which form a constituent, the two positions in a branching nucleus form a (left-headed) head-dependency relation. And predictably, this asymmetry is matched by a similar asymmetry at the segmental level: the strong head position can contain a headed expression whereas the weak dependent position only supports a non-headed expression – specifically, one of the three weak vowels [ɪ ʊ ə]. On this basis we expect to find just three types of diphthongs, grouped according to their terminal vowel.

(37) |I|-terminating |U|-terminating |A|-terminating
     [aɪ] *time*   [aʊ] *now*   [ɪə] *beer*
     [eɪ] *say*   [əʊ] *low*   [eə] *fair*
     [ɔɪ] *coin*   [ʊə] *tour*

This accounts for the full set of diphthongs in RP English. Let us examine each group in turn.

|I| *diphthongs*

The diphthongs [aɪ eɪ ɔɪ] all have non-headed |I| in their dependent position; notice that |I| is exactly the kind of expression we expect to find in a weak position, as it is short, simplex and non-headed. By contrast, the head position is strong enough to support headed segments, as the structures in (38) show.

(38) a. [aɪ] *time*   b. [eɪ] *say*   c. [ɔɪ] *coin*

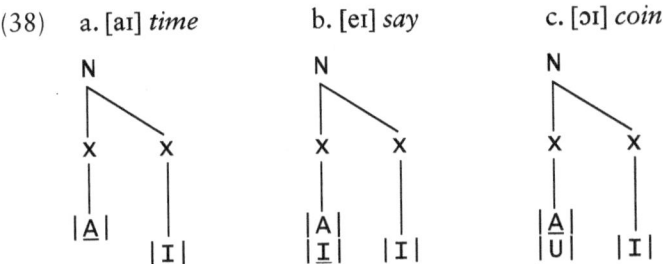

The starting point for [aɪ] varies noticeably between dialects; different realisations include [æɪ] in RP, [ɒɪ] in Australian English, [əɪ] in dialects of the south-west of England and [Ʌ̈ɪ] in Scottish English. But importantly, these variants are all phonologically similar since each contains |A|. In other words, [æ ɒ ə Ʌ̈] may be viewed as different phonetic interpretations of the same element structure. The main historical source of [aɪ] is Middle English [iː], which diphthongised to [əɪ] in the sixteenth century. Later, [əɪ] was reinterpreted as [ʌɪ] and then more recently as modern-day [aɪ]. Again, what unites these earlier forms is the presence of |A| in the first slot of the diphthong, non-headed in [əɪ] and headed in [ʌɪ] and [aɪ].

Diphthongs undergo vowel weakening in certain positions, just as monophthongs do. In the case of [aɪ] this is illustrated by alternations such as *der*[áɪ]*ve~der*[ɪ]*vátion* where, once again, the full vowel reduces to a minimal expression consisting of a single, non-headed element in a shortened nucleus. Because [aɪ] has two elements in its representation, there is a choice as to which one survives after reduction has taken place: a surviving |I| produces *der*[ɪ]*vátion* whereas a surviving |A| produces *der*[ə]*vátion*. Note that this process of [aɪ] → [ɪ] weakening has nothing to do with the historical process of tri-syllabic shortening exemplified by, for example, *cr*[áɪ]*me~cr*[í]*minal*. Unlike vowel reduction, tri-syllabic shortening cannot be considered a weakening process since it produces a stressed (and therefore, headed) short vowel.

Like [aɪ], [eɪ] varies in the quality of its starting vowel: the possibilities include RP [eɪ], 'refined' RP [ɛɪ] and Australian English [æɪ]. Notice that these variants all begin with a compound of |I| and |A|. In addition, there are some dialects which interpret the [eɪ] vowel as a monophthong, including Scottish English ([feːs] *face*) and dialects of northern England ([sɛː] *say*). Once again |I| and |A| are present, but in these cases interpreted simultaneously. Tyneside English provides yet another interpretation of the [eɪ] vowel, in which the diphthong ends in [ə] rather than [ɪ], as in *take* [teək]. This involves a reorganisation of the |I| and |A| elements, as shown in (39c).

(39) a. [æɪ] (Australia)   b. [eː] (Scotland)   c. [eə] (Tyneside)

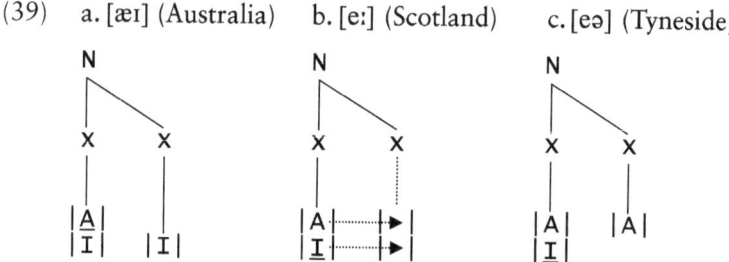

Instances of vowel weakening involving [eɪ] are rare. And those that do exist have become fossilised. For example, modern English *necklace* [néklǝs] was originally a compound of [nék] and [léɪs]. But as a result of applying the rules of compound stress, [léɪs] lost its stress and was reinterpreted as the unstressed form [lǝs]; and as a result, the vowel became short, headedness was lost, and part of the original element structure was suppressed, leaving in this case just a single |A|. This |A| is interpreted as the weak vowel [ə] in the present-day form [néklǝs].

Compared with [aɪ] and [eɪ], the diphthong [ɔɪ] does not vary much between dialects. Having said that, some varieties do have a closer starting vowel than others; for example, London English has [oɪ] rather than [ɔɪ]. Presumably these contain the same two elements but differ in headedness.

|U| *diphthongs*

RP has two |U| diphthongs, [aʊ] in *town* and [əʊ] in *home*. In both, the dependent position contains the weak expression |U|. They are represented as in (40).

(40)   a. [aʊ] *town*   b. [əʊ] *home*

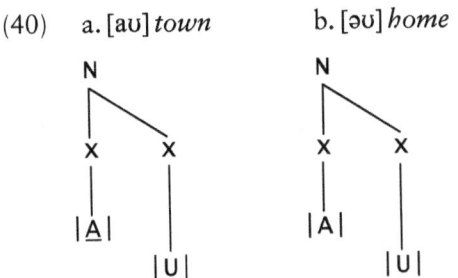

These two structures are very similar, differing only in headedness. We can be fairly certain that |A| is headed in [aʊ], because when we examine dialect pronunciations of this vowel we find that all variants have an |A|-headed vowel of some kind: examples include RP [aʊ], London English [æʊ] and 'refined' RP [ɑʊ]. Unfortunately, vowel weakening cannot be used to verify the structure of [aʊ] because this vowel does not usually reduce in unstressed positions.

We can be equally confident that |A| is non-headed in [əʊ]. The obvious clue is the schwa-like quality of the starting vowel, which we have already analysed as |A|. But there is also phonological evidence to consider. Historically, [əʊ] derives from two sources, Middle English [ɔː] (*no, home, ghost*) and Middle English [ɔu] (*know, soul, own*), both of which contain |A| and |U|. This gives us the structure we have proposed in (40b), assuming that both elements have survived into the present-day grammar. Meanwhile, there is also evidence from vowel weakening that [əʊ] contains |A|. In Tyneside English [əʊ] reduces to [ə] in weak syllables, for example *yellow* ['jelə] (cf. ['jeləʊ] in RP). And more generally there is the alternation [əʊ] ~ [ə] in, for example, *cust*[ə́ʊ]*dial* ~ *cust*[ə]*dy* and *pr*[ə́ʊ]*sody* ~ *pr*[ə]*sodic*. Because vowel weakening leaves behind a minimal expression containing just |A| (interpreted as [ə]), it follows that |A| must be present in the original full vowel [əʊ]. This |A| cannot be headed because [əʊ] is distinct from [aʊ], which does have headed |A|. Evidently, then, [əʊ] must have non-headed |A| in its strong position.

With a non-headed expression in its strong left-hand position, [əʊ] is unique among the English diphthongs – the other diphthongs all follow the convention of having a headed expression on the left and a non-headed one on the right. So clearly, [əʊ] does not conform to the general pattern. And yet this is not particularly surprising. Recall that a similar situation arose with the long monophthongs we analysed in §2.8.3, where we said that [iː uː ɑː ɔː] are all represented by headed expressions while [ɜː] has the non-headed structure |A|. And significantly, the rogue element is |A| in both cases. When discussing [ɜː] we noted that |A| may have a special status among the vowel elements, and now [əʊ] reinforces this same idea. The representations for [ɜː] and [əʊ] do suggest that |A| is inherently stronger than |I| or |U|, and it will be interesting to see whether ET can develop a means of expressing this in the grammar.

|A| diphthongs

Traditionally, RP is described as having three |A| diphthongs: [iə] in *beer*, [eə] in *fair* and [uə] in *tour*. (A fourth one, [ɔə] in *score*, is now obsolete.) These all have non-headed |A| in the dependent position of the branching nucleus. The |A| diphthongs are a feature of non-rhotic dialects like RP, and invariably occur in words with historical *r* in the spelling. They are represented as in (41).

(41) a. [iə]   b. [eə]   c. [uə]

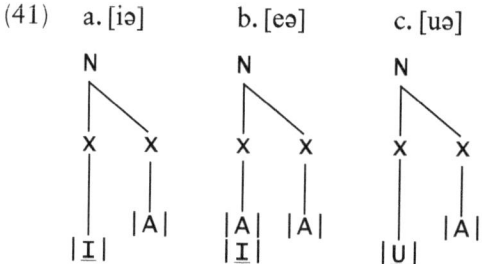

A characteristic of the |A| diphthongs is their tendency to become monophthongs. In the past this led to the vowel [ɔə] in *score* being reinterpreted as [ɔː]. It can also be seen in the widespread realisation of [eə] as [ɛː] in *fair*, as shown in (42a). We can speculate that this is driven by the desire to avoid interpreting |A| in the weak dependent position of the nucleus, since |A| is a naturally strong element. In some cases |A| is suppressed altogether, as shown in (42b); for example, Australian English [iə] in *beer* is regularly interpreted as [iː]. Another way to avoid interpreting |A| in the weak dependent position is to shift it to the strong head position, where it resides more naturally. The [uə] vowel in *poor* has undergone this change in Australia and New Zealand, where it is realised as [ɔː], and the same change is now taking place in British English too. This is illustrated in (42c).

(42) a. [eə] ~ [ɛː]   b. [iə] ~ [ɪː]   c. [uə] ~ [ɔː]

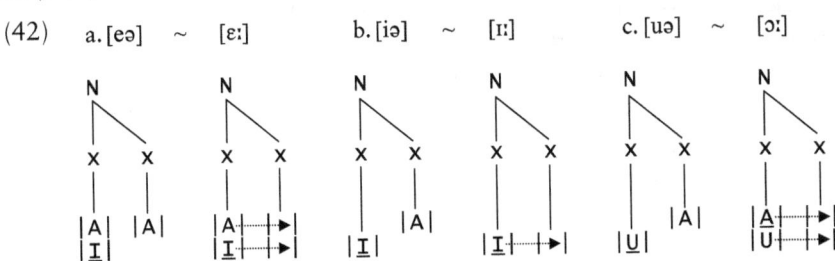

The |A| diphthongs are limited to non-rhotic dialects of English because they emerged as a result of the *r* loss process, which characterises these systems. The history and the representation of English *r* are discussed in Chapter 5.

2.9 SUMMARY

In this chapter we have seen how humans use the three acoustic patterns d*I*p, r*U*mp and m*A*ss to communicate information about vowels. These patterns act as acoustic cues to the presence of the abstract vowel elements |I U A|, which appear in vowel representations and characterise the phonological properties of vowel segments. |I U A| are interpretable alone or in combination. In languages with complex vowel systems, such as English, elements combine asymmetrically to form head-dependent relations within the segment. In the case of English we have noted that headed expressions are naturally strong and represent full vowels, whereas non-headed expressions are much weaker and naturally belong in weak positions such as unstressed syllables and the dependent position of a branching nucleus. In other words, the difference between heads and non-heads in segmental structure parallels a similar difference between heads and non-heads in prosodic structure. In fact this connection between segmental structure and prosodic structure is a central feature of ET. The idea is developed further in Chapter 5. Having described vowel structure in element terms, we next turn our attention to consonants.

FURTHER READING

Lass (1984) provides an overview of vowel system typology while Cruttenden (2001) offers a detailed survey of vowel realisations in different dialects of English. Quantal Theory is described in Stevens

(1989) and Dispersion Theory in Lindblom (1990). For an introduction to Dependency Phonology see Anderson and Ewen (1987). Discussions relating to the distribution of empty nuclei can be found in Charette (1991) and Scheer (2004). The data presented in this chapter are from the following sources: Hsin (2003) for vowel coalescence in Maga Rukai; Jones (1989) for monophthongisation in Middle English; Kubozono (2001) for monophthongisation in Japanese; Petterson and Wood (1987) for vowel weakening in Bulgarian; Simo Bobda (2007) for vowel realisation in varieties of African English.

REFERENCES

Anderson, John M. and Colin J. Ewen (1987), *Principles of Dependency Phonology*, Cambridge: Cambridge University Press.

Charette, Monik (1991), *Conditions on Phonological Government*, Cambridge: Cambridge University Press.

Cruttenden, Alan (2001), *Gimson's Pronunciation of English*, sixth edition, London: Arnold.

Harris, John (1994), *English Sound Structure*, Oxford: Blackwell.

Harris, John and Geoff Lindsey (1995), 'The elements of phonological representation', in J. Durand and F. Katamba (eds), *Frontiers of Phonology: Atoms, Structures, Derivations*, Harlow: Longman, pp. 34–79.

Harris, John and Geoff Lindsey (2000), 'Vowel patterns in mind and sound', in N. Burton-Roberts, P. Carr and G. Docherty (eds), *Phonological Knowledge: Conceptual and Empirical Issues*, Oxford: Oxford University Press, pp. 185–205.

Harris, John and Eno-Abasi Urua (2001), 'Lenition degrades information: consonant allophony in Ibibio', *Speech, Hearing and Language: Work in Progress* 13, 72–105.

Hsin, Tien-Hsin (2003), 'The mid vowels of Maga Rukai and their implications', *Journal of East Asian Linguistics* 12, 59–81.

Jones, Charles (1989), *A History of English Phonology*, London: Longman.

Kaye, Jonathan M. (1990) '"Coda" licensing', *Phonology* 7, 301–30.

Kubozono, Haruo (2001), 'On the markedness of diphthongs', unpublished manuscript, Kobe University.

Lass, Roger (1984), 'Vowel system universals and typology: prologue to theory', *Phonology Yearbook* 1, 75–112.

Lindblom, Bjorn (1990). 'Explaining phonetic variation: a sketch of the HandH theory', in W. Hardcastle and A. Marchal (eds), *Speech Production and Speech Modelling*, Dordrecht: Kluwer, pp. 403–39.

McMahon, April (2000), *Lexical Phonology and the History of English*, Cambridge: Cambridge University Press.

Petterson Thore and Sidney Wood (1987), 'Vowel reduction in Bulgarian and its implications for theories of vowel production: a review of the problem', *Folia Linguistica* 2–4, 261–79.

Scheer, Tobias (2004), *A Lateral Theory of Phonology*, Berlin and New York: Mouton de Gruyter.

Simo Bobda, Augustin (2007), 'Patterns of segment sequence simplification in some African Englishes', *World Englishes* 26.4, 411–23.

Stevens, Kenneth N. (1989), 'On the quantal nature of speech', *Journal of Phonetics* 17, 3–45.

Chapter 3
PLACE ELEMENTS IN CONSONANTS

3.1 Consonant–Vowel Unity

3.1.1 Shared Features

In Chapter 2 we saw how |I U A| function as the basic units of vowel structure. By referring to |I U A| and their headedness properties we can represent vowel contrasts and phonological processes involving vowels.

So far, nothing has been said about consonants. In *SPE*, different sets of features were used to describe consonants and vowels. And from a lay point of view this seems reasonable, particularly to speakers of languages with alphabetic writing systems, who are taught to distinguish between consonants and vowels from an early age. For example, English-speaking children learn spelling rules and play spelling games which differentiate between vowel letters and consonant letters. Students of phonetics are also encouraged to think of consonants and vowels in different terms: they learn that vowels are associated with an open vocal tract and a periodic sound wave, whereas consonants can be aperiodic and are produced with an obstructed vocal tract. Moreover, phonetic descriptions like this have influenced the development of phonological descriptions, which brings us back to *SPE* and its separate features for consonants and vowels.

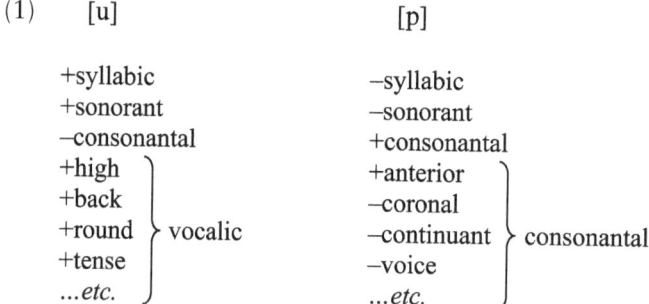

Petterson Thore and Sidney Wood (1987), 'Vowel reduction in Bulgarian and its implications for theories of vowel production: a review of the problem', *Folia Linguistica* 2–4, 261–79.

Scheer, Tobias (2004), *A Lateral Theory of Phonology*, Berlin and New York: Mouton de Gruyter.

Simo Bobda, Augustin (2007), 'Patterns of segment sequence simplification in some African Englishes', *World Englishes* 26.4, 411–23.

Stevens, Kenneth N. (1989), 'On the quantal nature of speech', *Journal of Phonetics* 17, 3–45.

Chapter 3

PLACE ELEMENTS IN CONSONANTS

3.1 Consonant–Vowel Unity

3.1.1 Shared Features

In Chapter 2 we saw how |I U A| function as the basic units of vowel structure. By referring to |I U A| and their headedness properties we can represent vowel contrasts and phonological processes involving vowels.

So far, nothing has been said about consonants. In *SPE*, different sets of features were used to describe consonants and vowels. And from a lay point of view this seems reasonable, particularly to speakers of languages with alphabetic writing systems, who are taught to distinguish between consonants and vowels from an early age. For example, English-speaking children learn spelling rules and play spelling games which differentiate between vowel letters and consonant letters. Students of phonetics are also encouraged to think of consonants and vowels in different terms: they learn that vowels are associated with an open vocal tract and a periodic sound wave, whereas consonants can be aperiodic and are produced with an obstructed vocal tract. Moreover, phonetic descriptions like this have influenced the development of phonological descriptions, which brings us back to *SPE* and its separate features for consonants and vowels.

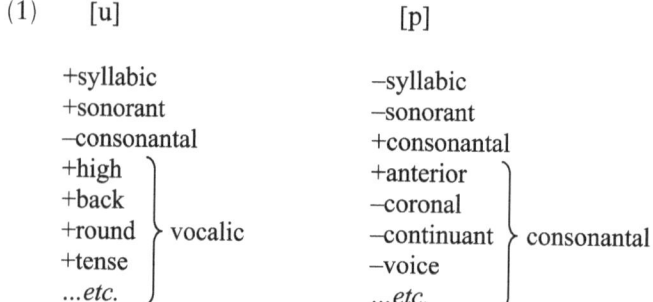

In the feature matrices in (1), the major class features [±syll], [±son] and [±cons] divide segments into consonants and vowels. But in order to describe a consonant or a vowel in full, we must refer to the relevant consonant or vowel features too: for example, [u] uses vowel features such as [±back], [±round] while [p] has consonant features such as [±cont], [±voice]. Because consonants and vowels are articulated differently, most consonant features are irrelevant to vowel descriptions and vice versa. It is true that some vowel features are responsible for creating consonant distinctions, for example velars are [+high] while uvulars are [−high]; but overall, the effect of using separate features is to present consonants and vowels as being different in kind.

The problem with this approach is that consonants and vowels actually have properties in common. This is clear from the way that assimilation can result in a property being shared between a consonant and a vowel. For example, in Mapila Malayalam a word-final empty nucleus is interpreted as the default vowel [ɨ], as shown in (2a). But when [ɨ] comes after a round vowel (2b) or a labial consonant (2c) earlier in the word, it is itself rounded to [u].

(2) a. [kaḍalɨ]   (*[kaḍal])   'sea'
       [ḍressɨ]   (*[ḍress])   'dress'

    b. [nuːru]   (*[nuːr], *[nuːrɨ])   'hundred'
       [onnu]   (*[onn], *[onnɨ])   'one'

    c. [ɕaːvu]   (*[ɕaːv], *[ɕaːvɨ])   'death'
       [jappu]   (*[japp], *[jappɨ])   'pound'

[ɨ] → [u] is an assimilation effect triggered by rounding or labiality in the same word. And because round vowels and labial consonants both act as triggers, they must share the same triggering property – and importantly, the same feature to represent that property. Yet traditional feature theories are unable to make a natural connection between vowel rounding and consonant labiality because they involve different features: labiality is represented by [+ant −cor] and rounding by [+round]. This gives the (false) impression that labiality and rounding have nothing in common, and that [ɨ] → [u] rounding is just an arbitrary change.

Some feature theories have responded to this problem by abandoning separate features for consonants and vowels, and instead using shared features which capture the properties that are common to consonants and vowels. The advantage of shared features is that they can make a non-arbitrary connection between a phonological process and its context. For example, if [+round] is used to represent labiality in consonants and also rounding in vowels, then the rounding process in (2) need no longer be treated as accidental: a vowel becomes [+round] when there is a [+round] segment in the context. If our goal is to model a grammar that can explain phonological behaviour rather than just describe it, then clearly there is an important role for shared features.

3.1.2 Shared Elements

Consonant–vowel unity is an important concept in ET too, where the same elements are used to represent consonants and vowels. This means we can expect to see the vowel elements |I U A| appearing in consonants as well as in vowels. It also means that other elements besides |I U A| should turn up in vowel representations. In fact, if our analysis of vowels in Chapter 2 had included properties such as nasalisation, pharyngealisation and tone, then we would have needed to employ consonant elements in addition to |I U A|. In Chapter 4 we will see how the consonant elements |ʔ H L| contribute to vowel representations, but for the moment let us focus on consonant structure, and in particular, on the role of |I U A| in describing consonant place.

We know that |I U A| are identified by their resonance properties, and that resonance is associated with vowel quality. But as we are about to see, the same resonance properties also provide information about place of articulation in consonants. So there are actually two ways of describing place distinctions: in articulatory terms the difference is indeed one of place, for example [p] has labial place, [ʃ] has palatal place, and so on; and in acoustic terms the difference is one of resonance, for example [p] has |U| resonance, [ʃ] has |I| resonance, and so on. Now, because elements represent acoustic patterns, it makes sense that we should classify consonants according to their acoustic properties. But because most readers are probably more familiar with traditional place labels like labial and palatal, we will also use these terms in this book. It should be remembered, however, that these labels refer to phonological classes and not to articulation. In ET, the way a segment is articulated is irrelevant to the way it is represented in the grammar.

As a result of employing shared elements, ET blurs the division between consonants and vowels, at least at the segmental level.

However, the consonant–vowel split is still expressed by syllable structure: vowels occupy the syllable nucleus while consonants belong in non-nuclear (onset or coda) positions. And this has an important implication for ET, namely, that if the same elements appear in consonants and vowels then each element expression must have at least two different interpretations – a vowel interpretation (when it is syllabified in a nucleus) and a consonant interpretation (when it appears outside the nucleus). As we will see, this dual interpretation can boost the grammar's ability to express natural classes of sounds.

3.2 Glides

3.2.1 Phonetic Properties

Using syllable structure as the criterion for distinguishing between consonants and vowels helps us to understand the nature of the glides [j w]. This is because glides and vowels are distinguished mainly by their distribution: vowels belong in the syllable nucleus and glides in non-nuclear positions. In other respects, they are remarkably similar. Notably, glides and vowels have almost the same segmental properties, suggesting that they contain the same features or elements. Let us therefore represent glides using the vowel elements |I U A|. Below we will consider the phonological evidence for this, but first let us look at the physical properties of glides.

Vowels and glides have much in common phonetically: both are produced with a relatively open vocal tract, and both can be identified from their formant structure. There are some minor differences between them too, such as a small difference in duration, but these are not important as far as linguistic information is concerned. So let us focus on the phonetic similarities between glides and vowels. As (3) shows, [i j] and [u w] form vowel–glide pairs, where the segments in each pair are represented by the same element. (Another vowel–glide pair [ə ɹ] will be described in Chapter 5.)

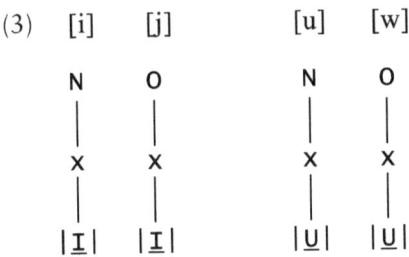

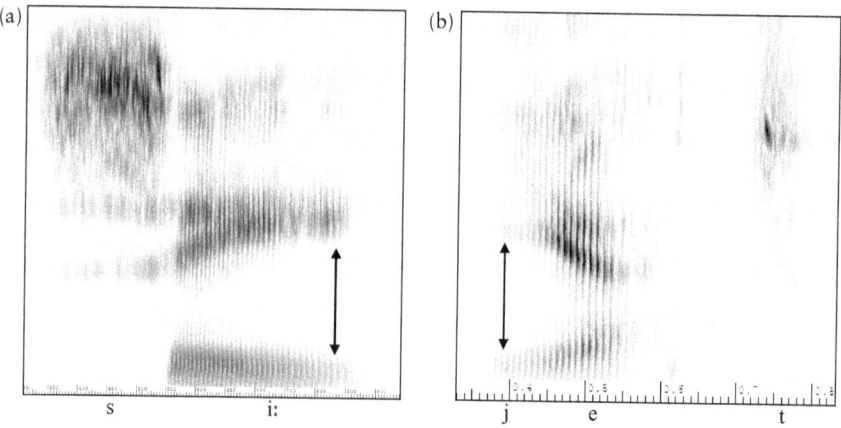

Figure 3.1 dIp *in* [i] *and* [j]. *(a) Spectrogram of see* [siː]; *(b) Spectrogram of yet* [jet]

Predictably, the segments in each pair also have similar acoustic patterns: the |I| segments [i j] both display a *dIp* pattern while the |U| segments [u w] both have *rUmp*. First, compare the formant patterns in the English words *see* [siː] and *yet* [jet], as shown in Figure 3.1. The vowel of *see* [siː] in Figure 3.1(a) has a high F2 which converges with F3 to create the *dIp* pattern associated with |I|. The arrow highlights the characteristic dip in energy between F1 and F2. Now look at Figure 3.1(b), which shows that [j] begins with the same *dIp* pattern before starting its transition into the next vowel. This acoustic similarity between [i] and [j] is no coincidence; it tells us that the same |I| element is present in both. Likewise, [u w] both display |U| resonance, as shown in Figure 3.2. The vowel of *you* [juː] in Figure 3.2(a) shows a concentration of energy at the lower end of the spectrum. This is the *rUmp* pattern associated with |U|. And as expected, [w] in Figure 3.2(b) produces the same pattern. As before, acoustic similarity suggests phonological similarity – [u] and [w] are different interpretations of the same |U| element. ET is able to make this association between acoustics and segmental structure because elements are linked to acoustic patterns in the speech signal. However, phonetic evidence alone is not enough to establish that [j w] are the consonant equivalents of [i u]. So let us now consider the phonological evidence.

3.2.2 Vowel/Glide Alternations

Although [j w] must be classified as consonants because they occupy the syllable onset, they nevertheless contain only vowel elements in

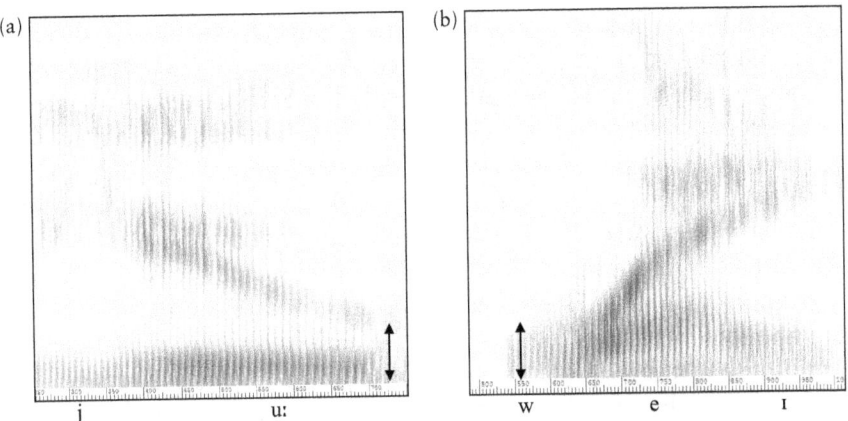

Figure 3.2 rUmp *in [u] and [w]. (a) Spectrogram of you [juː]; (b) Spectrogram of way [weɪ]*

their structure. And this makes them exceptional, since most consonants have one or more consonant elements in their structure (which will be introduced in Chapter 4). At the same time, this does explain why glides are considered to be the most vowel-like of consonants: if they are represented only by vowel elements, then we expect them to have acoustic properties similar to those of vowels. The absence of |ʔ H L| makes glides unstable, predisposing them to alternate with vowels. In Sanskrit, for example, the verb root *i-* 'go' is interpreted as [i] before a consonant (*i-tha* [itʰa] 'go-2.pers.pl.') and as [j] before a vowel (*i-anti* [janti] 'go-3.pers.pl.'). Clearly, the [i] ~ [j] alternation is purely phonological, since *i-* carries the same linguistic information whether it is pronounced as a vowel or a glide. In (4) we follow the convention of treating *i-* as a vowel, which is then reinterpreted as a glide when it is followed by another vowel. What we have therefore is a glide formation process driven by a preference for CV sequences over V.V sequences.

(4) a. [i-tha] 'go-2.pers.pl.'   b. [janti] 'go-3.pers.pl.'

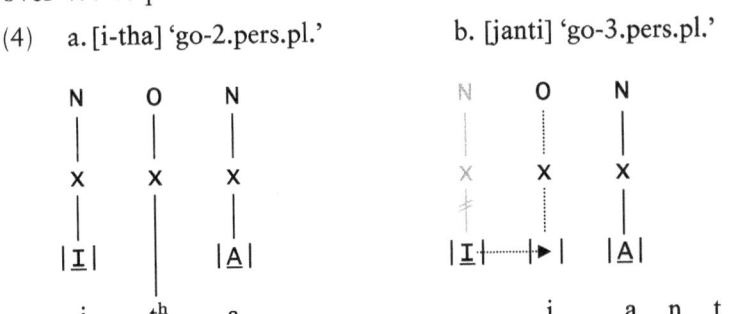

In (4a) the verb root with the structure |I| is interpreted as [i]. In (4b), however, the same interpretation would create an ill-formed vowel sequence *[ia], so it is avoided. Instead, |I| is interpreted as a glide in the adjacent onset, producing the form [janti] with a grammatical CV sequence [ja]. We need not be too concerned about where the onset position for [j] comes from; it makes no difference to our analysis whether it was introduced in order to accommodate [j] or whether it was already present in the structure. The point is that speakers must try to pronounce as much lexical information as possible, and they exploit the phonological structure however they can in order to do this.

Spanish also uses glide formation to eliminate vowel sequences. As in Sanskrit, it has an alternation involving the |I| segments [i] ~ [j], as shown in (5a); but additionally, there is an alternation between the |U| segments [u] ~ [w], as in (5b).

(5) a. [nérvio]   *nervio*   'nerve'
       [nervjóso] *nervioso* 'nervous (masc.)'

   b. [kontinuár] *continuar* 'continue'
       [kontínwa] *continua* 'continuous (fem.)'

In this case the alternations are conditioned by internal factors like stress and morphological structure, and also by external factors like speech rate. So for example, [j] is preferred in fast or casual speech (*mi amor* [mja.mor] 'my love'), while [i] occurs in more deliberate speech (*mi amor* [mi.a.mor] 'my love'). So far, we have only mentioned glides containing a single resonance element. But in some languages glides can have two elements. In French, for instance, |I U| can be interpreted as the front rounded vowel [y] (*pur* [pyʁ] 'pure') or as the corresponding glide [ɥ] (*huitre* [ɥitʁ] 'oyster'). [y] ~ [ɥ] alternation is observed in verbs such as [ty] *tue* 'kills', [tɥe] (*[tye]) *tuer* 'to kill'.

3.2.3 Glide Formation in English

Vowel/glide alternations show how the same element expression can be interpreted as a consonant or a vowel. But there is also a third possibility, illustrated by English, in which one expression is interpreted in both a nucleus and an onset, creating a vowel–glide sequence. This occurs medially in words with internal morphology (*high*[j]*est, go*[w]*ing*) and also within a phrase (*high* [j]*up, go* [w]*away*). The process reinterprets V.V sequences as V.CV sequences by extending the first vowel into the following onset position.

|I U A| AS PLACE ELEMENTS

(6) a. [i:] → [i:j] *ski*[j]*er*   [u:] → [u:w] *chew*[w]*y*
                    see [j]*out*   *through* [w]*it*

   b. [ɪ] → [ɪj] *happy*[j]*est*   [ʊ] → [ʊw] *Hindu*[w]*ism*
                  the [j]*end*   *to* [w]*eat*

   c. [aɪ] → [aɪj] *high*[j]*est*   [əʊ] → [əʊw] *go*[w]*ing*
                    high [j]*up*   *go* [w]*away*

Notice that the active |I| or |U| element may come from a full vowel (*ski*[j]*er*), from a weak vowel (*happy*[j]*est*), or from a vowel occupying the second slot in a diphthong (*high*[j]*est*). When it extends into the onset position it is interpreted as a headed element – recall that, in general, simplex expressions are headed by default. The glide formation process is illustrated in (7).

(7) a. *high up* [haɪ ˈjʌp]   b. *go away* [gəʊ wəˈweɪ]

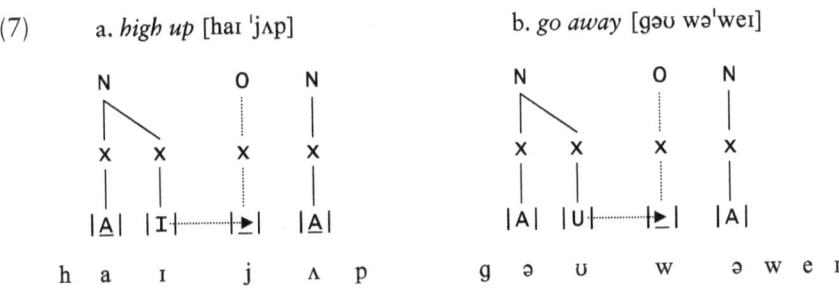

No new melodic material is introduced during glide formation because the glide element is already in the preceding nucleus. An advantage of analysing glide formation in this way is that we can extend it to another hiatus-breaking process in English, linking *r*. In Chapter 5 we will analyse linking *r* as glide formation involving the element |A|.

3.3 |I U A| as Place Elements

We have just seen how simplex |I| and |U| can be interpreted as the glides [j] and [w] respectively. But in fact, the vowel elements have a more general role in consonants too. In the remainder of this chapter we will learn how |I U A| function as place elements when they appear in compound expressions.

In §3.1 we stressed the importance of consonant–vowel unity for capturing segmental patterns, and noted that unified elements are central to the ET approach. However, some feature theories have also worked towards consonant–vowel unity too. The unified features listed in (8) are taken from the set of features employed by Clements and Hume (1995).

(8) [labial]   labial consonants and rounded vowels
    [coronal]   coronal consonants and front vowels
    [dorsal]   velar consonants and back vowels

Besides having intuitive appeal, unified features are able to express generalisations which appear arbitrary in *SPE*, where separate features were used for vowels and consonants. We can demonstrate this with a simple example of palatalisation in which [si] is reinterpreted as [ʃi]. From an *SPE* viewpoint, [ʃi] looks like a random variation on [si] because the theory cannot express any relation between the palatalised consonant [ʃ], which is [+cor −ant], and the triggering vowel [i], which is [+high −back]. But by employing the unified feature [coronal], which describes frontness in [i] and also palatality in [ʃ], we can analyse [si] → [ʃi] as a simple [coronal] assimilation. Recall that we made a similar point in §3.1.1 using the example of rounding and labiality in Mapila Malayalam. One shortcoming of the unified features in (8) is that they only describe place properties. This is partly because they are based on articulation, and articulatory properties other than place are not usually shared between consonants and vowels. This means that a feature system with unified place features must still use non-unified features in addition, in order to describe other segmental properties. For example, consonants (but not vowels) have manner features such as [continuant] while vowels (but not consonants) have aperture features such as [open]. In ET, on the other hand, consonant–vowel unity is maximised in the sense that all elements can potentially appear in consonants and vowels. This is consistent with our earlier point that any element is interpretable in any syllabic position.

Returning to |I| and |U| as place elements, we know that headed |I| is interpreted as the palatal glide [j]. Let us now generalise this by saying that headed |I| contributes palatal resonance to any consonant in which it appears. That is, headed |I| defines the natural class of palatals and is present in palatal and palatalised segments such as [ç ɟ ʃ kʲ ɲ j ʎ]. Note that, although sounds such as [ʃ] are phonetically palatoalveolar, they can be included in the class of headed |I| segments if it can be shown that they pattern with other palatals. The |U| element can be treated in a similar way. We know that headed |U| is associated with labiality, because in onsets it is interpreted as the labial glide [w]. Extending this to other consonants, we can say that headed |U| defines the natural class of labials, so it is present in labial and labialised consonants such as [ɸ b f kʷ m w β]. Notice that labiodentals like [f ɱ ʋ] can also be included in this class as long as they pattern with other labials. At this point it is worth noting that |I| and |U| have much in common with the features [acute] and [grave], which belong to the set of acoustic features proposed by Jakobson and Halle (§1.2): like the |I| element, [acute] is associated with a concentration of energy at higher frequencies, and like the |U| element, [grave] represents a concentration of low-frequency energy. And in the same way that [acute] and [grave] were originally devised as a pair of opposing features, there is a polar relation between |I| and |U| which we will explore in §5.3.1.

Before we look at the behaviour of |I U A| as place elements, it should be pointed out that this is an area where opinions differ. Like feature theory, ET comes in several versions, and although these different versions agree on most core ideas such as consonant–vowel unity and the need for monovalent elements, they disagree on certain issues including how to represent particular place contrasts. The role of headedness is also a matter for ongoing debate. The reader should be aware, therefore, that although the version of ET described in this book is backed by solid phonological evidence, alternative analyses and explanations will sometimes be possible. These will be mentioned where appropriate.

3.4 THE |I| ELEMENT

3.4.1 Palatals

The evidence that palatals contain headed |I̲| comes from assimilation processes in which palatal consonants interact with front vowels. Phonological effects like this indicate that both classes share the same headed |I̲| element. For example, in Ngiyambaa dental [d̪ n̪] are palatalised to [ɟ ɲ] respectively after [i] and [j], producing the alternations in (9). The diminutive suffix [-ɟul]~[-d̪ul] and the present tense marker [-ɲa]~[-n̪a] alternate according to the presence (9a) or absence (9b) of a preceding |I̲|.

(9) a. miri-ɟul   'dog'
       buraaj-ɟul   'child'
       d̪ari-ɲa   'disappear'

    b. mura-d̪ul   'spear'
       baamir-d̪ul 'tall'
       waṟa-n̪a   'stand'

Speakers produce the palatalised forms [-ɟul] and [-ɲa] as a result of allowing headed |I| to spread from a preceding [i] or [j]; and if there is no local |I| then we get non-palatalised [-d̪ul] and [-n̪a]. A similar pattern occurs in Slovak, where coronal [t d n l] palatalise to [c ɟ ɲ ʎ] before [j] or any of the |I| vowels [i e æ], as illustrated in (10).

(10) bara[n]   'ram'   bara[ɲ]-iar   'shepherd'
      hra[d]   'castle' hra[ɟ]-e   'castle' (locative singular)
      Egyp[t]   'Egypt'   Egyp[c]-[æ]n   'Egyptian'

In many languages, palatalisation produces the strident palatoalveolars [ʃ ʒ tʃ dʒ]. For example, some dialects of Brazilian Portuguese have developed [tʃ dʒ] realisations of [t d] before [i ɪ ĩ j]. Headed |I| is active here too, indicating that palatoalveolars also have headed |I| in their representation. As (11) shows, [t d] are not palatalised in other dialects of Portuguese.

(11)   *Brazilian (Rio)*   *European*
                Portuguese   *Portuguese*
      tipo   ˈtʃipʊ   ˈtipʊ   'type'
      arte   ˈahtʃɪ   ˈahtɪ   'art'
      patio   ˈpatʃju   ˈpatju   'yard'
      tinta   ˈtʃĩtə   ˈtĩtə   'paint'
      ditto   ˈdʒitʊ   ˈditʊ   'said'
      índio   ˈĩdʒju   ˈĩdju   'Indian'

There will be more to say about palatal resonance in §3.7.4. Also, in §3.8 we will discuss the relation between affricates such as [tʃ] and simple stops such as [t]. For the moment we will simply treat affricates as regular members of the stop series.

3.4.2 Coronals with |I|

In some languages, coronals and palatals form a natural class; that is, they have a similar distribution and pattern together in phonological processes. This suggests that, like palatals, coronals contain |I|. Of course, palatals and coronals also contrast, and later we will see how ET distinguishes them. But first let us consider the evidence for grouping palatals and coronals as a natural class of |I| segments. In Fèʔfèʔ-Bamileke we find the pattern of reduplication shown in (12).

(12) a. to   ti-to   'to punch'
         ben   pi-pen   'to accept'
         za   zi-za   'to eat'

b. si:m   si-si: (*sɨ-si:)   'to spoil'
    te:n   ti-te: (*tɨ-te:)   'to remove'
    cen   ci-cɛn (*cɨ-cɛn)   'to moan'

The vowel of the reduplicative prefix is usually [ɨ], shown in (12a). But [ɨ] is reinterpreted as [i] if the next syllable contains [i] or if the next syllable contains any front vowel from the set [i e ɛ] and the preceding consonant belongs to the unified class of palatals and coronals [t d s z n l c ɟ ʃ ʒ ɲ j], as in (12b). We know that the front vowels [i e ɛ] contain the |I| element, as do the palatals [c ɟ ʃ ʒ ɲ j]; but if palatals and coronals behave as a natural class then we can assume that the coronals [t d s z n l] must also contain |I|. This allows us to state the generalisation in Feʔfeʔ-Bamileke as follows: the prefix vowel is realised as [i] in the context of any |I| segment.

Korean is another language in which palatals and coronals behave as a single class. In syllables of the shape CjV, [j] cannot co-occur with a front vowel [i e ɛ], a palatal stop [c c' cʰ] or a coronal obstruent [t t' tʰ s s']. This renders syllables such as *[mje], *[cʰja] and *[t'ju] ungrammatical. By assuming that front vowels, palatals and coronals all contain |I|, it becomes possible to analyse this as a straightforward dissimilation: the |I| glide [j] cannot co-occur with another segment containing |I|. Coronals in Lahu also behave in a way which indicates that they contain |I|. (13a) shows the vowel system of Lahu, in which there is a distinction between front, central and back vowels. But interestingly, the central vowels [ɨ ə] never follow the palatals [tʃ tʃʰ ʃ j] or the alveolars [t tʰ ts tsʰ d n l]. In these contexts, [ɨ ə] are interpreted as [i e] respectively, as the forms in (13b) demonstrate.

(13) a. i   ɨ   u
          e   ə   o
          ɛ   a   ɔ

      b. ni   'look at, try doing'   (*nɨ,*nə)
          tí   'only'   (*tɨ,*tə)
          le   'substance questions'   (*lɨ,*lə)
          ʃí   'yellow, golden'   (*ʃɨ,*ʃə)
          gú-jiʔ   'mat'   (*jɨʔ,*jəʔ)

This pattern has now become lexicalised, but it appears to have resulted from an earlier vowel-fronting process in which |I| spread from the coronal or palatal consonant to [ɨ ə]. And if we take [ɨ ə] to have the same structures in Lahu as they have in English (§2.8.4), then we can represent the fronting process as in (14).

(14)   [ɨ] → [i]   [ə] → [e]

|I⃛▶| |I| I⃛▶| |I|
| | | | |A| |A|

The distribution of [ɨ ə] and [i e] in Lahu has a straightforward explanation if we assume that coronals as well as palatals contain the |I| element.

A similar vowel-fronting process took place in the history of Lhasa Tibetan, where [a o u] were reinterpreted as [ɛ ø y] when they acquired |I| from a following word-final coronal consonant. Later the word-final coronal dropped but the |I| resonance from this consonant was preserved in the preceding vowel. The effects of the process can be seen by comparing the Lhasa and Balti dialects of Tibetan in (15a). Unlike Lhasa, Balti has remained close to the written form of the language by resisting vowel fronting and final consonant deletion.

(15)   Written   Lhasa   Balti
           Tibetan   Tibetan   Tibetan
    a.   ras   rɛ̀ɛ   ras   'cloth'
           bal   phɛɛ   bal   'wool'
           chos   chøø̃   chhos   'religion'
           bod   phøø̃   bodh   'Tibet'
           jul   jyy   jul   'country'
           bdun   tỹỹ   bdun   'seven'

    b.   gjag   jaà   hjag   'yak'
           goŋ   qhõõ   'price'
           nub   nuù   nubkha   'west'

As with vowel fronting in Lahu, these vowel changes in Lhasa Tibetan result from the spreading of |I|. The process is illustrated in (16).

(16)   [a] → [ɛ]   [o] → [ø]   [u] → [y]

◀⃛I	I		◀⃛I	I		◀⃛I	I
A	|A| |A	|A|			
			|U	|U| |U	|U

As the examples in (15b) demonstrate, vowels did not change before labials or velars. From the fact that fronting took place only before coronals it is apparent that in Lhasa Tibetan, just as in Korean and

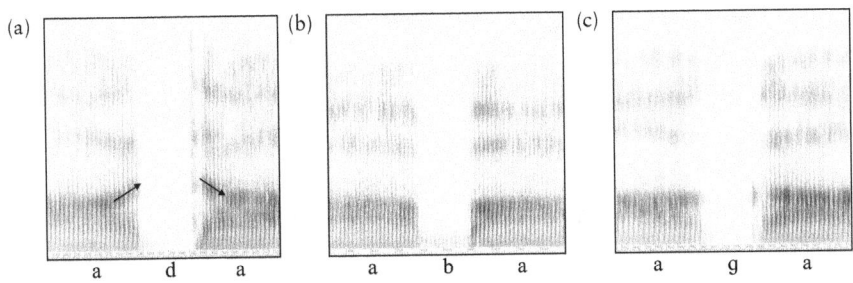

Figure 3.3 Formant patterns for [d], [b] and [g]. (a) Spectrogram of [ada]; (b) Spectrogram of [aba]; (c) Spectrogram of [aga]

Lahu, coronal resonance is represented by |I|. In these languages, coronals and palatals form a natural class of |I| segments.

Having seen that coronals can behave phonologically as |I| segments, we now turn to the phonetic evidence. There are some coronals that display the acoustic cues we associate with |I|, that is, a high F2 and a *dIp* spectral pattern. For instance, there are languages in which coronal stops are distinguished from labial and velar stops by their higher F2 transitions – compare the formant transitions for coronal [d] in Figure 3.3(a) with those for [b] in Figure 3.3(b) and [g] in Figure 3.3(c). In [d] F2 rises sharply during the transition from the preceding vowel and then falls again into the following vowel, as indicated by the arrows. No similar movement of F2 is observed in [b] or [g].

Some coronal fricatives also have a high F2, indicating that they too contain |I|. The formant pattern for [z] in Figure 3.4(a) is similar to the pattern for [d], with F2 rising into the consonant then falling again into the next vowel. The palatal fricatives [ʒ ʝ] in Figures 3.4(b) and 3.4(c) also show this pattern, but in the case of [ʒ ʝ] the movement of F2 involves bigger and more rapid changes in frequency. This exaggerated F2 pattern in the palatals carries the same linguistic information as before, the presence of |I|, but gives it greater prominence. In ET, acoustic prominence of this kind suggests a headed element – recall that the physical properties of a head are stronger than those of a non-head. We will therefore employ headedness to distinguish palatals from coronals, the difference in their headedness reflecting a difference in the strength of their acoustic cues: coronals have a high F2 represented by non-headed |I|, while palatals have an even higher F2 represented by headed |I|.

The difference in headedness between palatals and coronals mirrors a difference in their phonological character. Palatals are inherently strong as a result of being headed; and so they are often

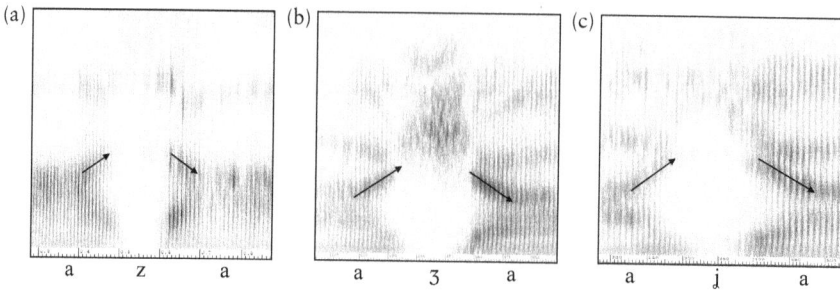

Figure 3.4 Formant patterns for [z], [ʒ] and [j]. (a) Spectrogram of [aza]; (b) Spectrogram of [aʒa]; (c) Spectrogram of [aja].

active in assimilation processes and remain palatal under most conditions. By contrast, coronals are weak because they are non-headed; this is clear from the way they are frequently targeted by phonological processes and tend to lose their coronal resonance through assimilation. Coronals, unlike palatals, are also favoured in weak (neutralising) contexts, which again can be explained by their non-headed status. This last point is demonstrated by a historical change in Mon, in which the word-final palatals [c ɲ] in Old Mon weakened to coronal [t n], respectively, in Middle and Modern Mon.

(17)   Old Mon   Middle/Modern Mon

       *tɗaːc   (t)ɗat   'to taste sweet'
       *klaːɲ   klan   'to lick'
       *duːɲ   dun   'bamboo'

There are at least two reasons for treating this sound change as a form of weakening. First, word-final position is a classic weakening context where most processes are of the lenition type. Second, the change from a headed palatal to a non-headed coronal involves a loss of headedness, which we have already analysed as a form of weakening – recall from Chapter 2 that vowel weakening always produces a non-headed expression, as in dr|A|ma → dr|A|matic. Similar examples are found in some Australian languages, where a contrast between palatal and coronal is neutralised in favour of coronal. For instance, Guugu Yimidhirr has a lexical contrast between palatal [ɲ] and coronal [n̪], but word-finally only non-headed [n̪] can appear (see also Ngiyambaa in §3.6.2).

From the observations we have made about coronals, it is tempting to conclude that coronals are always represented by non-headed |I|. But unfortunately, this turns out to be too broad a generalisation.

Although we have seen evidence that coronals have non-headed |I| in Lahu, Lhasa Tibetan, Korean and the other languages described above, it is not possible to extend this to all coronals in all languages. In fact, if we were to group all coronals together into a single category, we would obscure many of the phonological differences that exist between them. Compared with place categories such as labial and velar, which are fairly narrow and can be used unambiguously, coronal is a more general term covering a range of places including dental, alveolar, postalveolar, palatoalveolar and retroflex. And importantly, there are languages that make a contrast between some of these different types of coronals, which is something the grammar cannot capture if it represents all coronals uniformly as non-headed |I|. Furthermore, if we say that all coronals are represented in the same way, then we are, in effect, making the claim that coronals show the same behaviour in all languages, which is not the case. So at this point, all we can say is that |I| represents coronal resonance in some languages but not all. In §3.6.2 we will analyse another group of languages in which coronals pattern as |A| segments. Before that, we turn our attention to the natural class of |U| consonants.

3.5 The |U| Element

3.5.1 Labials

As we have noted, |U| represents labial resonance not just in the labial glide [w] but also in other labial consonants. We know that labials contain |U| because in many languages they interact with round vowels, which are represented by the same element |U|. For example, we have seen that Mapila Malayalam has an assimilation process in which |U| spreads from a labial consonant or a round vowel to a word-final empty nucleus (§3.1.1). This empty nucleus must be phonetically realised, because the language does not allow consonants in word-final position. Recall that the empty nucleus is usually interpreted as the default vowel [ɨ] (18a), but if the word contains a labial consonant (18b) or a round vowel (18c), [ɨ] acquires |U| and is rounded to [u].

(18) a. pal   [palɨ]   'milk'
        pand   [pandɨ]   'shake'

    b. japp   [jappu]   'pound'
       isla:m [isla:mu] 'Islam'

c. unn   [unnu]   'dine!'
    onn   [onnu]   'one'

Whether the source of |U| is a consonant (19a) or a vowel (19b), the assimilation process is the same: |U| extends along its tier to the empty nucleus where it is interpreted as a round vowel. (Note that [m] in (19a) also contains the nasal element |L|, which will be described in Chapter 4.)

(19)   a. [islaːmu] 'Islam'   b. [unnu] 'dine!'

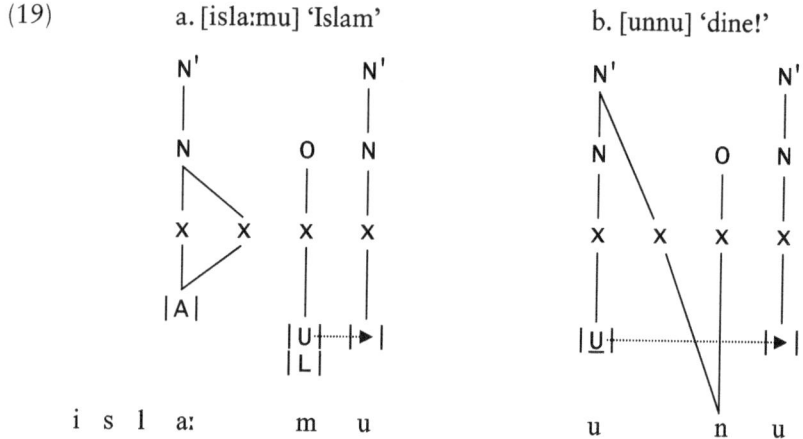

A similar |U|-spreading process occurs in Garifuna. As in Mapila Malayalam, a word-final empty nucleus must be pronounced; in this case the default realisation is [i] (*inglés* [i'glesi] 'English'). But after a labial [p b m f w] the default vowel becomes [u] (*pásam* ['pasamu] 'possum'), again as a result of |U| from the labial consonant being interpreted as a round vowel in the empty nucleus. Notice that in Garifuna the |U| class includes the labiodental [f].

Cantonese confirms that labial consonants and round vowels both have |U|. This language has a distributional restriction preventing |U| from occurring more than once in a morpheme (most morphemes in Cantonese consist of one syllable). Segments with |U| include the labials [p m f w], the labialised velar stop [kʷ] and the round vowels [o u ø y]. The condition bans morphemes containing two labials, hence *[pim] *[fap], and morphemes in which a labial consonant follows a round vowel, hence *[om] *[øp]. Sequences such as *[fø] and *[kʷy] are also ungrammatical, though the condition does allow a labial onset to be followed by a back vowel, e.g. [mo] 'fog'. Loanwords and onomatopoeic words are not subject to this co-occurrence restriction.

3.5.2 Velars

In some languages, velars and labials pattern together as a natural class. This suggests that velars, like labials, contain |U|. It may be a little surprising to learn that velars and labials share the same resonance element, given that they are so different in articulation. But in fact there is a long tradition of treating velars and labials as related categories. There are two reasons for this: first, we see labials and velars interacting phonologically, and second, they have acoustic properties in common. For example, Jakobson's feature [grave] that we mentioned in §3.3 describes sounds which have most of their energy in the lower part of the spectrum; [grave] therefore brings together the 'peripheral' categories of labial and velar whilst excluding the 'medial' categories of palatal and dental, which are [acute]. The same groupings can be expressed using standard articulatory features by employing a geometry such as the one shown in (20), where a peripheral node dominates [labial] in labial consonants and [dorsal] in velar consonants.

(20)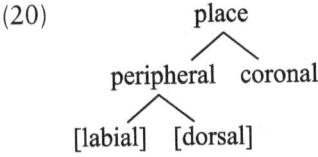

The peripheral node makes it possible to refer to non-coronals as a group without having to involve the negative feature [−coronal] − which is a useful development, as most feature theories now consider [coronal] to be monovalent. This allows the grammar to describe processes which target labials and velars but not coronals. For example, consonant weakening in Old English affected voiced labial stops (*beber* [bever] 'beaver') and voiced velar stops (*būgan* [buːɣan] 'bow') but not voiced coronals (*hydan* [hydan] (*[hyðan]) 'hide').

In ET terms, labials and velars form a natural class of |U| segments. (Note that not all versions of ET analyse labials and velars in this way. According to one tradition, labials are viewed as |U| segments while velars have empty or unspecified resonance − see, for example, Harris and Lindsey (1995).) Later we will see how the grammar distinguishes between labial |U| and velar |U|, but first let us consider the phonological reasons for grouping labials and velars as a natural class. Many languages show fossilised evidence of earlier sound changes involving an active class of labials and velars. In fifteenth-century Korean, for example, [ɨ] was rounded to [u] before [m p pʰ k kʰ]. And if we assume that |U| is present in labial and velar consonants, as well as in round vowels, the process can be understood as a simple assimilation: [ɨ] rounds to [u] by acquiring |U| from a following labial [m p pʰ] or velar [k kʰ]. The process created forms such as ətip [ətup] 'dark' and təik [təuk] 'more'. As expected, vowels were unchanged before coronals or palatals.

There is also evidence that labials and velars pattern together in English. We know from the spelling of words such as *climb* and *sing* that the homorganic clusters [mb] and [ŋg] were once pronounced morpheme-finally (in general, current spelling reflects Middle English pronunciation). But by the end of the sixteenth century these clusters had reduced to [m] and [ŋ] respectively, giving [klaɪm(b)] and [sɪŋ(g)]. Although the loss of final [b] predates the loss of final [g], we can assume that both are examples of the same effect, namely, the simplification of voiced clusters containing |U|. First the labial cluster [mb] reduced to [m], and then at a later time the velar cluster [ŋg] reduced to [ŋ]. Because other clusters were unaffected – coronal [nd] (*mend, wind*) and palatal [ndʒ] (e.g. *range, singe*) have survived into modern English – we can understand this as a pattern which specifically targeted the class of |U| segments. Lardil is another system in which |U| consonants pattern as a group. Labials and velars in Lardil have a limited distribution, occurring only before a vowel ([pirŋen] 'woman') or a homorganic consonant ([ɲampit] 'humpy'). This means that |U| consonants cannot appear word-finally, which explains alternations such as [ŋalu(k)] ~ [ŋaluk-in] 'story'. And because labials and velars behave in parallel, the grammar needs a way of referring to them as a natural class.

The labial–velar relationship is also evident from historical changes in which labial consonants have become velars and vice versa. For example, velar–coronal sequences became labial–coronal sequences during the development of Romanian from Latin.

(21) | Latin | Romanian | |
|---|---|---|
| la[k]tem | la[p]te | 'milk' |
| no[k]tem | noa[p]te | 'night' |
| pe[k]tus | pie[p]t | 'chest' |
| o[k]to | o[p]t | 'eight' |
| li[ŋ]num | li[m]n | 'wood' |

The shift from velar to labial in Romanian may be understood as a reinterpretation process rather than as a substitution. That is, consonants containing |U| were interpreted as having velar resonance by Latin speakers, but reinterpreted as having labial resonance by

Romanian speakers. And there is a possible acoustic explanation for this. Much of the acoustic information about consonant place is contained within the transition phase from consonant to vowel. But because [k] is followed by a consonant and not by a vowel in Latin words such as [laktem] 'milk', this information is masked and therefore difficult for listeners to recover. And if the cues for velar resonance are weak, listeners run the risk of misinterpreting them as something acoustically similar, such as labial resonance. Even in pre-vowel contexts it is possible for listeners to confuse velars and labials, owing to the acoustic similarity between these categories. In other words, there is nothing arbitrary about the reinterpretation of velars as labials; by taking the acoustic facts into consideration we can understand it as a plausible historical change.

The reinterpretation process can also work in the opposite direction, producing velars from labials. When Arapaho developed from Proto-Algonquian, for example, *p was reinterpreted as k and *k in the proto-language was mostly lost, hence [éétóókúh] 'big tooth' in Arapaho from Proto-Algonquian *[keʔtaːpitʃi]. As a result of the loss of *k, the proto-language contrast between labials and velars neutralised to velar in Arapaho. Again, this demonstrates how velars and labials tend to interact to the exclusion of other consonants, which in turn supports the idea that velars and labials are phonologically related. And from the evidence we have reviewed so far, it appears that this relation is based on the presence of a shared |U| element.

If labials and velars both contain |U|, then we expect them to show similar acoustic properties. Indeed, it was acoustic similarity that led Jakobson to use the feature [grave] as a means of bringing together labials and velars as a single class. We have already noted that [grave] overlaps with |U|, both being associated with a predominance of low-frequency energy. This energy pattern produces the falling spectral slope called *rUmp*, which serves as a cue for the |U| element. Now, we know that this pattern occurs in round vowels and labial consonants; but we also find the same pattern in velars, confirming that they too have |U| resonance. Figures 3.5(a) and 3.5(b) show the spectral profiles of [k] and [p] when released into a following [ə]. Clearly, labials and velars have the same falling *rUmp* pattern. But in most grammars labials and velars are contrastive, so we need a way of distinguishing them. As with palatals and coronals, this can be done through headedness: headed |U̲| is interpreted as labial resonance and non-headed |U| as velar resonance. In this way, labials and velars are formally related, and at the same time phonologically distinct.

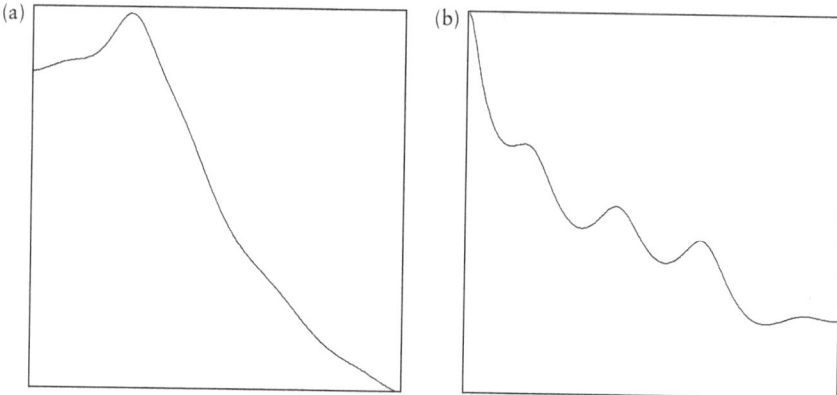

Figure 3.5 Spectral profiles of [k] and [p]. (a) Spectral pattern of [k]; (b) Spectral pattern of [p]

But why should it be labials rather than velars which are headed? In §3.4.2 we noted that the inherent weakness of coronals is a reflection of their non-headedness – they are regularly targeted by assimilation processes and occur in weak positions because they are non-headed. But interestingly, in some languages it is velars rather than coronals which behave in this way, indicating that velars are also weak and non-headed. For example, Selayarese has a reduplication process in which velar [ŋ] is the target of place assimilation.

(22) pekaŋ → peka[m]pekaŋ   'hook'
      soroŋ → soro[n]soroŋ   'push'
      jaɲaŋ → jaɲa[ɲ]jaɲaŋ   'loose'
      keloŋ → kelo[ŋ]keloŋ   'sing'

The fact that velar resonance can be overridden by another resonance property suggests that velarity is relatively weak in this language. And as we have seen, ET uses non-headedness to represent phonological weakness of this kind. Moreover, Selayarese is not an isolated case; in Chukchi velar [ŋ] undergoes place assimilation too, as the alternations in (23) show.

(23) [təŋ-əɬʔ-ən]   'good'
      [tam-waɣərɣ-ən]   'good life'
      [ten-leut]   'good head'

Midi French also illustrates the weakness of velars. This dialect permits sequences of vowel plus nasal stop, for example [lɑmp] *lampe* 'lamp' (cf. Standard French [lɑ̃p] with a nasalised vowel). The nasal stop in Midi French assimilates in place to a following consonant, as in (24a); if no consonant follows, it is interpreted as [ŋ] word-finally (24b) or as [n] before a vowel (24c).

(24) a. bɑŋk   *banque*   'bank'
          lɑmp   *lampe*   'lamp'
          lɑntœr   *lenteur*   'slowness'

     b. bɔŋ   *bon*   'good'   (cf. Standard French [bɔ̃])
          savɔŋ   *savon*   'soap'   (cf. Standard French [savɔ̃])

     c. bɔnœr   *bonheur*   'happiness'
          savɔne   *savonner*   'to lather'

What is significant here is the distribution of velar [ŋ], which appears in word-final position, a universally weak context. Assuming that weak positions are generally associated with weak segments, we can infer that velar resonance is also weak. The grammar formalises this by representing velar resonance as non-headed |U|.

The difference in strength between headed labials and non-headed velars can also be seen in Skikun, an Atayalic dialect of Formosan. In Skikun a shift from labial to velar is currently taking place in word-final position. The change is still in progress, having spread through the lexicon more extensively in younger speakers than in older speakers. In words with a final labial, older speakers typically produce labial [p m] while younger speakers show a tendency to produce velar [k ŋ] instead.

(25)   *Older speakers*   *Younger speakers*
         talap   talak   'eaves'
         mgop   mgok   'share one cup'
         kmiyap   kmiyak   'catch'
         tmalam   tmalaŋ   'taste'
         cmom   cmoŋ   'wipe'
         qinam   qinaŋ   'peach'

Again, it is significant that the change from labial to velar occurs word-finally, a prosodically weak position which favours weak segments. Like Midi French, Skikun reveals a difference in strength between labials and velars, in that strong (headed) labials are giving way to weak (non-headed) velars. Once the change is complete, the contrast between labials and velars will have neutralised word-finally. The direction of neutralisation in Skikun is typical in the sense that the weaker alternant (in this case, velar) survives.

The syllable coda is also a weak position where segmental contrasts can easily be lost. In Caribbean dialects of Spanish the contrast between [p] and [k] can be neutralised to [k] in codas. This happens particularly in casual speech, as illustrated in (26a). Compare this with the regular forms shown in (26b), where the [k] vs. [p] contrast is maintained in codas.

(26) a. *conce*[k]*to*   'concept'   b. *conce*[p]*to*
     rece[k]*tor*   'receptor'   *rece*[p]*tor*
     pe[k]*si*   'Pepsi'   *pe*[p]*si*
     a[k]*titud*   'aptitude'   *a*[p]*titud*

The fact that neutralisation produces [k] rather than [p] suggests that velar is the weaker of the two. And in ET we express this weakness using headedness. By analysing labial-to-velar weakening in terms of the loss of headedness, it parallels the palatal-to-coronal weakening described in §3.4.2 as well as some of the examples of vowel reduction such as [ɑː] → [ə] that we analysed in Chapter 2.

To summarise, there are phonological and acoustic reasons for supposing that labials and velars form a natural class of |U| segments. And to distinguish them, we refer to headedness: labials have headed |U| and velars have non-headed |U|. In some languages, velars display their non-headedness by behaving as typical weak segments: that is, they act as assimilation targets, they are favoured in weak positions, and they emerge as the outcome of neutralisation. Headedness therefore functions as a contrastive property within the |U| class, just as it does within the |I| class where it distinguishes palatals from coronals. Next we turn to the role of |A| in consonants.

3.6 The |A| Element

3.6.1 Gutturals

Naturally, place categories represented by |A| should display the acoustic properties of |A|. And we know from Chapter 2 that these include a high F1 and a *mAss* energy pattern. These are the properties associated with guttural consonants, in particular the pharyngeals [ħ ʕ] and to a lesser extent the uvulars [q ɢ χ ʁ]. On this basis we can assume that the pharyngeals [ħ ʕ] and perhaps the uvulars contain |A|. Although pharyngeal consonants are not very common, they are a feature of several language groups including Semitic (which includes Arabic), Caucasian and Salish. If pharyngeal resonance is represented by |A|, then we can expect pharyngeals to be linked phonologically with low vowels, which are also represented by |A|. Let us review the phonological and acoustic evidence for a class of |A| segments comprising pharyngeal consonants and low vowels.

The presence of |A| in gutturals is confirmed by the way these segments interact with vowels containing |A| – especially low vowels, in which |A| is headed. For example, in Standard Arabic the distribution of [a] is partly controlled by the presence of gutturals. Arabic verb stems are formed by taking a verb root – a consonant sequence such as *ktb* 'write', *fʕl* 'do', *ʃrb* 'drink' – and inserting vowels that add grammatical or semantic information. There are five thematic vowel classes, the thematic vowel being the final vowel of the stem. Here we focus on the 'a–a' class because verb roots are assigned to this class on phonological grounds (rather than on lexical or semantic grounds, for example). The label 'a–a' indicates that [a] is the thematic vowel in the perfective and also the imperfective forms. The thematic vowels are underlined in (27).

(27) [faʔa̱l]   'do (perf.)'
      [jafʔa̱l] 'do (imperf.)'

In one study, 94 per cent of verbs in the 'a–a' class were found to have a guttural consonant next to the thematic vowel [a], which is too disproportionate to be accidental. Rather, it suggests that vowels are lowered to [a] when they appear next to a guttural. This comes about through a process of |A| sharing in which the guttural's resonance element |A| spreads from the consonant to the neighbouring vowel. There are other Semitic languages which also support the claim that gutturals contain |A|. Like Standard Arabic, Tiberian Hebrew has a process of vowel lowering triggered by gutturals. As (28a) shows, the word-final pharyngeals [ʕ ħ] give an [a]-like quality to a preceding vowel. The process is also responsible for vowel alternations such as those in (28b).

(28) a.   *moːħ*   [moaħ]   'marrow'
           ʃuːʕ   [ʃuaʕ]   'cry'

      b.   [eː] ~ [a]: [ʃaːmeːʕuː] 'they heard'
                        [ʃaːmaʕ]   'he heard'
           [uː] ~ [ua]: [ruːħiː]   'my spirit'
                        [ruaħ]   'spirit'

Vowel lowering takes place in Lebanese Arabic too. This system allows an empty nucleus to be phonetically interpreted as [i] in order to break up illicit consonant sequences (*kitf* [kitif] 'shoulders', *naml* [namil] 'ants'). But when [i] is realised next to a guttural it is interpreted as [a] (*fiʕr* [ʃiʕar] 'poetry', *dʒarḥ* [dʒaraħ] 'wounding'), which again is the result of |A| spreading from consonant to vowel. Evidently, pharyngeal consonants have a natural tendency to appear in low-vowel contexts, and ET formalises this relation by using |A| to represent both.

Traditionally, pharyngeals are classified as obstruents and denoted by the fricative symbols [ħ ʕ]. But in reality these segments are often interpreted as frictionless continuants, typically approximants or glides. This is true in some Salish languages, where pharyngeals sound like sonorants and also pattern phonologically with other sonorants. In Salish, sonorant consonants including pharyngeals come in two forms, plain and glottalised, all of which are reinterpreted as vowels in certain contexts.

(29)   *Glide*   *Vowel*   *Resonance*
       [j] ~ [j']   [i] ~ [iʔ] |I|
       [w] ~ [w']   [u] ~ [uʔ] |U|
       [ʕ] ~ [ʕ']   [ɑ] ~ [ɑʔ] |A|
       [ʕʷ] ~ [ʕʷ']   [ɔ] ~ [ɔʔ] |A U|

Predictably, [j j'] correspond to the vowels [i iʔ] while [w w'] correspond to [u uʔ]. And because the pharyngeals [ʕ ʕ'] contain |A| resonance, their corresponding vowel is [ɑ]. Also predictable is the pattern involving the labialised pharyngeals [ʕʷ ʕʷ']. These have two resonance properties, pharyngeal |A| and labial |U|, which combine in the expected way to create the mid vowel [ɔ].

So far we have focused on pharyngeals, but uvulars can also behave as |A| segments. In Montana Salish, pharyngeals and uvulars both have a lowering effect on certain vowels: *e* is lowered to [a] and *u* to [o] when a pharyngeal or a uvular consonant appears later in the word. This is evidently another example of |A| assimilation between consonant and vowel, from which we can infer that uvulars as well as pharyngeals contain |A|. In the same language, |A| also spreads from a uvular to a following [i], colouring the vowel by raising F1 and lowering F2. Speakers reproduce this colouring effect as a schwa on-glide, as in *laq'i* [laq'ᵊi] 'sweat bath'. In other Salish languages too there are uvulars that pattern with pharyngeals. For example, vowel lowering in Thompson is triggered by uvular, pharyngeal and emphatic consonants, as in *ʔuqʷeʔ* [ʔoqʷeʔ] 'drink'. Notice that in Thompson, as well as in other languages such as Shuswap and

Tamazight Berber, the natural class includes emphatics, which we have to assume are |A| consonants too. The phonology of emphatics is explored in Bellem (2007), and we will have nothing further to say about them here. However, in §3.7.2 we will examine the representation of uvulars in more detail.

3.6.2 Coronals with |A|

We have seen that an element can be realised differently according to whether it is headed or non-headed. For example, |U| may be labial (headed) or velar (non-headed) while |I| may be palatal (headed) or coronal (non-headed). And in this section we will conclude that the same applies to the |A| element too: pharyngeal resonance is represented by headed |A| and coronal resonance by non-headed |A|. Now, coronals and pharyngeals are quite different in articulatory terms, and therefore, quite different in feature terms too. But they do have acoustic properties in common, which is a good reason for analysing them as different interpretations of the same element. Of course there are phonological reasons too, which we will examine in a moment.

Using |A| to represent coronal does not contradict what we said about |I| coronals in §3.4.2. This is because ET recognises two different kinds of coronals, |I| coronals and |A| coronals, and languages are divided according to which of the two they employ. At first this may seem a little odd, since we do not expect to find two different elements representing the same category – in fact, it goes against our intuitions about how a generative grammar works. It is important to realise, however, that |A| coronals and |I| coronals are not the same category; they have different representations because they display different phonological behaviour. The term 'coronal' is often used in a way which (wrongly) implies that coronal consonants form a single, clearly defined place category. But as we have already noted, 'coronal' serves as a cover term for a range of place categories including dental, alveolar, alveopalatal, palatoalveolar and retroflex. As usual, we need not be concerned about the small articulatory differences that may exist between these categories. What is important is the fact that some of them can be contrastive in the same language, which requires them to have distinct representations. In other words, it is not enough to recognise just one general class of coronals, or to employ just the |I| element to represent coronal resonance. The grammar must be able to refer to several kinds of coronals, and the |A| element makes this possible.

By recognising both |I| and |A| as coronal elements, we can capture the fact that some coronals behave phonologically like |I| segments while others behave as though they contain |A|. In §3.4.2 we looked at languages where coronals pattern as |I| segments, so let us now focus on languages with |A| coronals. As we will see in Chapter 5, *r* sounds such as [ɹ r ɽ] often behave as |A| segments. This is illustrated by coronal *r* in Munster Irish, a language which distinguishes between plain consonants such as [p f ʃ h] and their palatalised equivalents [pʲ fʲ ʃʲ hʲ]. Usually, palatalisation shows up not just on the consonant itself but also on neighbouring segments – compare plain *asal* [asəl] 'donkey' with palatalised *asail* [asilʲ] 'donkey (genitive)' (palatalisation marks the genitive case in Munster Irish). Coronal *r*, which alternates between a trill and a tap in Munster Irish, also comes in plain [r] ~ [ɾ] and palatalised [rʲ] ~ [ɾʲ] forms. And from the distribution of the plain trill [r] and the plain tap [ɾ] we can see that [ɾ] is a weakened version of [r], since [r] is found in strong (word-initial) positions and [ɾ] in weak (word-final and intervocalic) positions. Cyran (1997) analyses this as a difference in headedness in which trilled [r] is represented as headed |A̲| and flapped [ɾ] as non-headed |A| – which helps explain another fact about *r* distribution, namely, the absence of palatalised [rʲ] word-initially. In this position a plain trill [r] is possible (*rí* [riː] 'king') but a palatalised trill [rʲ] is not, hence *[rʲiː]. At first, this looks like just an arbitrary fact about trills, but on closer inspection we find that it is part of a more general pattern, because there are also certain vowels that cannot be palatalised either – specifically, those vowels containing headed |A̲|. As (30) shows, vowels containing non-headed |A| can palatalise whereas vowels with headed |A̲| cannot.

(30) a. *cnoc* [knok] 'hill'   b. *cat* [kɑt] 'cat'
         cnoic [knikʲ] 'hill (genitive)'   *cait* [kɑtʲ] 'cat (genitive)'

[o] (= |U̲ A|) in [knok] (30a) palatalises to [i] in [knikʲ] 'hill (genitive)' because it has non-headed |A|, whereas [ɑ] in [kɑt] (30b) is unchanged in [kɑtʲ] 'cat (genitive)' because it is represented by headed |A̲|. It is as though headed |A̲| blocks the palatalisation process, which provides useful evidence to support our representations for *r*: flapped [ɾ] (non-headed |A|) palatalises but trilled [r] (headed |A̲|) does not. Note that we may informally refer to *r* sounds as glides because, like [j w ɥ], they have only a vowel element in their structure.

Rhotics are represented by |A| in other languages too. We know this because they cause vowel lowering in adjacent vowels; this can be achieved either by spreading |A| or by promoting an existing |A|

from non-headed to headed. For example, in Acadian French [ɛ] optionally lowers to [a] before *r* (*certain* [sɛrtɛ̃]~[sartɛ̃] 'certain'), and in Southern Swedish a high mid vowel [øː] (= |I U A|) becomes a low mid [œː] (= |I U A̲|) before *r* (*att dö* [døː] 'to die', *jag dör* [dœːr] 'I die'). Other coronals besides *r* can have |A| resonance too. For example, in dialects of Bedouin Arabic |A| is present in all the coronal sonorants [r l n]. Furthermore, these pattern with the gutturals to form a natural class of |A| segments: short [a] raises to [i] in open syllables, as in (31a), but remains [a] next to a guttural consonant (31b) or a coronal sonorant (31c).

(31) a. [kitab] (*[katab])   'he wrote'
        [difan] (*[dafan])   'he buried'

    b. [saħab]   'he pulled'
       [ħamal]   'he carried'

    c. [sarag]   'he stole'
       [balas]   'he denounced'
       [ʃanag]   'he beheaded'

In §3.6.1 we saw how |A| is active in consonant–vowel interactions in Arabic, and now we have another illustration of this. Here, |A| from a guttural [ħ] or a coronal [r l n] is interpreted as [a] in the preceding nucleus, thereby blocking the [a] → [i] raising process. Now, one question that arises is this: why should coronal sonorants have this effect when obstruents such as [t d s ʃ] do not (hence [kisar] but *[kasar])? One reason may be that coronal obstruents do not belong to the |A| class; that is, perhaps they do not produce [a] because they do not contain |A|. It is important to realise that, just because some coronals in a language contain |A|, it is not necessarily the case that all coronals will be represented by |A|. For instance, it may be that [r l n] behave as |A| segments whereas in the same system [s z t d] behave as |I| segments. Just because two sounds appear to have the same phonetic place of articulation, it does not always follow that they have the same phonological properties.

On this point ET departs from most feature theories, in which it is assumed that a direct relation exists between a segment's phonological properties and its articulatory properties. For example, in the standard model all dental sounds [d̪ s̪ n̪ ...] have, by definition, the same place features and should therefore be grouped together as a phonological class. The same goes for all alveolars, all postalveolars, and so on. There are two problems with this approach. First, it may not be consistent with the linguistic facts: sometimes an articulatory grouping does not coincide neatly with a phonological grouping, as demonstrated by Bedouin Arabic. And second, traditional place labels like dental and alveolar are not always reliable as a way of identifying segmental categories. To see this, consider how coronals are pronounced in English and French. Conventionally, English coronals are described as alveolar and French coronals as dental, but in reality the situation is not as straightforward as this. One study has shown that English speakers produce alveolar *l* and dental *l* in approximately equal numbers, and that about one third of English 'alveolar' *t*, *d*, *n* tokens are actually produced as dentals. Meanwhile, French *l* is mostly alveolar rather than dental, and less than half the tokens of French 'dental' *s*, *z* are actually dental. It appears that phonetic labelling can be more abstract than we might think, which means that these labels cannot be relied upon for identifying phonological classes. As we have noted several times already, we can only determine how a segment is represented by observing its phonological behaviour. Returning to the question of coronals, we cannot assume that two coronals are represented by the same resonance element just because they appear to have the same phonetic place property – it may be that one contains |I| and the other |A|. This appears to be the case in Bedouin Arabic. It is also true of the Australian language Ngiyambaa, which we consider next.

As Table 3.1 shows, Ngiyambaa has five consonant places: labial and velar are both represented by |U|, which leaves |I| and |A| to represent the three coronal categories labelled dental, alveolar and alveopalatal. Note that voicing is not distinctive in this language, so the stops [b ḏ d dʲ g] may be alternatively written as [p t̪ t tʲ k]. All consonants in Ngiyambaa contrast word-medially, but in other positions their distribution is restricted. The alveolars [d n l r ɹ] are

Table 3.1   Consonants in Ngiyambaa

Category	labial	dental	alveolar	alveopalatal	velar
Resonance	|U|	|I|	|A|	|I|	|U|
	b	ḏ	d	dʲ	g
	m	n̪	n	ɲ	ŋ
			l		
			r		
	w		ɹ	j	

the only consonants that cannot appear in word-initial position, but on the other hand, they are the only ones that are permitted word-finally. The alveolars therefore behave as a natural class and must be assigned a unique representation. The |A| element is appropriate here for two reasons. First, the class includes the rhotics [r ɹ], which are typically associated with |A|. And second, in this system the alveolars are phonologically distinct from the dentals and alveopalatals, and it is apparent that these both have |I| resonance. Specifically, dental [d̪] and alveopalatal [dʲ] are in complementary distribution word-initially, which suggests that they are phonologically related and form another natural class. The conditions controlling the choice between [d̪] and [dʲ] are complex, but generally speaking we get alveopalatal [dʲ] in palatal contexts (before [i] or another palatal consonant: [dʲiːr] 'spirit of dead person', [dʲiːɲdal] 'lick') and dental [d̪] elsewhere ([d̪uːr] 'man', [d̪arij] 'disappear'). And because palatal resonance is represented by the |I| element, it makes sense to view alveopalatals and dentals as a natural class of |I| segments in this language. We will distinguish them by headedness: following our earlier analysis of Mon (§3.4.2) let us assume that alveopalatals are headed and dentals non-headed. Overall, what the phonology of Ngiyambaa demonstrates is that we need to recognise two types of coronals, dental |I| and alveolar |A|. They may be phonetically similar, but they are phonologically distinct.

3.6.3 Retroflexes

Ngiyambaa is unusual in having three contrastive stops in the coronal region. It is far more common to find languages with just a single coronal stop, such as Rotokas with [t], or with a two-way coronal contrast, such as Bulgarian with [t tʲ]. However, even more unusual than Ngiyambaa are languages with four coronal stops, which exist among the Dravidian languages (Tamil with [n̪ n ɳ ɲ]) and the languages of Australia (Aranda with [t̪ t ʈ tʲ], Pitta-Pitta with [l̪ l ɭ ʎ]). Interestingly, these large coronal systems all contain one of the retroflex consonants [ʈ ɖ ɳ ɭ ɽ], and moreover, this retroflex often patterns phonologically with alveolars. Adding this to what we already know about (alveo)palatals and dentals, we arrive at the set of representations shown in (32). Here coronal divides into two classes, |I| coronals and |A| coronals, each of which then further divides on the basis of headedness.

(32)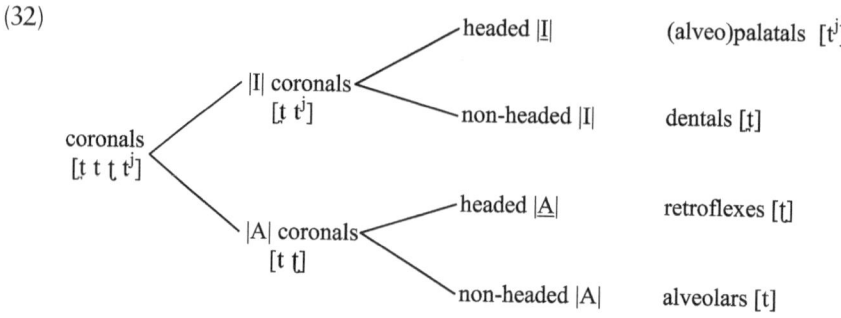

Some feature theories employ [±distributed] to distinguish the |I| and |A| classes in (32): (alveo)palatal and dental are [+distributed] because they are produced with a laminal (tongue blade) articulation while retroflex and alveolar are [−distributed] because they are apical (tongue tip) articulations. For several reasons there is no element equivalent to [±distributed] in ET. One reason is that [±distributed] is an articulatory feature (referring to the length of oral constriction), so it has no place in an element system based on acoustic patterns. Another reason is that [±distributed] is bivalent, so its negative value [−distributed] can function as an active property; this is at odds with ET's commitment to monovalency. A third reason is that [±distributed] is irrelevant to vowels, so it does not belong in a theory where consonant–vowel unity is an underlying principle. However, these issues are avoided if we use |I| and |A| to represent separate coronal categories. Both are intrinsically positive, and in addition, both conform to consonant–vowel unity because they each appear in consonant and vowel expressions. There are several points concerning (32) that we still need to address, however.

Most importantly, we need phonological evidence for a natural class of retroflexes and alveolars. Hall (1997) summarises this evidence, and here we pick up on just two of his examples. In Lardil, the retroflexes [ʈ ɳ ɽ] and the alveolars [t n l r] have a similar distribution, as these are the only consonants to appear word-finally, for example [miyaɽ] 'spear', [pirŋen] 'woman'. Following (32), this can be expressed as a simple generalisation: |A| consonants are permitted in word-final position whereas |I| and |U| consonants are not. Consonants with |I| and |U| resonance are therefore not interpreted when they are lexically word-final or when they become word-final following vowel apocope.

(33) [wuṭaltʲ(i)]→[wuṭal] (*[wuṭaltʲ]) 'meat' (following vowel apocope)
[ŋaluk]   →[ŋalu] (*[ŋaluk])   'story'

Toda is another language in which retroflexes and alveolars pattern together as a natural class of |A| segments. Not only are these segments banned from word-initial and stem-initial position, but their distribution is also restricted word-finally: in disyllabic words a single final consonant must be a retroflex [ṭ ḍ ṇ ṭ ḷ] (34a), an alveolar [t d l] (34b), or a rhotic (34c). The same consonants pattern together in final CC clusters too: one of them must occupy the first C slot whereas they are all banned from appearing in the second C slot (34d).

(34) a. [kopaṇ] 'butterfly'
 b. [elal] 'easy'
 c. [uθur] 'gums'
 d. [sobuḷm] 'wages'
    [ogodj] 'bazaar'
    [kuborm] 'manure'

Clearly, distributional patterns like these are helpful in establishing a natural class of |A| segments comprising retroflexes and alveolars. In some languages, however, retroflexes and alveolars are contrastive, and must therefore have distinct representations. This can be expressed by a difference in headedness: retroflex resonance is represented by headed |A| and alveolar resonance by non-headed |A|. As headed expressions, retroflex consonants display the kind of phonological behaviour we associate with strong segments, that is, they generally trigger phonological processes rather than undergo them. For example, unlike alveolars they are not usually targeted by weakening or assimilation, but instead retain their resonance properties in weak contexts. Moreover, retroflexes are more often found in prosodically strong positions. This is true in languages such as Wambaya, where retroflexes and alveolars contrast word-internally (35a) but are neutralised word-initially (35b) in favour of retroflex.

(35) a. [ḍ] vs. [d]: [guḍa] 'to be sick'
              [guda] 'stone'
    [ḷ] vs. [l]: [buḷindʲa] 'to smoke'
              [bulindʲa] 'algae'
    [ṇ] vs. [n]: [gaṇmaŋga] 'jaw'
              [ganmami] 'to get close'

 b. [ḍ] (*[d]) [ḍididʲa] (*[dididʲa]) 'to carry'
    [ḷ] (*[l]) [ḷaŋga] (*[laŋga]) 'north'
    [ṇ] (*[n]) [ṇawu] (*[nawu]) 'to sit on, stand on'

As we will see in §5.2.4, word-initial position is universally strong and attracts phonologically strong segments. This indicates that retroflex resonance is stronger than alveolar resonance, in turn suggesting that retroflex has headed |A|. In some cases an initial retroflex is lexically retroflex, and in other cases it is a retroflex interpretation of an alveolar, as in *didid^{j}a* [ɖidid^{j}a] 'to carry'. We can be sure that *didid^{j}a* begins lexically with alveolar [d] because in Wambaya lexical information is revealed during reduplication, as illustrated by the example in (36).

(36) a. [ɖidid^{j}a] 'to carry'
 b. [ɖi-didid^{j}a] 'carry (dur.)'

In (36a) alveolar [d] strengthens to a retroflex [ɖ] in order to match the strength of its word-initial position. Speakers do this by reinterpreting non-headed |A| (alveolar) as headed |A̲| (retroflex). On the other hand, in reduplicated forms such as (36b) no strengthening takes place at the beginning of the stem *didid^{j}a* because [d] is now word-internal and can therefore be interpreted as an alveolar. Notice, however, that the reduplicated consonant in the prefix is interpreted as a retroflex [ɖ] because it is word-initial. This example from Wambaya illustrates a very common phonological effect whereby a segment is interpreted in a way that reflects the strength or weakness of its prosodic position. This issue is taken up in §5.2.

If retroflex and alveolar are linked phonologically, then we expect them to be linked acoustically too. And predictably, they show similar spectral patterns in that both have an energy peak in the central region of the spectrum. This is the *mAss* energy pattern associated with the |A| element. However, listeners are able to distinguish between retroflex and alveolar resonance by focusing on their formant frequencies, particularly on F3, since retroflexes have an unusually low F3 to distinguish them from other coronal sounds. There are several things that speakers can do to lower F3 including rounding the lips, retracting the tongue body and moving the tongue towards the post-alveolar region in order to create an apical contact. And although the precise articulation of retroflexes varies from one language to another, they are all interpreted by implementing some combination of these articulatory devices to reproduce the target acoustic cue, a low F3.

Retroflex consonants are typologically uncommon, occurring in only about 11 per cent of languages. This is not unexpected, however, if we consider that the vowel-like nature of |A| makes this element unsuited to functioning as a consonant element, particularly in its headed (and therefore, even more vowel-like) form. In some languages, such as those shown in (37), retroflexes have developed from *r*C sequences across morpheme boundaries. This is unsurprising too, given that the *r* glide is also represented by |A| (§5.1.2).

(37) a. Norwegian [sʉːʈ]   (sʉr-t)   *surt*   'sour AGR'
                   [baːɳ]   (bar-n)   *baren*   'bar DEF-SG'
                   [ʋoɭi]   (ʋor-li)   *vårlig* 'spring-like'
                   [bruːʂ]   (brur-s)   *brors*   'brother POSS'

     b. Swedish   [fœːʈ]   (før-t)   *fört*   'brought SUP'
                   [fœːʂ]   (før-s)   *förs*   'is brought PASS'
                   [fœːˈʂɔrg] (før-sorj) *försorg* 'taking care'
                   [fœːˌʈɯːr] (før-tɯr) *förtur* 'priority'

The forms in (37) illustrate how [t d s n l] have merged with *r* to produce retroflexes; we can assume that [t d s n l] acquired |A| from *r*, and that this |A| was interpreted in its headed form as retroflex resonance in the new element compound. The fact that |A| is headed in the resulting compound is a reflection of the strong position in which it finds itself. From an information point of view, the retroflexes in (37) are prominent because they are all morpheme-initial. Although we tend to focus on word-initial position as a strong context, we should not forget that morpheme-initial and foot-initial are also important for linguistic information. So although [ʈ ɳ ɭ ʂ] in (37) may at first appear to occupy weak positions – that is, word-final in [fœːʈ], word-medial in [ʋoɭi] – these positions turn out to be strong when we take morphology into account. To further illustrate the point, the sequence *rd* in Swedish has the weak realisation [rd] foot-internally (*garde* [ˈgɑr.də] 'guard') but the strong realisation [ɖ] foot-initially (*gardist* [gɑ.ˈɖist] 'guardsman'). Retroflexes have developed from *r*C sequences in other languages besides Norwegian and Swedish, including Cham ([tr] > [ʈ], [sr] > [ʂ]) and Watjarri ([r-t] > [ʈ]).

You may have noticed that retroflex resonance and pharyngeal resonance have the same representation, headed |A|. And of course, this can only be correct if there are no languages with a lexical contrast between retroflex and pharyngeal place. If this is the case, then the representations we have proposed can stand. In fact, by assigning retroflexes and pharyngeals the same structure we are actually making the claim that these categories cannot be contrastive in the same system. But on the other hand, if we find languages with a genuine contrast between retroflex and pharyngeal place, then some revisions will be required; for example, in a language with |I| coronals but no |A| coronals it may be feasible to assign non-headed |A| to retroflexes and headed |A̲| to pharyngeals. For the moment, however, let us assume that headed |A̲| is interpreted as retroflex or pharyngeal, depending on the language. After all, both have strong phonological motivation: in languages such as Wambaya retroflexes form a natural class with alveolars, which are thought to have |A|; and in languages such as Arabic pharyngeals interact with low vowels, which we know contain |A|.

This level of uncertainty about how certain classes are represented can give the impression that ET is rather vague. Actually, this vagueness highlights the point that representations in ET are specific to a given sound system – that is, they apply to individual languages and not to languages in general. So for instance, [t] in one system may have a different representation from [t] in another system. This is because elements represent the phonological properties of a segment but not their articulatory properties; and just because two languages have a segment which sounds like [t], for instance, it does not guarantee that [t] is linguistically the same in both systems. This is clear from the way dental/alveolar resonance is represented by |I| in some languages and by |A| in others.

3.6.4 Summary

Table 3.2 summarises what we have said so far about the interpretation of |I U A| in consonants. Each resonance property in the table is numbered and then described below.

1. Headed |I̲| is present in palatals. In most languages these are phonetically alveopalatal or palatoalveolar, often [ʃ ʒ tʃ dʒ].
2. Non-headed |I| represents coronals (dental or alveolar) in some languages with a single coronal class, but see 8.
3. Non-headed |I| specifically defines the class of dentals in languages where dentals contrast with |A| coronals (alveolars) but also pattern with palatals.
4. Headed |U̲| represents labials (including labiodentals such as [f v] – see §3.7.1).
5. Non-headed |U| represents velars (including front velars such as [c ɟ ç ʝ] – see §3.7.3).
6. Headed |A̲| represents the class of gutturals, typically realised as pharyngeal.

Table 3.2 Resonance properties of |I U A|

		Resonance property	Examples
|I|:			
headed	|I̲|	1 palatal	most languages
non-headed	|I|	2 coronal (dental or alveolar)	Lahu
		3 coronal (dental)	Ngiyambaa
|U|:			
headed	|U̲|	4 labial	most languages
non-headed	|U|	5 velar	most languages
|A|:			
headed	|A̲|	6 pharyngeal	Arabic
		7 coronal (retroflex)	Wambaya
non-headed	|A|	8 coronal (dental or alveolar)	English
		9 coronal (alveolar)	Lardil

7. Headed |A| can represent retroflexes in languages where retroflexes pattern with alveolars but also contrast with dentals.
8. Non-headed |A| represents coronals (dental or alveolar) in some languages with a single coronal class, but see 2.
9. Non-headed |A| specifically defines the class of alveolars in languages with a contrast between |A| coronals (alveolars) and |I| coronals (dentals).

Once again we are left with the impression that ET is rather vague and unsystematic in the way it represents consonant place. But if we look beyond this variation and focus on just the core characteristics of I U A|, then we can define their general resonance properties as in (38).

(38) |I| palatals and some coronals
      |U| labials and velars
      |A| gutturals and some coronals

Table 3.3 shows how these properties are matched with traditional consonant categories. The table contains some gaps, and our remaining task is to find suitable representations for labiodental, palatovelar and uvular place. As we will see in the next section, these all have complex resonance.

Table 3.3 Consonant categories with simplex resonance

labial	labio-dental	dental	alveolar	retroflex	palatal	palato-velar	velar	uvular	pharyngeal
[p ɸ]	[f ɱ]	[t ts s θ]	[ṭ ṣ]	[tʃ j]	[c ç]	[k x]	[q χ]	[ħ ʕ]
|U|		|I| or |A|	|A|	|I|		|U|		|A|

3.7 Complex Resonance

3.7.1 Labiodentals

In §3.5.1 we noted that labials and labiodentals show similar phonological behaviour because they both contain headed |U|; for example, [p b m f w] form a natural class in Garifuna. But labials and labiodentals can also contrast, so they must have distinct representations. If both have headed |U|, and if labials are simplex, then labiodentals must contain headed |U| plus another element. In this case the additional element is |A|, so labiodental resonance is represented as |U A|.

The presence of |A| affects not only the acoustic quality of labiodentals but also their phonological character. For instance, by treating labiodental as complex resonance, we can understand what happens when labials and labiodentals neutralise. Some dialects of Catalan, such as Valencian and Balearic, maintain a contrast between labial *b* and labiodental *v*, whereas in other dialects this contrast has neutralised to *b*. For example, compare the form *enveja* [eɱˈvedʒa] 'envy' in the non-neutralising dialect of Valencian with the corresponding form *enveja* [əmˈbɛʒə] in the neutralising dialect of Eastern Catalonia, where labiodentals have been reinterpreted as labials. When place categories merge in this way, the outcome is usually the simpler or less marked member of the pair. And in ET, simplex resonance is less marked than complex resonance – recall that vowel weakening leaves a simplex segment (§2.8.4). This suggests that labials are less complex and less marked than labiodentals. The neutralisation which took place in Eastern Catalonia may be understood as a simplification process involving the loss of |A|.

3.7.2 Uvulars

Now consider uvular resonance, another of the gaps in Table 3.3. Like labiodentals, uvulars such as [q χ] have complex resonance. Uvular segments show a strong tendency to pattern with velars, which indicates that they, like velars, contain non-headed |U|. But because some languages have a contrast between velars and uvulars, the two must still be phonologically distinct. The phonetic characteristics of uvulars suggest that these segments also belong among the back consonants, and some feature theories have tried to show this by including uvulars in the [guttural] class. To express the same idea in ET we have to assume that uvulars contain headed |<u>A</u>|, because headed |<u>A</u>| is the closest equivalent to the feature [guttural] (§3.6.1). This gives us a natural class of |A| segments comprising low vowels, pharyngeals and uvulars. And if uvulars are guttural consonants that also pattern with velars, then it follows that they must be compounds of |A| and |U|. In Quechua the |A| element appears to be phonologically active in uvulars, as these sounds have a lowering effect on vowels. Since vowel lowering involves the addition of |A|, we may treat this effect as a process in which |A| spreads from a uvular to an adjacent nucleus. Quechua has only three lexical vowels *a i u*, which appear freely in words that do not contain uvulars, as shown by the forms in (39a). But next to a uvular, [i u] are reinterpreted as [e o] respectively, as shown in (39b).

(39) a. [api]   'take'
        [suti]   'name'
        [karu]   'far'

    b. [qori] (*[quri])   'gold'
       [waleχ] (*[waliχ])   'poor'
       [seɴqa] (*[siɴqa])   'nose'

    c. [pisi]   'little'
       [pise-qa]   'little-TOPIC'

The lowering effect of uvulars is also responsible for alternations such as in (39c). The structures in (40) illustrate the active behaviour of |<u>A</u>| in the phonology of Quechua (only resonance properties are shown).

(40) a.   [qori] 'gold'   b.   [pise-qa] 'little-TOPIC'

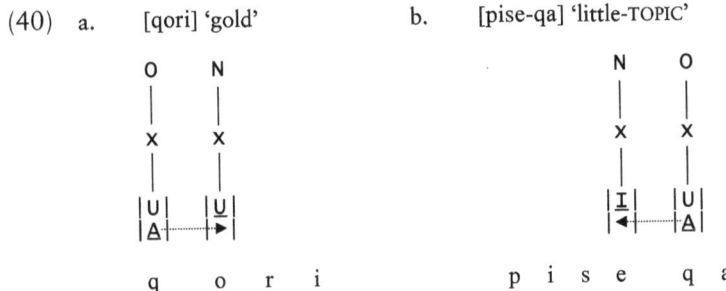

Mongolian is another language which allows us to see inside the structure of uvulars. This language has a pharyngeal harmony system which classifies words as either pharyngeal or non-pharyngeal. In general the velars [ŋ x g] appear in non-pharyngeal words, and they alternate with the uvulars [N χ ɢ], which belong in pharyngeal words.

(41) Non-pharyngeal   Pharyngeal
      [cʰoːŋ] ~ [cʰõː] 'few' [ɔN] ~ [ɔ̃]   'year'
      [sux]   'axe'   [aχ]   'elder brother'
      [gir]   'house' [ɢar]   'hand'

Pharyngeal words have a dark acoustic quality that speakers reproduce by retracting (the root of) the tongue – compare, for example, the rich and sonorous retracted vowels [a ʊ ɔ] we find in pharyngeal words with the brighter non-retracted vowels [i e u o] in non-pharyngeal words. As (41) shows, pharyngeal harmony controls the distribution of uvulars and velars, which appear in pharyngeal and non-pharyngeal domains, respectively. From this we can assume that uvulars in Mongolian are the retracted (pharyngealised) counterparts of velars. This is true phonetically, since uvulars are indeed acoustically darker and are produced further back in the vocal tract than velars. But it is also true phonologically, since velars are represented by |U| whereas uvulars have the structure |U A|. The additional |A| element in uvulars is responsible for the darker acoustic quality and more retracted (guttural) articulation of these sounds.

One remaining question is whether the |A| in uvulars is always headed, giving |U A̱|, or whether the non-headed structure |U A| may also be grammatical in some languages. It seems that |U A̱| and |U A| are both possible, which means that the structure of uvulars must be determined on a language by language basis. We can regard uvulars with non-headed |U A| as velar segments that have been modified by the addition of |A|. The |A| element gives them a darker acoustic quality; in articulatory terms, this means that they are more retracted than regular velars. For example, when velars assimilate to a low/back vowel, as in the English word *call* [kɔːl] (cf. *came* [keɪm]), their resonance takes on the characteristics of |U A|. By contrast, uvulars represented by the headed expression |U A̱| have more in common with pharyngeals because of their headed |A̱|. We can expect them to display some of the phonological characteristics of pharyngeals while at the same time being lexically distinct from them. In Nootka, uvulars and pharyngeals pattern as a natural class: both cause a following high vowel to lower, as in *qitʃin* [qetʃɪn] 'louse', *huːjiɫ* [hoʊjiɫ] 'over there on the floor'. In addition, they cause a preceding [i iː] to be produced with a schwa off-glide, as in *siqmis* [sɪᵊqmɪs] 'pus', *tsiːʕitɬ* [tsiːᵊʕetɬ] 'to ask permission'. Both effects involve an active |A| element, and because |A| is headed in pharyngeals we can assume that in Nootka it is also headed in uvulars. Predictably, the low vowels [a aː] are unaffected by a neighbouring uvular or pharyngeal consonant; after all, if |A̲| spreads to a vowel which already contains |A|, then no change should take place.

3.7.3 Palatovelars

The remaining gap in Table 3.3 is the category that includes the sounds [c ɟ ç ʝ]. Although these segments are typically described as palatals, we will refer to them here as palatovelars or front velars, in order to distinguish them from the |I| segments called palatals, such as [ʃ tʃ ʒ dʒ ɲ ʎ j], which typically have a palatoalveolar articulation. Like the |I| palatals, the palatovelars show a prominent *dIp* spectral pattern, indicating that they contain headed |I̲|. But because palatovelars behave independently of palatals, they must have different representations. Like labials and labiodentals, palatals and palatovelars differ in complexity: palatals have a single |I| element whereas palatovelars have |I| plus another element. In this case the additional element is |U|. We know this because in some languages palatovelars pattern with velars, which contain |U|, whereas palatals do not. We will therefore represent palatovelar resonance as |I̲ U|, which combines headed |I̲| (palatal) with non-headed |U| (velar). Earlier we pointed out that |I| and |U| do not combine easily because they have conflicting acoustic properties. And this is reflected here in the fact that the non-affricated palatovelar stops [c ɟ] and their corresponding fricatives [ç ʝ] are relatively rare in the languages of the world.

Again, we should be cautious about taking phonetic symbols at face value, as there are languages with segments which are transcribed as [c ɟ] but which actually behave and sound like the palatal affricates [tʃ dʒ] – and should therefore be represented with simplex |I̲|. Similarly, there are cases where the fricatives written as [ç ʝ] may be more accurately transcribed as [ʃ ʒ]. In §3.4.2 we noted that Korean has the palatals [c cʼ cʰ], the choice of symbols implying that these sounds are non-affricated stops. And yet they are regularly analysed as stridents, often being described as palatoalveolar affricates ([tʃ tʃʼ tʃʰ]) or alveolo-palatal affricates ([tɕ tɕʼ tɕʰ]). Similarly, the Sanskrit consonants that are transcribed as [c cʰ ɟ ɟʰ] were most likely pronounced as affricates, as they correspond to the affricates

Table 3.4 Consonants in Yanyuwa

	labial	coronal				palatovelar	velar
		dental	alveolar	retroflex	palatal		
Stops	b	d̪	d	ɖ	dʲ	ɟ	g
Nasals	m	n̪	n	ɳ	nʲ	ɲ	ŋ
	|U|	|I|	|A|	|A|	|I|	|I U|	|U|

[tʃ tʃʰ dʒ dʒʰ] in descendant languages such as Gujarati. The point here is that, although some languages are reported to have [c ɟ ç ʝ], these sounds should sometimes be written as [tʃ dʒ ʃ ʒ] and should be represented with a simplex headed |I|. In short, genuine examples of [c ɟ ç ʝ] are probably rarer than we are led to believe.

Nevertheless, there are at least some languages which employ the non-affricated stops [c ɟ] and/or the non-strident fricatives [ç ʝ] as contrastive segments, so we must classify these sounds as a distinct place category; we will call this category palatovelar. Yanyuwa is one of several Australian languages with a place contrast between palatovelar and velar. This language distinguishes no fewer than seven consonant places in stops and nasals, as Table 3.4 shows. Like Aranda and some of the other Australian languages mentioned in §3.6.3, Yanyuwa has a four-way place contrast among coronals. In addition to this four-way coronal contrast there is a distinction between labial and velar and also a fairly unusual contrast between velar [g ŋ] and palatovelar [ɟ ɲ]. The palatovelars are described as being produced 'with the back of the tongue touching the hard palate, producing a dorso-palatal stop and nasal' (Dixon 1980: 141), which is consistent with the ET view that these segments have complex (palatal and velar) resonance (the symbols [gʲ ŋʲ] could be used as an alternative to [ɟ ɲ] if we wanted to highlight the dual nature of palatovelar resonance). Garawa and Djingili are languages spoken in the same region of Australia as Yanyuwa, and these too have a contrast between velar and palatovelar. It has been suggested that palatovelars may have evolved from sequences of [k] + [j] and [g] + [j] across a morpheme boundary, and certainly, this would support the representation of palatovelars as a combination of |I| and |U|.

Yanyuwa is typical of Australian languages in having no fricatives. So to observe the behaviour of the palatovelar fricatives [ç ʝ] we must look to other language groups. Hall (1997) presents evidence from several languages to indicate that palatovelar [ç ʝ] should not be classified as coronal segments. One of these is the North-West Caucasian language Bzhedukh, which has a large fricative series that includes the palatovelars [ç çʰ]. In this language only certain consonants may appear at the beginning of a consonant sequence, the choice being restricted to labials (42a), the voiceless uvular fricative (42b) and voiceless coronal obstruents (42c).

(42) a. ps, bɣ, p'tɕ' ...
 b. χs, χs̞ ...
 c. tɕ, s̞ʷt, sχ, sʰtʰ, ɕt, ɕχ, s̞k, ɬf, ɬχʷ ...

Importantly, the palatovelars [ç çʰ] are excluded from the set of coronals in (42c), thus ruling out sequences such as *[çk] and *[çʰtʰ]. And as we have just seen, ET is able to keep palatovelars distinct from coronals by treating them as complex (palatalised) velars. This reflects another aspect of their behaviour in Bzhedukh, where velars and palatovelars form a natural class of segments – both are banned from the first consonant in a sequence.

German provides further evidence that palatovelar resonance is represented as |I U|. In German, palatovelar [ç] and velar [x] (sometimes described phonetically as uvular [χ]) are in complementary distribution: [ç] comes after vowels containing |I| (43b) while [x] appears after all other vowels (43a).

(43) a. [dax]   Dach 'roof'   b. [dɛçɐ]   Dächer 'roofs'
     [gɛʁɔxən] gerochen 'smelt'   [ʁiːçən]   riechen 'to smell'
     [flʊxt]   Flucht 'escape (n.)'   [flyçtən] flüchten 'to escape'

In other words, [ç] is a phonologically conditioned (palatalised) version of [x] while [x] itself represents the elsewhere case. As (44b) illustrates, velar [x] is interpreted as palatovelar [ç] when it interprets a headed |I| from the preceding vowel. And when palatal |I| combines with velar |U| the result is palatovelar resonance represented as |I U|. Only resonance properties are shown in (44).

(44) a. [dax] Dach 'roof'   b. [dɛçɐ] Dächer 'roofs'

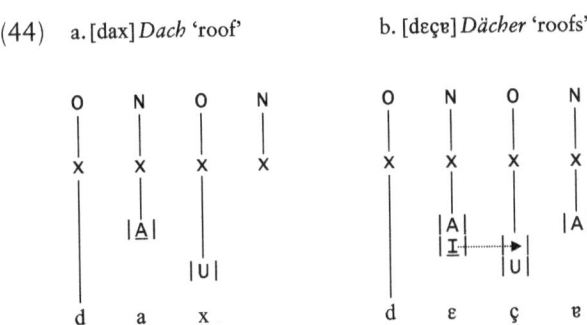

It is clear that palatovelars and velars are phonologically related, and this is represented in the grammar by a shared |U| element. But because palatolvelars also contain headed |I|, we can expect to see them behaving like palatal consonants too. This is what happens in Margi, a language in which palatal [ʃ ʒ ɲ] and palatovelar [c ɟ ç ʝ] behave as a natural class. This language is known for having a minimal vowel system consisting of just two contrastive vowels, low [a] and non-low [ɨ]. In the final form of words the non-low vowel is interpreted as [ɯ], but in non-final forms it alternates between [i] and [ə] in a predictable way: after [ʃ ʒ ɲ c ɟ ç ʝ] we get [i] (45a) while [ə] appears elsewhere (45b).

(45)   *Final form*   *Non-final form*
a.   [çɯ̀]   [çì]   'to tear'
    [hə̀cɯ̀]   [hə̀cì]   'to care for'
    [ɲɯ̀]   [ɲì]   'to fill'
    [ʃɯ́]   [ʃí]   'to spin'
    [ʒɯ̀]   [ʒì]   'to claim first'

b.   [kákádɯ̀]   [kákádə̀]   'book'
    [sɯ̀]   [sə̀]   'thing'
    [défɯ́]   [défə́]   'mush'

[ɨ] is interpreted as [i] when a palatal or palatovelar consonant occupies the preceding onset. And because these categories both have headed |I|, we can take [i] to be the result of a simple assimilation in which headed |I| spreads from the consonant to [ɨ], which is reinterpreted as the palatal vowel [i].

Putting together the evidence from Margi, German and Yanyuwa, we can be fairly certain that palatovelar resonance is represented by |I U|. This structure identifies a natural class comprising the fricatives [ç ʝ] and the non-affricated stops [c ɟ]. With this, we now have element structures to represent the major consonant place categories in Table 3.3, which is repeated in its completed form as Table 3.5. By now it should be clear that these structures are to be understood as abstract phonological categories, and that we can expect some

Table 3.5   Simplex and compound consonant categories

labial	labio-dental	dental	alveolar	retroflex	palatal	palato-velar	velar	uvular	pharyngeal
[p ɸ]	[f m̥]	[t ts s θ]	[t ʂ]	[tʃ j]	[c ç]		[k x]	[q χ]	[h ʕ]
|U|	|U A|	|I| or |A|	|A|	|I|	|I U|		|U|	|U A|	|A|

phonetic variation in the way each one is interpreted in individual languages. Even when two segments appear to have phonetically the same place property, it does not always follow that they will show the same phonological behaviour. For example, a dental stop in one language may have different phonological properties – and therefore, a different representation – from a dental stop in another language.

It is easy to view this kind of vagueness as a weakness of the ET approach, because it limits the theory's ability to make universal claims about how representations are phonetically realised. But in reality, it is simply a consequence of the fact that elements are based on phonological patterns rather than on articulation. The phonological classes in Table 3.5 are modelled on linguistic behaviour, which does not always coincide with place of articulation labels like palatal, labiodental and so on. If we chose to follow the standard model and assumed that there is a regular correspondence between phonological classes and articulatory labels, then we would obscure the fact that phonetically similar segments can sometimes differ phonologically. You may wish to compare the ET approach described here with feature theories in which a particular articulatory feature is universally associated with a particular phonological place category. This may be sufficient for describing articulation, but it does not tell us much about phonology.

3.7.4 Palatals Again

Although we have assigned element representations to all the place categories in Table 3.5, one issue still remains. Recall that, in aiming to achieve consonant–vowel unity, ET assumes that the same structural units are present in consonants and vowels. You may have noticed, however, that the combination of |I| and |A| is missing from Table 3.5 despite turning up frequently in vowel systems. This is unexpected and deserves further discussion. If |I A| were to exist as a consonant place category, then presumably it would be associated with the coronal/palatal region, as this is where |I| and |A| predominate. So let us examine the possibility that |I A| could represent a place category that we have not yet considered.

In fact there are some versions of ET which already use the compound |I̲ A| to represent the class of palatoalveolars [tʃ dʒ ʃ ʒ]. However, in §3.4 we analysed these as |I̲| segments because, despite being phonetically palatoalveolar, they behave phonologically as palatals. And this is backed up by palatalisation processes of two kinds.

One kind targets dentals and alveolars such as [t s], which are reinterpreted as [tʃ ʃ]. This happens in, for example, British English ([tjuːn] ~ [tʃuːn] *tune*) and dialects of Brazilian Portuguese ([ahtɪ] ~ [ahtʃɪ] *arte* 'art'). Another kind of palatalisation targets velars, which are also reinterpreted as [tʃ ʃ], as in Italian *medici* [meditʃi] 'doctors' (cf. *medico* [mediko] 'doctor'). In effect, coronal palatalisation and velar palatalisation are different forms of the same process, as both involve an active headed |I̳| element and both produce the headed |I̳| segments [tʃ ʃ]. And there is no doubt that [tʃ ʃ] are represented by |I̳| because they acquire their resonance properties from the triggering segments [i j], which contain only |I̳|. We can rule out the possibility that [tʃ ʃ] have complex resonance – say, |I̳| combined with an |A| element already in the target segment – because coronal targets (with |I| or |A|) and velar targets (with |U|) have different resonance elements but they all palatalise to [tʃ ʃ]. Velar palatalisation in Italian can be represented as in (46b).

(46) a. *medico* [mediko] 'doctor'   b. *medici* [meditʃi] 'doctors'

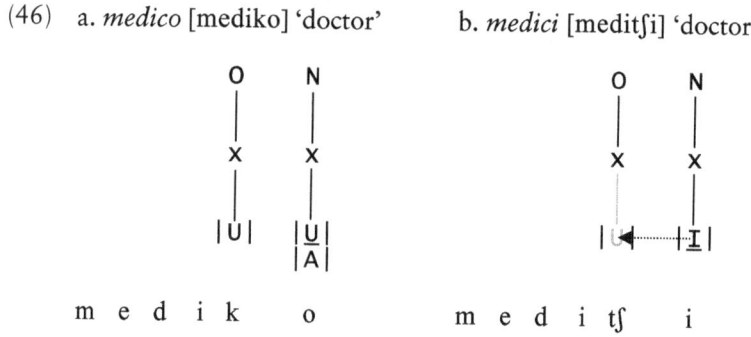

Adding the plural marker *-i* causes velar [k] to be reinterpreted as palatal [tʃ]. This happens when headed |I̳| extends from *-i* to the preceding onset and displaces the resonance element already there. There are two reasons why the original |U| is overridden: first, it is non-headed and therefore relatively weak compared to the active element |I̳|; and second, the elements |U| and |I| do not combine in Italian – recall that this is universally a marked combination.

Unfortunately, not all cases of palatalisation can be analysed in the way just described. In Polish, for example, palatalisation is a complex and idiosyncratic phenomenon that is best captured by a set of related processes rather than by a single generalisation. Four such processes are shown in (47), each triggered by a following [i] or [ɛ]. In (47a) coronal [t d] palatalise to alveopalatal [tɕ dʑ], but in (47b) they are interpreted as [ts dz]. Then in (47c) velar [k g] are palatalised to [c ɟ] (written [kʲ gʲ] in some sources), while in (47d) they become [tʃ dʒ].

(47) a. t → tɕ   d → dʑ
         [vata]   'cotton wool'   [mɔda]   'fashion'
         [vatɕɛ] 'cotton wool, dat.loc.' [mɔdʑɛ] 'fashion, dat.loc.'

     b. t → ts   d → dz
         [lɔt]   'flight'   [rada]   'advice'
         [lɛtsɛ] 'I fly'   [radzɛ] 'I advise'

     c. k → c   g → ɟ
         [rak]   'crab'   [taŋgɔ] 'tango'
         [racɛm] 'crab, instr.sg.'   [taɲɟɛm] 'tango, instr.sg.'

     d. k → tʃ   g → dʒ
         [bɔk]   'side'   [muzgu] 'brain'
         [bɔtʃɛk] 'side, dim.'   [muʒdʒɛk] 'brain, dim.'

According to (47), Polish has at least five place categories in the coronal/palatal region (not all of which are necessarily contrastive – recall that ET is concerned with linguistic information in general, not just contrastive information). And although more data are needed before we can be certain how they are represented, some possible structures are given in (48). These representations are based on the assumption that the processes in (47) are all palatalisations of one kind or another, each involving an active |I| element.

(48) a. [t,d] |A|
     b. [ts,dz] |A I|
     c. [tʃ,dʒ] |I|
     d. [tɕ,dʑ] |A I̲|
     e. [c,ɟ] |I̲ U|

Assuming that [t d] are |A| coronals in Polish, palatalisation to [ts dz] and also palatalisation to [tɕ dʑ] can be analysed as |I| spreading in which the original |A| is preserved. The result is the headed compound |A I̲| in [tɕ dʑ] (49a) and the non-headed compound |A I| in [ts dz] (49b). When [k g] are palatalised to [c ɟ], the active |I| element spreads to form a compound with the original |U|, as shown in (49c). And finally, the palatalisation of [k g] to [tʃ dʒ] proceeds as in Italian, where the velar's |U| element is suppressed when |I̲| spreads. This is shown in (49d).

(49)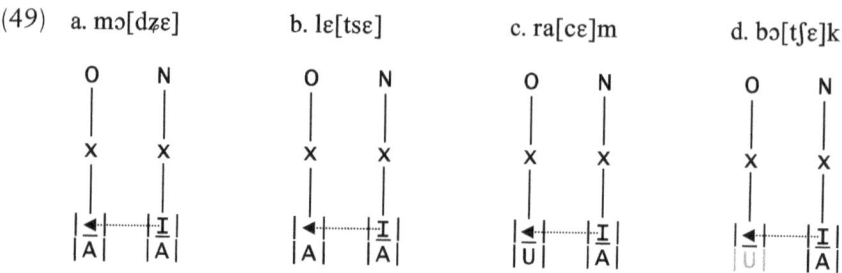

These representations are speculative, but nevertheless they demonstrate how it should be possible for |I| and |A| to combine as a place category. And with several divisions within the coronal/palatal region, Polish seems a likely system to include this combination. We will therefore add |I̲ A| to the table of consonant resonance structures, giving us the set shown in Table 3.6. Here the segments [tɕ ɕ] are given to illustrate how |I̲ A| might be interpreted, but it should be stressed that the phonetic quality of these sounds will vary between languages.

Table 3.6 Consonant place categories

labial	labio-dental	dental	alveolar	retroflex	alveolo-palatal	palatal	palato-velar	velar	uvular	pharyngeal
[p ɸ]	[f m̪]	[t ts s θ]	[ṭ ṣ]	[tɕ ɕ]	[tʃ ʃ]	[c ç]	[k x]	[q χ]	[ħ ʕ]
|U|	|U A|	|I| or |A|	|A|	|I̲ A|	|I|	|I̲ U|	|U|	|U A̲|	|A|

3.8 A Note on Affricates

So far we have not distinguished between simple stops such as [p t̪ c q] and affricated stops such as [pf] and [tʃ]. In fact, ET assumes that they are phonologically identical, differing only in the way they are phonetically interpreted: simple stops have a short, sometimes inaudible release phase whereas affricated stops have a more prolonged release phase accompanied by audible resonance. There is a long tradition of including affricates within the class of stops. For example, Jakobson, Fant and Halle (1952) analyse affricates as strident stops – that is, as stops which bear the additional feature [+strident]. In practice, this approach runs into problems when it comes to describing some of the less common affricates such as [tθ] and [kx], as these are phonetically non-strident. Nevertheless, the idea that affricates should be treated as stops is still a widely accepted one. One reason for this is that stops and affricates sometimes pattern as a natural class. In Turkish, for instance, both are devoiced in syllable-final position whereas fricatives are not. And in Zoque both

Table 3.7 Plosive–affricate complementarity

labial	labio-dental	dental or alveolar	retroflex	alveolo-palatal	palatal	palato-velar	velar	uvular
|U|	|U A|	|I| or |A| or |I A|	|A|	|I A|	|I|	|I U|	|U|	|U A|
ɸ	f	s θ	ṣ	ɕ	ʃ	ç	x	χ
p		t	ṭ			c	k	q
	pf	ts		tɕ	tʃ			

undergo postnasal voicing while fricatives remain voiceless. Another reason for analysing affricates as stops is that we rarely find a contrast between affricates and stops at the same place of articulation. Clements (1999) refers to this as plosive–affricate complementarity. As Table 3.7 shows, stops and affricates are mutually exclusive; affricates appear where there are gaps in the stop system, so if there is already a stop at a particular place of articulation then we do not usually find an affricate as well. This suggests that stops and affricates are distinguished by their resonance (place) properties rather than by their laryngeal (manner) properties. It also suggests that stops and affricates form a single series, otherwise there is no way of explaining the absence of simple stops in certain place categories. We have, therefore, a system in which each fricative is paired with a corresponding stop or affricate, allowing us to view fricative–affricate pairs such as [f]–[pf] and [ɕ]–[tɕ] on a par with fricative–stop pairs such as [ɸ]–[p] and [ṣ]–[ṭ].

But there is still the question of why we get stops at some places of articulation and affricates at others. One reason may be to do with speech perception. The simple stops [p t ṭ c k q] have resonance cues that can be recovered from their short release burst; for example, when [p] is released into a following vowel it is perceived unambiguously as a labial. However, some other stops have place cues that are less easily perceived and can only be transmitted if speakers make an effort to reinforce them. For instance, a labiodental stop is almost indistinguishable from bilabial [p] unless its resonance cues are exaggerated. Speakers do this by enhancing its release burst to the point where it takes on the character of a fricative [f], from which listeners can recover the cues for labiodental resonance. And by interpreting a labiodental stop as the affricate [pf], its resonance cues become perceptually distinct from those of bilabial [p]. The remaining affricates in Table 3.7 can be analysed in the same way. The stops that are paired with [s] and [θ] are again perceptually similar, and as a result, liable to be confused; indeed both are usually transcribed using the same symbol [t]. However, in some languages they are made perceptually distinct by affricating one ([s]–[ts]) but not the other ([θ]–[t]). Meanwhile the two palatal fricatives [ɕ] and [ʃ] have corresponding stops that listeners would have difficulty distinguishing if they were both produced as simple non-affricated stops. So in order to make their resonance cues stronger and easier to perceive, they are produced as the affricates [tɕ] and [tʃ] respectively. By contrast, the simple stops [p t ʈ c k q] have resonance cues that are unambiguous, and therefore, recoverable from their stop bursts alone. They can remain as simple stops because speakers have no need to emphasise their place properties. Interestingly, [p t ʈ c k q] are optionally affricated to [pɸ tθ ts̪ cɕ kx qχ] in some languages. These affricates are rare, however, presumably because they are unnecessary from a perceptual point of view.

In this chapter we have described the role of the vowel elements |I U A| in consonants. Next, we continue our description of consonant representations by introducing the three consonant elements |ʔ H L|.

Further Reading

Most versions of ET analyse velars as having empty resonance, as described in Harris and Lindsey (1995). However, for arguments that labials and velars are treated as a natural class, see recent work by Judith Broadbent, Daniel Huber, Kuniya Nasukawa and Phillip Backley, and Tobias Scheer. The feature geometry approach is motivated in Rice and Avery (1991), while Clements and Hume (1995) present the case for unified features. The phonology of retroflex consonants is discussed in Hamann (2003), and phonetic labelling in French and English is surveyed in Dart (1991). The motivation for analysing affricates as stops is discussed in Clements (1999), Rubach (1994) and Kehrein (2002).

The data presented in this chapter are from the following sources: Ćavar and Hamann (2003) for Polish; Cho (1991) for Korean; Cristófaro-Silva and Guimarães (2009) for Brazilian Portuguese; Dillon (2001) for Wambaya; Dixon (1980) for Yanyuwa; Donaldson (1980) for Ngiyambaa; Emeneau (1984) for Toda; Flemming (2002) for Lahu and Mapila Malayalam; Flemming, Ladefoged and Thomason (2008) for vowel colouring in Montana Salish; Hagiwara

(1993) for Garifuna; Hall (1997) and Hoffmann (1963) for vowel alternations in Margi; Hume (1994) for Cantonese and Ngiyambaa; Ihiunu and Kenstowicz (1994) for Bedouin Arabic; Kenstowicz (1994) for Lardil; Labov (1994) for Skikun; McCarthy (1994) for pharyngeals in Arabic; Mithun and Basri (1986) for Selayarese; Pulleyblank (2003) for the vocalisation of sonorants in Salish; Rice (1994) for the development of Arapaho from Proto-Algonquian; Rubach (1993) for Slovak; Svantesson, Tsendina, Karlsson and Franzén (2005) for pharyngeal harmony in Mongolian.

References

Bellem, Alex (2007), 'Towards a comparative typology of emphatics: across Semitic and into Arabic dialect phonology', PhD dissertation, School of Oriental and African Studies, University of London.

Čavar, Małgorzata and Silke Hamann (2003), 'Polish velar and coronal palatalization – its perceptual background', in P. Kosta, J. Blaszczak, J. Frasek, L. Geist and M. Zygis (eds), *Investigations into Formal Slavic Linguistics*, Berlin: Peter Lang Verlag, pp. 31–48.

Cho, Young-Mee Yu (1991), 'On the universality of the coronal articulator', in C. Paradis and J-F. Prunet (eds), *The Special Status of Coronals: Internal and External Evidence*, San Diego: Academic Press, pp. 159–77.

Clements, George N. (1999), 'Affricates as non-contoured stops', in O. Fujimura, B. Joseph and B. Palek (eds), *Proceedings of LP '98: Item Order in Language and Speech*, Prague: The Karolinum Press, pp. 271–99.

Clements, George N. and Elizabeth Hume (1995), 'The internal organization of speech sounds', in J. A. Goldsmith (ed.), *The Handbook of Phonological Theory*, Cambridge, MA and Oxford: Blackwell, pp. 245–306.

Cristófaro-Silva, Thaïs and Daniela Guimarães (2009), 'Patterns of lenition in Brazilian Portuguese', in F. Kügler, C. Féry and R. van de Vijver (eds), *Variation and Gradience in Phonetics and Phonology*, Berlin: Mouton de Gruyter, pp. 141–62.

Cyran, Eugeniusz (1997), *Resonance Elements in Phonology: A Study in Munster Irish*, Lublin, Poland: Wydawnictwo Folium.

Dart, Sarah (1991), *Articulatory and Acoustic Properties of Apical and Laminal Articulations* (UCLA Working Papers in Phonetics 79), Los Angeles: UCLA Phonetics Laboratory.

Dillon, Caitlin (2001), 'Neutralization and reduplication interactions in Wambaya: an OT analysis', *Indiana University Linguistics Club Working Papers Online*.

Dixon, Robert (1980), *The Languages of Australia*, Cambridge: Cambridge University Press.

Donaldson, Tamsin (1980), *Ngiyambaa*, Cambridge: Cambridge University Press.
Emeneau, Murray (1984), *Toda Grammar and Texts*, Philadelphia: American Philosophical Society.
Flemming, Edward (2002), *Auditory Representations in Phonology*, New York and London: Routledge.
Flemming, Edward, Peter Ladefoged and Sally Thomason (2008), 'Phonetic structures of Montana Salish', *Journal of Phonetics* 36, 465–91.
Hagiwara, Robert (1993), 'Predictability in Garifuna vowel alternations: a problem for Radical Underspecification', in D. Silverman and R. Kirchner (eds), *Papers in Phonology* (UCLA Occasional Papers in Linguistics 13), Los Angeles: Department of Linguistics, University of California, pp. 49–59.
Hall, T. Alan (1997), *The Phonology of Coronals*, Amsterdam: John Benjamins.
Hamann, Silke (2003), *The Phonetics and Phonology of Retroflexes*, Utrecht: LOT Press.
Harris, John and Geoff Lindsey (1995), 'The elements of phonological representation', in J. Durand and F. Katamba (eds), *Frontiers of Phonology: Atoms, Structures, Derivations*, Harlow: Longman, pp. 34–79.
Hoffmann, Carl (1963), *A Grammar of the Margi Language*, London: Oxford University Press.
Hume, Elizabeth (1994), *Front Vowels, Coronal Consonants and their Interaction in Nonlinear Phonology*, New York: Garland.
Ihiunu, Peter and Michael Kenstowicz (1994), 'Two notes on Igbo vowels', unpublished manuscript, MIT.
Jakobson, Roman, Gunnar M. Fant and Morris Halle (1952), *Preliminaries to Speech Analysis*, Cambridge, MA: MIT Press.
Kehrein, Wolfgang (2002), *Phonological Representation and Phonetic Phasing: Affricates and Laryngeals*, Tübingen: Niemeyer.
Kenstowicz, Michael (1994), *Phonology in Generative Grammar*, Oxford: Blackwell.
Labov, William (1994), *Principles of Linguistic Change*, vol. 1: *Internal Factors*, Oxford: Blackwell.
McCarthy, John (1994), 'The phonetics and phonology of Semitic pharyngeals', in P. Keating (ed.), *Phonological Structure and Phonetic Form: Papers in Laboratory Phonology III*, Cambridge: Cambridge University Press, pp. 191–233.
Mithun, Marianne and Hasan Basri (1986), 'The phonology of Selayarese', *Oceanic Linguistics* 25, 210–54.
Pulleyblank, Edwin (2003), 'Non-contrastive features or enhancement by redundant features?', *Language and Linguistics* 4.4, 713–55.
Rice, Keren (1994), 'Peripheral in consonants', *Canadian Journal of Linguistics* 39, 191–216.

Rice, Keren and Peter Avery (1991), 'On the relationship between laterality and coronality', in C. Paradis and J-F. Prunet (eds), *The Special Status of Coronals: Internal and External Evidence*, San Diego: Academic Press, pp. 101–24.

Rubach, Jerzy (1993), *The Lexical Phonology of Slovak*, Oxford: Clarendon Press.

Rubach, Jerzy (1994), 'Affricates as strident stops in Polish', *Linguistic Inquiry* 25, 119–43.

Svantesson, Jan-Olof, Anna Tsendina, Anastasia Karlsson and Vivan Franzén (2005), *The Phonology of Mongolian*, Oxford: Oxford University Press.

Chapter 4

MANNER ELEMENTS IN CONSONANTS

4.1 Introduction

In Chapter 3 we saw how consonant place is represented by the vowel elements |I U A|. We now turn to those aspects of consonant structure that traditionally come under the headings manner and voice. Feature theories typically describe consonant manner using features such as [±cont] and [±nasal], while voicing (or, more generally, laryngeal) properties are captured by [±voice], [±spread glottis] and [±constricted glottis]. In ET there is no clear division between manner and laryngeal properties; collectively they are represented by the consonant elements |ʔ H L|.

Most consonants are actually a combination of vowel and consonant elements: the vowel elements |I U A| provide resonance while the consonant elements |ʔ H L| add non-resonance properties such as occlusion, aspiration, frication, voicing and nasality. So in a sense, consonants are not entirely consonantal; rather, they are a fusion of vowel and consonant properties. (One version of Dependency Phonology builds on this idea by proposing that segments are combinations of just two elements, C(onsonant) and V(owel).) To capture this aspect of segment structure, scholars traditionally invoke the notion of sonority and arrange segments on a sonority scale, a segment's position on the scale determining the extent of its vowel-like and/or consonant-like character. Sonority values are therefore expressed in relative terms rather than absolute terms, for example, 'α is more/less sonorous than β'. There is no doubt that sonority offers a convenient way of capturing segmental patterns. But as Harris (2006) explains, its usefulness is limited because it cannot easily explain why those patterns are the way they are. Its problem is one of circularity: the sonority scale derives from a set of observations about how segments are grouped into syllables and words, but at the same time, the distribution of individual segments is accounted for by referring to their position on the sonority scale. For this reason, ET does not base phonological generalisations on sonority. However, it does assume that most segments are a blend of vocalic and consonantal properties, which it formalises by allowing vowel elements |I U A| and consonant elements |ʔ H L| to combine in the same structure. Let us now examine the consonant elements |ʔ H L| in detail, beginning with the stop element |ʔ|. Like |I U A|, consonant elements represent information-bearing patterns in the speech signal and may be either headed or non-headed.

4.2 The |ʔ| Element

4.2.1 Stops

The stop element |ʔ|, also known as the occlusion element, is present in segments which involve a sudden and sustained drop in acoustic energy. On a spectrogram, this reduction in energy appears as an empty vertical slice. Speakers cause a reduction in acoustic energy by momentarily interrupting the airflow – that is, by making a complete closure somewhere in the oral cavity or at the glottis. In Figures 4.1(a–c) there is a drop in energy during the hold phase of the stop sounds [p d ʔ]. Although the |ʔ| element is characterised by an absence (or near absence) of speech signal activity, it carries positive linguistic information because it functions as a cue to the identification of stops.

The oral stop [p] has the structure |U ʔ| (voicing properties are omitted – these will be described in §4.3 and §4.4). This structure has two elements and therefore combines two speech signal patterns: headed |U| provides labial resonance while |ʔ| marks a drop in energy, and together they are interpreted as a labial stop. Now, if we remove the place element from |U ʔ| then we are left with just |ʔ|, essentially a placeless stop. This is phonetically interpreted as a glottal stop [ʔ],

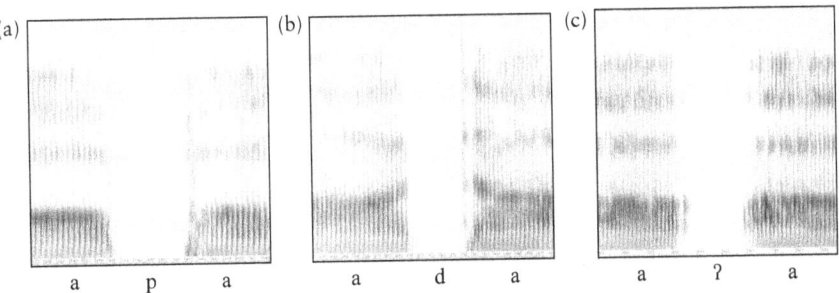

Figure 4.1 Energy pattern of |ʔ|. (a) Spectrogram of [apa]; (b) Spectrogram of [ada]; (c) Spectrogram of [aʔa]

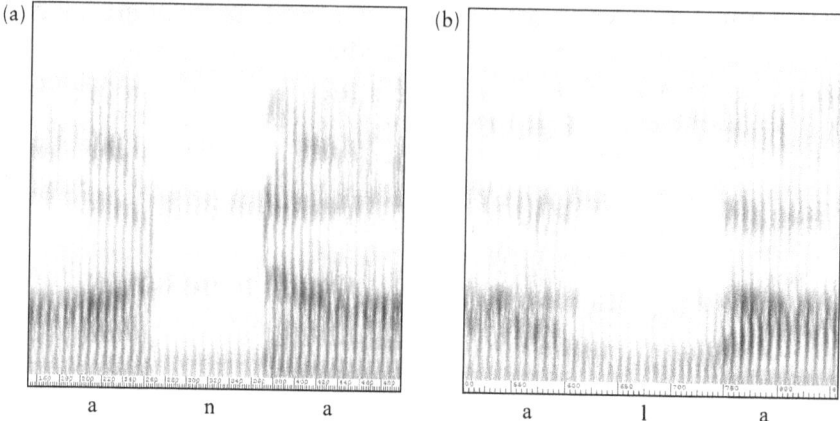

Figure 4.2 *Energy pattern of nasals and laterals. (a) Spectrogram of [ana]; (b) Spectrogram of [ala]*

as this is the easiest way for speakers to produce a drop in acoustic energy without any accompanying oral resonance. What this tells us is that ET does not consider glottal to be an active place property – there is no such thing as a glottal resonance element, for instance. Instead, glottal may be understood as the phonetic result of having no resonance element, and therefore, no specification for oral place.

Like oral stops, nasals such as [m ŋ N] and laterals such as [l ɭ ɫ ʎ] are produced with some occlusion in the oral cavity. And again this appears on the spectrogram as a drop in acoustic energy, suggesting that nasals and laterals also contain |ʔ| in their representation (see Figure 4.2). However, remember that a segment's element structure is based primarily on its phonological behaviour, not its acoustic properties. So we can only be sure that nasals and laterals contain |ʔ| if we see them patterning with oral stops. This is what happens in Basque, where oral stops, nasals and laterals form a natural class of |ʔ| segments. As (1) shows, the |ʔ| segments [p t k l n] cause a preceding oral stop to delete. Presumably, this is done to avoid contiguous |ʔ| segments.

(1) *bat paratu*   [ba paratu]   'put one'
     arront lapurre [arron lapurre] 'a total thief'
     bat naka   [ba naka]   'one by one'

In the same context affricates also lose their |ʔ| element and are reinterpreted as fricatives, as in *hots-bat* [hos-bat] 'a cold'. Korean is another language in which nasals and laterals pattern with oral stops; for example, a word-final consonant must be from the class [p t k l m n ŋ].

Not all languages behave like Basque and Korean, however. There are some in which nasals and/or laterals do not contain |ʔ|. For instance, nasals lack |ʔ| in Samish; this is clear from the way they pattern with |ʔ|-less fricatives rather than with oral stops. In this language geminate stops and affricates are pronounced as sequences of two separate articulations, as in (2a), whereas geminate fricatives and nasals are produced as long consonants, as in (2b).

(2) a. [ʔitʰtʰ]   'to sleep'
       [ʔəmatʰtʰxʷ]   'seat somebody'
       [sŋetʃtʃ]   'lagoon'

    b. [tʰsasːən]   'I'm poor'
       [sʔasəsː tən' seləs]   'palm of your hand'
       [pʰənːuxʷəŋ]   'Matia Island'

On the other hand, in Frisian it is the lateral consonant [l] which lacks |ʔ|. [n] in the verbal prefix *in-* agrees in place with a following stop, as shown in (3a), but not with a following fricative or liquid (3b). The difference between the two contexts comes down to the presence of |ʔ| in (3a) versus its absence in (3b): that is, [l] does not trigger place assimilation because it does not contain |ʔ|. When assimilation fails to take place, the [n] of *in-* is reinterpreted as nasality on the preceding vowel, as in [ĩlɪzə] (*[inlɪzə]) 'to preserve'.

(3) a. in-pɑkə   [impɑkə]   'to wrap up'
       in-gɪən   [iŋgɪən]   'to enter'

    b. in-fɑlə   [ĩfɑlə]   'to fall in'
       in-ʋɛɲə   [ĩʋɛɲə]   'to live with one's parents'
       in-lɪzə   [ĩlɪzə]   'to preserve'

In a recent study, coronal nasals such as [n n̪ ɲ] and laterals such as [l l̪ ʎ] were found to behave as |ʔ| segments (in feature terms, [–continuant] segments) in about half the languages surveyed and as |ʔ|-less segments ([+continuant]) in the remaining half. So in ET we should find nasals and laterals being represented with and without |ʔ| in roughly equal proportions. As always, we need to consider the phonological behaviour of the segments concerned in order to decide one way or the other, so the structure of nasals and laterals must be established on a language by language basis. We return to the representation of nasals in §4.4.1 and to the representation of laterals in Chapter 5.

4.2.2 Ejectives

In complex expressions the difference between headed |ʔ| and non-headed |ʔ| is linguistically important: non-headed |ʔ| represents the class of plain stops, as we have just seen, while headed |ʔ| represents the class of ejectives. Let us look at the reasons for assuming that ejective stops have headed |ʔ|.

In Chapter 2 we saw how headedness can make a vowel element stronger and more prominent, particularly in compounds; for example, |A| is more prominent in [æ] |A̲ I| than in [e] |A I̲| because in [æ] it is headed. The same applies to consonant elements, meaning that expressions with headed |ʔ| should display more prominent stop-like characteristics than expressions with just non-headed |ʔ|. This prominence shows up as a lengthened or exaggerated period of low energy, which is what we observe in ejective stops such as [k' t' q']. In fact there are two strong cues to help listeners identify ejectives. One is this lengthened period of reduced energy and the other is their glottalic release burst, which is quite distinct from the pulmonic burst we get in plain stops. To reproduce the acoustic cues for an ejective stop, speakers must first make two closures in the vocal tract, one somewhere in the oral cavity, at the lips or the velum, for instance, and another at the glottis. Next, the larynx must be raised in order to compress the column of air which has become trapped between these two closures. Finally, while the glottis is closed the oral closure is released with an audible burst. Ejectives usually have a louder release burst than plain stops because air pressure behind the oral closure is greater. So glottal closure is clearly a key feature of ejectives, which is expressed phonologically through headedness: the class of ejectives is marked by headed |ʔ|.

Around 15 per cent of the world's languages make a distinction between plain and ejective stops, including many languages of the Americas such as Navajo, Klamath and Quileute. In these systems the headedness of |ʔ| is therefore phonologically significant. (4) shows examples from Montana Salish to illustrate how the distinction between [p] and [p'] is represented. It is reported that ejective [p'] in this language is produced with a considerable time lag between oral release and glottal release. This makes the glottalic character of [p'] more easily perceptible and therefore helps listeners to recover the linguistic information carried by headed |ʔ|.

(4)   [páʕas]   [p] = |U̲ ʔ| 'face is pale'
       [p'aʕáp]   [p'] = |U̲ ʔ̲| 'grass fire'

Note that ejective release can also be a feature of affricates. For example, the ejective series in Montana Salish contains affricates as well as stops, as in [ts'áɫt] 'it's cold'. In ET affricated stops are considered to be structurally no different from regular stops (§3.8).

In some languages, the difference in headedness between plain stops with non-headed |ʔ| and ejective stops with headed |ʔ̲| manifests itself as a difference in phonological strength; that is, ejectives are favoured in strong prosodic positions and plain stops in weak positions. One such language is Maidu, where ejective [p' t' k'] weaken to plain [p t k] before a consonant.

(5) a. jèp'ím kawáju   'stallion'   b. jèpsí   'men'
       batám hit'í   'butter'   hítpe   'fat'
       bolók'om soló   'moccasin'   bolókti 'put on shoes'

Because the ejectives in (5a) precede a vowel they are syllabified in an onset; this context is sufficiently strong to allow [p' t' k'] to be interpreted in full. Compare this with (5b), where the same segments are reinterpreted as plain [p t k] because they occupy a weaker pre-consonantal position. So in this language the headedness of |ʔ| is sensitive to syllabic position: headed |ʔ̲| is permitted before a vowel, but elsewhere it weakens to non-headed |ʔ| by losing its headed status in order to conform to the grammar of the language. Speakers interpret this weakened structure as a plain stop. The behaviour of stops in Maidu provides another example of consonant weakening involving a loss of headedness – recall from Chapter 3 that resonance elements undergo this form of weakening too.

Although headed |ʔ̲| usually defines ejectives, other interpretations are also possible. In fact, because |ʔ| is a unit of phonological structure and not a phonetic property, we can expect to find some cross-linguistic variation in the way it is realised. In Korean, headed |ʔ̲| defines the series of stops variously described as fortis, glottalised or tense, which are produced with a glottal constriction. Although Korean fortis stops are not produced in exactly the same way as ejectives, their phonological behaviour suggests that they too have headed |ʔ̲|; sometimes they are even transcribed as [p' t' tʃ' k'] to highlight their ejective-like nature. Korean makes a contrast between plain [p t tʃ k] and fortis [p' t' tʃ' k'] before a vowel but, as in Maidu, this becomes neutralised elsewhere in favour of the plain series. For example, (6b) shows how fortis [k'] alternates with plain [k] in the verb *tak'*- 'polish'.

(6) a. mək-   'eat'   b. tak'-   'polish'
       [mək-ə]   'to eat'   [tak'-a]   'to polish'
       [mək-k'o]   'eat (conj.)'   [tak-k'o]   'polish (conj.)'

The [k'] ~ [k] alternation is another example of a weakening effect controlled by headedness. Before a vowel the headed expression |U ʔ| is prosodically strong and can be interpreted in full as an ejective [k'], as in [tak'-a] 'to polish'. But pre-consonantal position is weaker, so the same expression |U ʔ| must itself weaken from headed to non-headed. And when |U ʔ| weakens to |U ʔ|, speakers reinterpret it as a plain [k], as in [tak-k'o] 'polish (conjunctive)'.

4.2.3 Implosives

Most feature theories use the feature [±constricted glottis] to distinguish ejectives from plain stops: ejectives are [+constricted glottis] and plain stops [−constricted glottis]. Implosives such as [ɓ ɗ ʄ] are also marked [+constricted glottis], which allows ejectives and implosives to be grouped together as a natural class of glottalic consonants. To express the same natural class in ET we have to assume that implosives, like ejectives, have headed |ʔ|. This is appropriate, given that implosives display a prolonged and prominent span of low acoustic energy similar to that of ejectives. In some languages such as Swahili, implosives are simply phonetic variants of regular voiced stops. But in other languages they behave independently of the voiced series, and therefore require a distinct representation. In Kimatuumbi, for example, implosives (but not voiced stops) are banned from nasal–stop clusters, hence [kitʊʊmbɪ] (*[kitʊʊmɓɪ]) 'hill'. And in Zina Kotoko the voiced stops (but not the implosives) function as depressor consonants, causing the tone on a following vowel to lower; so verb roots with a lexical H tone preserve their tone after an implosive ([n-ɗə́v-à] 'put') but lose their H tone after a voiced stop ([m-ban-à] (*[m-bán-à]) 'bathe').

Ejectives and implosives form a natural class of headed |ʔ| segments, but there still remains the question of how to distinguish between them. In ET the difference is taken to be one of voicing: ejectives are voiceless and therefore pattern with other voiceless obstruents whereas implosives are voiced and belong to the same class as other voiced obstruents. The fact that [ɓ ɗ ʄ] alternate with the voiced stops [b d g] in Kimatuumbi, and not with [p t k], reinforces the point. The representation of voicing contrasts will be described later in this chapter. For the moment let us just say that ejectives have headed |ʔ| plus a voicelessness element called |H|, while implosives have headed |ʔ| plus a voicing element called |L|.

Having seen how |ʔ| functions in representations, let us compare this element with its feature equivalents. The contrasts we have described can be expressed just as easily using traditional features; for example, we could have used [–cont] instead of non-headed |ʔ| and [+constricted glottis] in place of headed |ʔ|. And if our only goal were to represent lexical contrasts, then it would not really matter whether we used features or elements. But segmental phonology is about more than just describing contrasts. For instance, it should be able to explain why sounds form certain natural classes and behave in predictable ways. In this sense, ET has the advantage of being able to refer to the same element in two different forms, headed and non-headed; each form captures a different natural class, but at the same time the two classes are inherently related because they have an element in common. In the case of |ʔ| we can express a relation between the class of ejectives and the class of stops because both are represented by the stop element. On the other hand, with features it is difficult to show this relation directly. One option is to employ a feature geometry in which features are related structurally; for example, Clements and Hume (1995) treat [constricted glottis] as a dependent of the laryngeal node, as shown in (7).

(7)
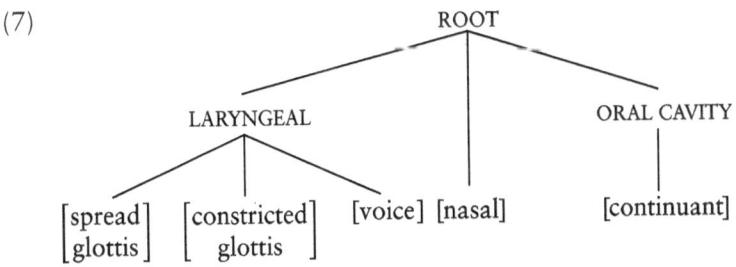

However, even this approach encounters a problem, in that it is difficult to express a formal link between stops and ejectives because [–cont] and [+constricted glottis] belong to separate nodes. According to (7) there is no grammatical connection between these features because one attaches to the laryngeal node and the other to the oral cavity node (or in some other models, to the manner node). Clearly it is important to look beyond the familiar criteria of contrast and alternation when evaluating systems of segmental representation.

4.2.4 Laryngealised Vowels

So far we have only described |ʔ| in consonants. But because ET allows any element to occupy any syllabic position, we can expect to find languages in which even |ʔ|, the most consonant-like element, is present in vowels. One such language is Jalapa Mazatec, which makes a distinction between the plain (modal voice) vowels [i æ a o u] and the laryngealised (creaky voice) vowels [ḭ æ̰ a̰ o̰ ṵ]. In the following examples tone is omitted.

(8) a. *Modal voice*   b. *Creaky voice*
       [ja] 'tree'   [ja̰] 'he carries'
       [nt^hæ] 'seed'   [ndæ̰] 'buttocks'
       [si] 'dirty'   [sḭ] 'holiday'
       [su] 'lukewarm'   [tʃṵ] 'blouse'

Laryngealised vowels are produced with creaky voice, in which the vocal folds are open along only part of their length; this opening is sufficient to produce voicing, but at the same time it results in a series of irregularly spaced glottal pulses. Impressionistically, this gives creaky vowels a jittery quality. Furthermore, vocal fold vibration tends to be slower in creaky voice than in modal voice, so individual voicing pulses are noticeably further apart. In the spectrograms in Figure 4.3, each vertical striation marks a single glottal pulse; notice how the pulses produced during creaky voice (Figure 4.3(a)) are widely spaced whereas the pulses for modal voice (Figure 4.3(b)) are more closely packed together.

We know that |ʔ| is responsible for creaky voice because some

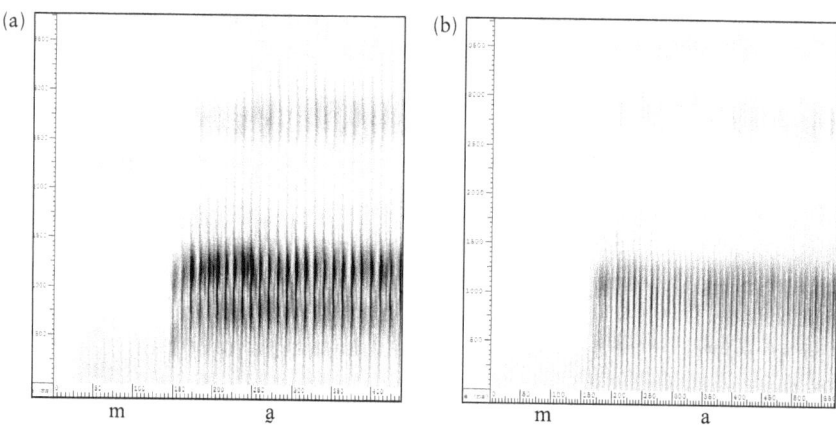

Figure 4.3 Glottal pulses in creaky and modal voice. (a) Spectrogram of [ma̰] (creaky voice); (b) Spectrogram of [ma] (modal voice)

THE |ʔ| ELEMENT

languages show a phonological link between creakiness in vowels and occlusion in consonants. For example, Capanahua has an alternation between Vʔ. (vowel plus coda [ʔ]) in strong syllables and V̰ (laryngealised vowel) in weak syllables. A syllable in Capanahua is strong if two conditions are met: first, it must be the first syllable in the morpheme, and second, it must occupy the head of a metrical foot. Counting from the left, odd-numbered syllables are usually strong and even-numbered syllables are usually weak, since foot structure is left-headed in this language and most roots are disyllabic.

(9) a. Vʔ. (in strong syllables)

ʔiʔbu-riʔbi   (ʔiʔ.bu)(riʔ.bi)   [ʔiʔ.bu.riʔ.bi]
owner also   'the owner, too'

pi-ma-riʔbi-i   (pi.ma)(riʔ.bi).ʔi   [pi.ma.riʔ.bi.ʔi]
eat CAUS again PRES   '(he) makes (him) eat again'

tuʔku-taʔ-ki   (tuʔ.ku)(taʔ.ki)   [tuʔ.ku.taʔ.ki]
frog EVID DECL   'it is a frog'

b. V̰ (in weak syllables)

ʔatapa-riʔbi   (ʔa.ta)(pa.riʔ).bi   [ʔa.ta.pa.rḭ.bi]
hen also   'the hen, too'

tuʔku-ma-taʔ-ki   (tuʔ.ku)(ma.taʔ).ki   [tuʔ.ku.ma.ta̰.ki]
frog NEG EVID DECL   'it is not a frog'

ʔuʔčiti-taʔ-ki   (ʔuʔ.či)(ti.taʔ).ki   [ʔuʔ.či.ti.ta̰.ki]
dog EVID DECL   'it is a dog'

In strong syllables a |ʔ| in coda position is interpreted as [ʔ], hence *riʔ.bi* [riʔ.bi] 'also' in (9a), illustrated in (10a). But in weak syllables |ʔ| cannot be interpreted in a coda; instead it is incorporated into the preceding nucleus, forming a laryngealised vowel, for example *riʔ.bi* [rḭ.bi] 'also' in (9b), illustrated in (10b).

(10) a.   *riʔ.bi* [riʔbi] (strong)   b.   *riʔ.bi* [rḭbi] (weak)

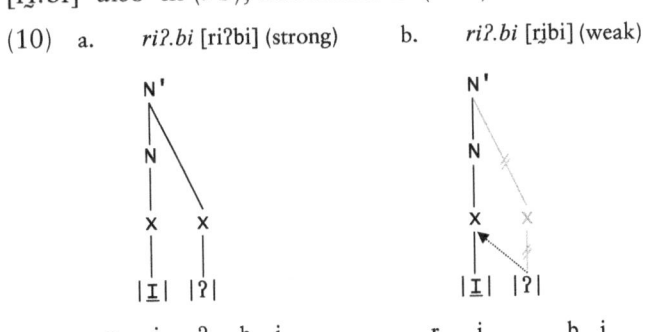

As (10) shows, strong syllables in Capanahua may contain a coda consonant [ʔ] whereas weak syllables may not. Yet although the expression |ʔ| is not interpretable in a weak syllable, the |ʔ| element itself is not lost; instead it is interpreted in the adjacent nucleus along with any vowel elements already present. Combining |ʔ| with |I U A| in a nucleus produces a vowel with creaky voice. Hence, |I ʔ| in (10b) is interpreted as [ḭ]. Further evidence of the link between |ʔ| and creaky voice can be found in other languages too, particularly those of the Americas. Cayuga displays a coalescence process similar to the one in Capanahua, where a coda [ʔ] merges with a preceding unstressed vowel to produce a laryngealised vowel. And in Hupa long vowels are interpreted with creaky voice if an ejective stop occupies the following coda position. So although we have reason to think of the |ʔ| element as belonging naturally in consonants, there is also evidence that it contributes to the structure of vowels too.

Let us summarise the characteristics of |ʔ|. In consonants, |ʔ| maps onto the speech signal as a sharp reduction in acoustic energy; this is produced by an oral or glottal closure which interrupts the airflow. Non-headed |ʔ| is present in oral stops such as [b t̪ q] as well as, in some languages, nasals and laterals. Meanwhile, headed |ʔ| is found in ejectives such as [t' tʃ' p'] and implosives such as [ɓ ɗ ɠ]. The stop element is also present in laryngealised vowels such as [ḛ a̰ o̰ː a̰ḭ]. As a single element, |ʔ| is pronounced as a glottal stop [ʔ]. In this section we have seen that the stop element plays an important role in the representation of consonants, as well as a marginal role in vowel representations. But to fully understand the function of |ʔ| in sound systems, we need to consider how it combines with the two remaining consonant elements, |H| and |L|. The nasality element |L| will be introduced in §4.4. Before that, we examine the noise element |H|.

4.3 The |H| Element

4.3.1 Frication

The |H| element has the effect of raising fundamental frequency, and is present in segments displaying aperiodic noise energy. Aperiodic noise is produced by high-frequency acoustic energy which is distributed fairly randomly across the upper part of the spectrum. It is therefore distinct from periodic energy, which is associated with clearly defined formants of the kind we see in vowels and other

THE |H| ELEMENT   125

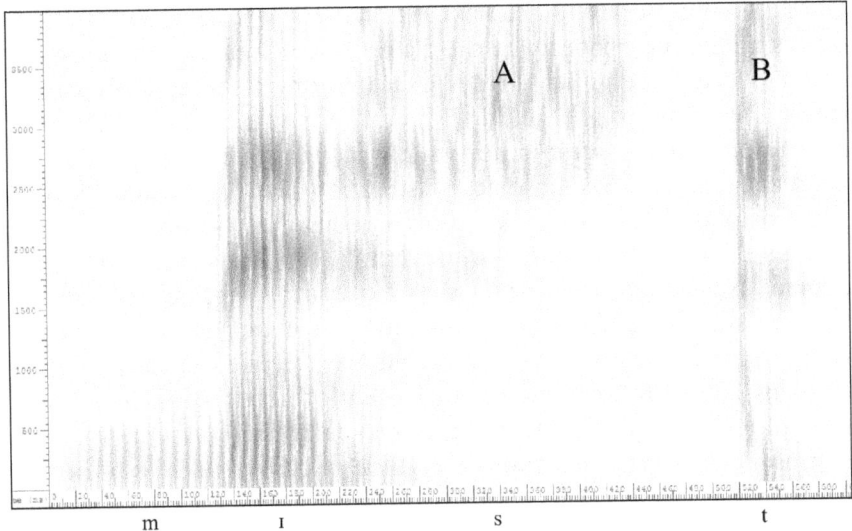

Figure 4.4 Spectrogram of missed ['mɪst]

sonorants. There are two kinds of aperiodic noise, continuous and transient. Continuous noise is produced when turbulent air passes through a narrow constriction. This creates a hissing sound which, in speech, is perceived as frication in fricatives. On the other hand, transient noise involves a sudden burst of energy which can be produced by clapping your hands, coughing, or in speech, by releasing a stop. The English word *missed* ['mɪst] shown in Figure 4.4 displays both continuous and transient noise. The transition from [ɪ] to [s] is marked by a switch from periodic to aperiodic energy. The aperiodic energy in [s] produces the continuous noise that characterises fricatives, shown in the upper part of the spectrogram as an area of dense irregular shading (labelled A). Then, following the hold phase of [t], there is another span of aperiodic energy (labelled B); this is much shorter in duration, and produces the transient noise we associate with the release burst in stops. Both types of noise are represented by the same |H| element; [s] and [t] therefore have the representations shown in (11). Voicing properties are not shown.

(11) a. [s] *Acoustic properties*   b. [t] *Acoustic properties*

　　　　|A| coronal resonance　　　　|A| coronal resonance
　　　　|H| noise (frication),　　　　|H| noise (burst), raised F0
　　　　　　 raised F0　　　　　　　　|ʔ| reduction in energy

The presence of |H| in fricatives is uncontroversial; after all, frication is a defining property of the class of fricatives. But the presence of |H| in stops requires further explanation. A possible objection to the idea that stops contain |H| is that the presence or absence of an audible release burst is not usually contrastive in stops; that is, languages do not make a lexical distinction between released [p t k] and unreleased [p̚ t̚ k̚]. We should remember, however, that elements are units of linguistic information, not units of contrast. Of course, linguistic information usually *is* contrastive, but it need not be. Sometimes elements carry information which is important for perception, for example, which is the case here. The release burst in stops is rich in acoustic cues to place of articulation, making it phonologically significant. For this reason we will assume that |H| is present in stops, even though audible release is not a contrastive property.

4.3.2 Consonant Weakening

There are also phonological reasons for assuming that released stops contain |H|. In weak positions consonants are susceptible to weakening, which involves the loss or suppression of some of their elements. As we saw with vowels in §2.5.2, when an element is suppressed it fails to be pronounced, but it may leave behind other elements which can still be phonetically interpreted. In fact the weakening process often exposes any remaining elements, making them more easily identifiable. For example, in most dialects of Spanish the voiced stops [b d g] weaken to [β ð ɣ] between vowels.

(12)   [b] ~ [β]:   *bota*   [bota]   'boot'
                    la bota   [la βota]   'the boot'
       [d] ~ [ð]:   *dota*   [dota]   'he equips'
                    la dota   [la ðota]   'he equips her'
       [g] ~ [ɣ]:   *gota*   [gota]   'drop'
                    la gota   [la ɣota]   'the drop'

When a stop weakens to a fricative, it loses its oral occlusion, that is, the |ʔ| element is suppressed. But because the outcome of this process is a fricative, which contains |H|, we have to assume that |H| was already present in the original stop. This is illustrated in (13), where shading indicates a suppressed element. Obstruent voicing has been omitted.

(13)   [g]*ota* 'drop'   [g] = |U H ʔ|
       la [ɣ]*ota* 'the drop' [ɣ] = |U H ʔ|

In segments such as [g], where |H| and |ʔ| are both present, |H| represents transient noise and is interpreted as an audible release burst. Interpreting |H| as continuous noise (frication) is not an option here because frication is not compatible with occlusion: speakers cannot produce the prolonged high-frequency energy needed for frication at the same time as producing the drop in energy needed for |ʔ|. But when |ʔ| is suppressed, the barrier to frication is removed and the weakened expression |U H ʔ| can be interpreted with continuous noise: the combination of |H| (continuous noise) with |U| (velar resonance) produces a velar fricative [ɣ]. Stop-to-fricative weakening, or spirantisation, is very common cross-linguistically. In some languages it affects the entire stop system; for example, in Tiberian Hebrew [p t k b d g] weaken to [f θ x v ð ɣ]. And in other languages it targets stops only at certain places of articulation; for example, in Quechua [k q] weaken to [x χ].

Although spirantisation is perhaps the most common form of stop weakening, other weakening processes are also possible. In the dialect of Spanish spoken in Western Andalusia the stops [b d g] may spirantise to [β ð ɣ], as in (12), or they may weaken further to the approximants [β̞ ð̞ ɣ̞]. Since [β̞ ð̞ ɣ̞] are frictionless continuants, they presumably lack |H| as well as |ʔ|, as shown in (14).

(14)   ['deβan] 'let them owe'   [β] = |U H ʔ|
       ['tejðe] (mountain name)   [ð] = |A H ʔ|
       ['rjeɣo] 'I water'   [ɣ] = |U H ʔ|

Suppressing |H| and |ʔ| leaves just a resonance element remaining. And as we saw in Chapter 3, a single resonance element in an onset is realised as a glide. The approximants [β̞ ð̞ ɣ̞] in (14) do indeed have the character of glides. Of course, in linguistic terms it makes no difference whether speakers produce an approximant [β̞ ð̞ ɣ̞] or a fricative [β ð ɣ], since the two are phonologically equivalent – both are weakened versions of the original stop. So it should not be surprising to find that segments resulting from weakening processes often show some degree of phonetic variation. For example, when [b] weakens to a continuant the resulting sound could fall anywhere within the range [β]–[β̞]–[ʋ]–[w]; the choice may be down to external factors such as register or speech rate, or it may simply reflect the preferences of individual languages or even different dialects of the same language.

We now know that weakening processes cause elements to be suppressed, leaving any remaining ones still interpretable. We also know that stops and fricatives are structured as follows:

Stops resonance |I U A| + noise |H| + occlusion |ʔ|
Fricatives resonance |I U A| + noise |H|

From this, we can anticipate how stops and fricatives might behave in weak positions, because weakening always produces an expression containing a subset of the elements from the original segment. For example, we correctly predict the weakening effects in (15)–(20).

(15) Spirantisation Target: stops
  Realisation: fricatives
  Suppressed: |ʔ|
  Interpreted: resonance, |H|
  Example: [b] → [β] (|U H ʔ| → |U H ʔ|)

Table 4.1 Spirantisation

	Strong		Weak	Context	Examples
Northern Corsican	[b d g]	→	[β ð ɣ]	V__V	[a βokka] 'the mouth' (cf. [bokka] 'mouth')
Quechua	[k q]	→	[x χ]	__.C	[ʎixʎa] (*[ʎikʎa]) 'small shawl'
Assamese	[pʰ tʰ bʱ]	→	[ɸ θ β]	__#	[loβ] (*[lobʱ]) 'greed'
Nez Perce	[t]	→	[s]	__n,w	[ˈjuʔs-ne] 'poor (obj.)' (cf. [ˈjuʔt] 'poor')

(16) Non-release Target: stops
  Realisation: unreleased stops
  Suppressed: |H|
  Interpreted: resonance, |ʔ|
  Example: [p] → [p̚] (|U H ʔ| → |U H ʔ|)

Table 4.2 Non-release

	Strong		Weak	Context	Examples
Korean	[p pʰ]	→	[p̚]	__C/#	[pap̚] 'rice' (cf. [papin] 'rice (topic)') [sup̚] 'forest' (cf. [supʰin] 'forest (topic)')
	[k kʰ k']	→	[k̚]		
English	[p t k]	→	[p̚ t̚ k̚]	__.C	[ˈæk̚tə] *actor*, [ˈfit̚nəs] *fitness*

THE |H| ELEMENT   129

	Strong		Weak	Context	Examples
Malay	[p b]	→	[p̚]	__#	[serba:p̚] *sebab* 'reason'
	[t d]	→	[t̚]	__#	[abat̚] *abad* 'century'
Laotian	[p t k ʔ]	→	[p̚ t̚ k̚ ʔ̚]	__#	[dɑk̚] (*[dɑk]) 'deep'
					[cet̚] (*[cet]) 'seven'

(17) Glottaling to [ʔ]   Target: stops
                         Realisation: [ʔ]
                         Suppressed: resonance, |H|
                         Interpreted: |ʔ|
                         Example: [k] → [ʔ]   (|U H ʔ| → |U̶ H̶ ʔ|)

Table 4.3 Glottaling

	Strong		Weak	Context	Examples
Toba Batak	[p t k]	→	[ʔ]	__C	[ganuʔ tan] 'every year' (cf. [ganup] 'every')
Arbore	[t' tʃ' k' ɓ ɗ]	→	[ʔ]	__C	[dʒéʔ-lo] 'this scorpion' [dʒéɗ] 'scorpion'
Malay	[k]	→	[ʔ]	__C/#	[soraʔ] 'shout' (cf. [sorak-i] 'shout (trans.)')
English (London)	[p t k]	⟩	[ʔ]	__#	[læɪʔ] *late*, [lʊʔ] *look*

(18) Debuccalisation to [h] Target: stops, fricatives
                             Realisation: [h]
                             Suppressed: resonance, (|ʔ|)
                             Interpreted: |H|
                             Example: [x] → [h]   (|U H| → |U̶ H|)

Table 4.4 Debuccalisation

	Strong		Weak	Context	Examples
Spanish	[s]	→	[h]	__#	[toh] *tos* 'cough (noun)' (cf. [toser] *toser* 'to cough')
Páes	[x]	→	[h]	non-initial	[jáʔha] (*[jáʔxa]) 'ladle' [háʔⁿda]~[xáʔⁿda] 'equal'

	Strong	Weak	Context	Examples
Miami-Illinois	[θ ʃ ç x] →	[h]	before an obstruent	[tohpone] 'table' (Proto-Algonquian *[ato-xpoweni])
Kanakuru	[k]	→ [h]	V__V	[garak] 'okra', [garah-i] 'the okra'

(19) Vocalisation Target: stops, fricatives
                  Realisation: glides
                  Suppressed: |ʔ|, |H|
                  Interpreted: resonance
                  Example: [p] → [w]   (|U̱ H ʔ| → |U̱ H ʔ|)

Table 4.5 Vocalisation

	Strong	Weak	Context	Examples
Kanakuru	[p t]	→ [w ɹ]	V__V	[jaŋkat] 'lice', [woi jaŋkaɹ u] 'not lice'
Warndarang	[b ɟ]	→ [w j]	V__V (redupl.)	[ɹaɽi-ɹaɽi] 'to do continuously' (*[ɹaɽi-ɹaɽi])
Shoshone	[m] [n]	→ [w̃] → [j̃]	V(h)__V	[níw̃ɨ] (*[nímɨ]) nümü 'person' [wíh̃ju] (*[wíhnu]) wihnu 'then'
Axininca Campa	[k p]	→ [j w]	V__	[porita] 'small hen' [no-woritati] 'my small hen'

(20) Tapping to [ɾ] Target: coronal stops
                     Realisation: [ɾ]
                     Suppressed: |ʔ|, |H|
                     Interpreted: coronal (|I|)
                                    resonance
                     Example: [t] → [ɾ]   (|I H ʔ| → |I H ʔ|)

Table 4.6 Tapping

	Strong	Weak	Context	Examples
English (Australia)	[t]	→ [ɾ]	V__V	[ˈwɔːɾə] water, [ˈgɒɾə] got to
Low German	[d t]	→ [ɾ]	V__V	[ˈvaːɾə] Water 'water' [ˈbeːrn] bäden 'to pray'
Tagalog	[d]	→ [ɾ]	V__V	[pa-tawaɾ-in] 'forgive' (cf. [tawad] 'forgiveness')
Taiwanese	[t]	→ [ɾ]	V__V	[kʰuɾa] (*[kʰuta]) 'little hole'

Weakening processes like these tell us a good deal about how individual elements are interpreted. This is because they often leave just a single element remaining, and we can hear the phonetic quality of that remaining element when the weakened segment is pronounced. The processes in (17)–(20) all produce simplex expressions, allowing us to assign phonetic values to individual elements as shown in Table 4.7. The examples shown in (a)–(d) confirm the following element interpretations, which we have already discussed:

|?| = [?]   drop in energy, no accompanying resonance
|I̲| = [j]   palatality, no accompanying consonant properties
|U̲|= [w]   labiality, no accompanying consonant properties
|A|= [ɹ]   coronality, no accompanying consonant properties

So let us focus on the remaining examples in (e)–(g). As (e) shows, when |H| stands alone it is interpreted as a glottal fricative [h]. But because glottal segments have no active resonance (§4.2.1), we may also view [h] as bare frication, that is, frication with no accompanying consonant properties. This matches our earlier description of |H| as aperiodic noise, since acoustic noise roughly corresponds to articulatory frication. (Note that, in reality, single |H| is rarely interpreted without some kind of resonance, since |H| tends to copy the resonance properties of a neighbouring vowel. As a result, [h] displays different vowel colourings according to its context, creating alternations such as [hi] ~ [çi], [hu] ~ [ɸu], [ha] ~ [ħa], and so on.) Example (e) in Table 4.7 is illustrated by Spanish, where a coronal fricative [s] |A H| ([toser] *toser* 'to cough') weakens to [h] |A̲ H| ([toh] *tos* 'cough (n.)') when the coronal element |A| is suppressed word-finally. The surviving |H| is interpreted as pure frication, i.e. [h]. Note that single |H|, like single |?|, has a similar interpretation whether it is headed or not: |H̲| and |H| are both realised as [h]. The debuccalisation process shown in (e) of Table 4.7 is represented as in (21).

(21) a.   [toser] *toser* 'to cough'   b.   [toh] *tos* 'cough (n.)'

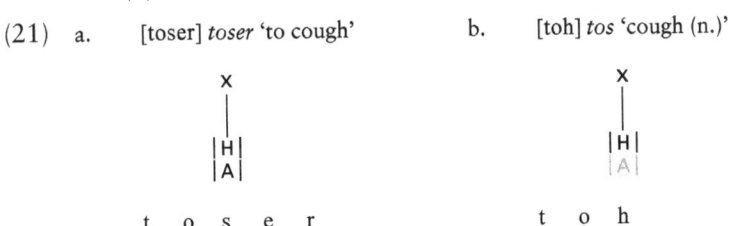

Turning to the weakening processes in (f) and (g) of Table 4.7, these are examples of vocalisation in which all consonant properties are suppressed to leave just a resonance element remaining. And

Table 4.7 Interpreting single elements

		Interpretation process			Example
a.	|ʔ|	[ʔ]	glottaling	[k] → [ʔ] (= |U̱ H ʔ|)	London English: [lʊʔ] *look*
b.	|I|	[j]	vocalisation	[ɟ] → [j] (= |I̱ H ʔ|)	Warndarang: [jaɟi-jaɟi] 'to do continuously'
c.	|U|	[w]	vocalisation	[p] → [w] (= |U̱ H ʔ|)	Axininca Campa: [no-woritati] 'my small hen' (cf. [porita] 'small hen')
d.	|A|	[ɹ]	rhoticisation	[t] → [ɹ] (= |A H ʔ|)	Tyneside English: [ˌgeɹəˈweː] *get away*
e.	|H|	[h]	debuccalisation	[s] → [h] (= |A H|)	Spanish: [toh] *tos* 'cough' (cf. [toser] *toser*)
f.	|U|	[ɯ]	vocalisation	[g] → [ɯ] (= |U H ʔ|)	Icelandic: [saːɣa]~[saːya] *saga* 'story'
g.	|I|	[ɾ]	tapping	[t] → [ɾ] (= |I H ʔ|)	Australian English: [ˈwɔːɾə] *water*

because it occupies a non-nuclear position, the surviving resonance element is realised as a glide. In (f) it is velar resonance that remains, non-headed |U| being interpreted as the velar glide [ɰ]. The example [saːɰa]~[saːɣa] *saga* 'story' shows how intervocalic [g] in Icelandic optionally weakens in this way. The weakening effect is illustrated in (22a). Meanwhile (g) shows how |I| coronals weaken to a coronal tap when all other elements are suppressed, as in Australian English ['wɔːɾə] *water*. In other words, [ɾ] is the phonetic interpretation of a single non-headed |I|. The tapping process is represented as in (22b).

(22) a. [saːɰa] *saga* 'story' b. ['wɔːɾə] *water*

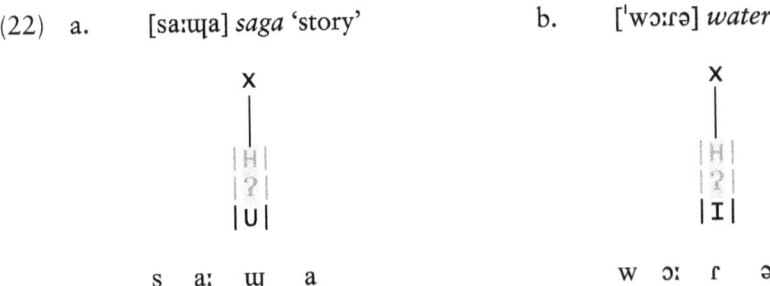

It is interesting to note that the tapping process in (22b) is observed in some varieties of English (Irish, Australian, General American) but not others (Welsh, southern British). One way of accounting for this difference is to assume that [t d] are represented as |I| coronals in tapping dialects but as |A| coronals in non-tapping dialects. If [t d] have the structure |I H ʔ| then they can weaken to |I| (= [ɾ]) as in (22b). This is what happens in Australian English. But if [t d] are represented as |A H ʔ| then tapping is not an option because there is no |I| element in the original stop that could be interpreted as a coronal tap. However, in non-tapping dialects [t d] may undergo other forms of weakening instead, as the structures in (23) illustrate.

(23) a. glottalisation   b. debuccalisation   c. rhoticisation
         (London)   (Liverpool)   (Tyneside)

         put [pʊʔ]   *what* [wɒh]   *get it* [geɹ ɪt]

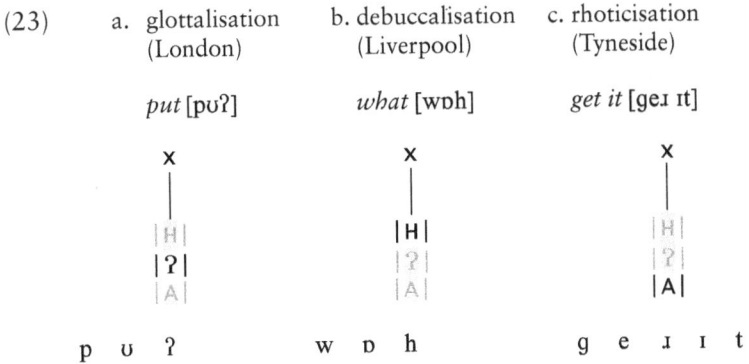

4.3.3 Voicelessness

Having seen how ET handles consonant weakening, let us return to our description of the |H| element. We have seen how |H| is interpreted as noise energy, either continuous (in fricatives) or transient (in stop bursts). But in some languages, |H| can also be interpreted another way – as voicelessness or aspiration, in which case it is normally headed. English is one language where headed |H̲| functions as a voicelessness or aspiration element, and as such, it can represent the so-called 'voicing' contrast in pairs such as *b–p*. This does not mean that we can treat |H| as the ET equivalent of the standard feature [±voice], however. In fact ET does not attempt to replicate [±voice], as this feature has a questionable status in the grammar. The problems associated with [±voice] are widely recognised, not just in ET but in most feature theories too. In this section we look at the reasons for rejecting the feature [±voice], and then see how ET represents voicing (or more appropriately, laryngeal) contrasts.

Traditionally, [±voice] applied to any language with a two-way laryngeal contrast, dividing obstruents into two sets, a [+voice] set [b d g ʒ ð . . .] and a [–voice] set [p t k ʃ θ . . .]. Like other features, [±voice] was assumed to be universal in the sense that [+voice] and [–voice] had the same phonetic values in all languages. Similarly, the phonemic symbols used to refer to segments were also thought to be universal, for example, *b* stood for a voiced labial stop in any language, *p* stood for any voiceless labial stop, and so on. However, we now know that [+voice] and [–voice] are not used consistently across languages, so a *b–p* contrast in one language is not necessarily the same phonologically as a *b–p* contrast in another language. Labels such as 'voiced' and 'voiceless' are therefore misleading, as are symbols such as *b* and *p*. To see this, let us compare the English stop system *p t k b d g* with what appears to be the same system *p t k b d g* in French. In both languages *p–b*, *t–d* and *k–g* create minimal pairs, suggesting that both systems have a voicing contrast in stops. But in fact only French uses voicing to distinguish between *b d g* (voiced) and *p t k* (voiceless). For English we must refer to some other property, namely aspiration, to separate *b d g* from *p t k*; this is because the entire stop series *p t k b d g* is voiceless (and it might therefore be more accurate to write it as *p t k b̥ d̥ g̊* or even *pʰ tʰ kʰ b̥ d̥ g̊*).

If French has a laryngeal contrast based on voicing while English has one based on aspiration, then two different properties must be involved and two independent features required. The privative feature [voice] is appropriate for French, with [voice] being present in *b d g* but not in *p t k*. Because *p t k* lack a voicing feature, they are represented as neutral or unspecified for voicing. The voicing contrast in French is exemplified in (24).

(24) a. [pat] *patte* 'paw'   [   ]   voicing begins at stop release
     b. [bat] *batte* 'bat'   [voice] voicing throughout stop closure

The phonological contrast in (24) between voiced and neutral stops has a direct phonetic correlate: stops with [voice] are produced with voicing lead, in which the vocal folds vibrate during the hold phase of the stop, while in neutral stops vocal fold vibration begins when the stop is released, that is, at the beginning of the following vowel. Now compare this with the laryngeal pattern in English, where the privative feature [spread glottis] is sometimes used to represent aspiration. This feature is present in *p t k* but not in *b d g*. So in English it is the *b d g* series rather than the *p t k* series which is phonologically neutral and lacks a laryngeal feature. The relevant contrast in English is illustrated in (25).

(25) a. [bæt] (or [b̥æt])   *bat* [   ]   voicing begins at stop release

     b. [pæt] (or [pʰæt])   *pat* [spread   voicing begins after stop
                                    glottis]   release

Again, this phonological contrast has a phonetic correlate: in neutral stops vocal fold vibration coincides with stop release, as it does in French, while in stops with [spread glottis] there is voicing lag – a gap between stop release and the start of vocal fold vibration in the following vowel. This delay in the onset of voicing produces a short period of voicelessness which, in some contexts, is interpreted as aspiration. The laryngeal patterns for French and English are schematised in (26), where the shading indicates vocal fold vibration.

(26)

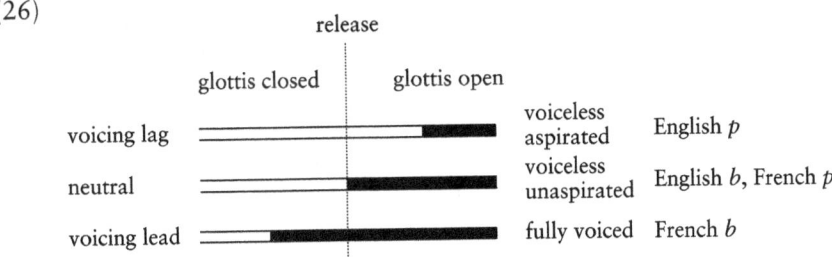

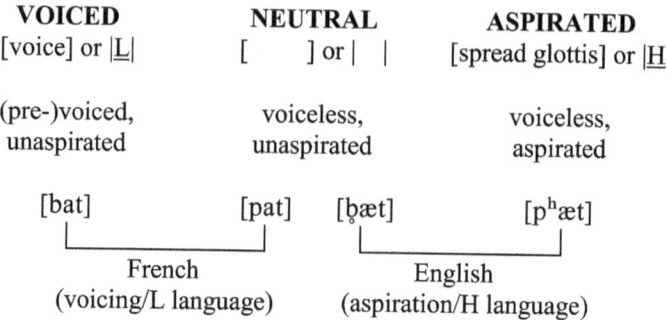

Figure 4.5 Typology of two-way laryngeal distinctions

It is clear that an approach using [±voice] cannot represent the laryngeal contrasts of both French and English as they are depicted in (26). It fails to recognise that voicing is irrelevant in English stops, and that the French neutral stops *p t k* and the English neutral stops *b d g* are similar phonetically and, as we shall see, phonologically. If we were to employ the feature [±voice] here, it would force us to assign French neutral *p* (24a) and English neutral *b* (25a) to different phonological classes: French neutral *p* would have to be 'voiceless' or [−voice] and English neutral *b* would be 'voiced' or [+voice]. Yet the linguistic facts contradict this, because both behave as phonologically neutral segments. Evidently, traditional feature theories are rather loose in their use of the feature [±voice] and the labels voiced and voiceless.

To represent the laryngeal properties of French and English in a way that captures the phonological differences between these languages, two features must be involved because two different laryngeal contrasts need to be described: neutral versus voiced (French) and neutral versus aspirated (English), as shown in Figure 4.5. The features [voice] and [spread glottis], which we have been using to represent the categories voiced and aspirated, have near equivalents in ET: let the headed |L| element stand for obstruent voicing and headed |H| stand for aspiration. French, which has |L| as its active laryngeal element, belongs to the group of L languages or 'voicing languages'; other L languages include Spanish, Russian, Japanese and Dutch. Meanwhile, English with headed |H| belongs to the group of H languages or 'aspiration languages'; other H languages include German, Swedish and Korean. All languages with a two-way laryngeal contrast belong to one of these two groups.

As Figure 4.5 shows, neutral stops have neither |L| nor |H|; that is, they are unspecified for laryngeal properties. The absence of a laryngeal element in these segments means that they are inactive as far as their laryngeal properties are concerned; after all, 'neutral' cannot be deleted, nor can it become active in processes such as assimilation. By contrast, |L| in voicing languages does behave actively in phonological processes, as does |H| in aspiration languages. In fact the only reliable way of determining whether a language has |L| or |H| is to observe which of these two elements is phonologically active. In §4.4.2 we will examine the active behaviour of |L| in voicing languages, but first let us review the evidence for an active headed |H| element in aspiration languages.

English is a good example of an H language because it displays clear phonological patterns involving headed |H|. These patterns are likely to be familiar to readers already, but it is worth repeating them here to illustrate the active behaviour of headed |H|. The first pattern is sonorant devoicing that occurs in branching onsets, for example *pride* [pr̥aɪd], *fly* [fl̥aɪ]: when a stop or fricative with headed |H| is followed by one of the sonorants [l r w j], |H| spreads to the sonorant and causes it to devoice.

(27)   a. *pride* [pr̥aɪd]   b. *bride* [braɪd]

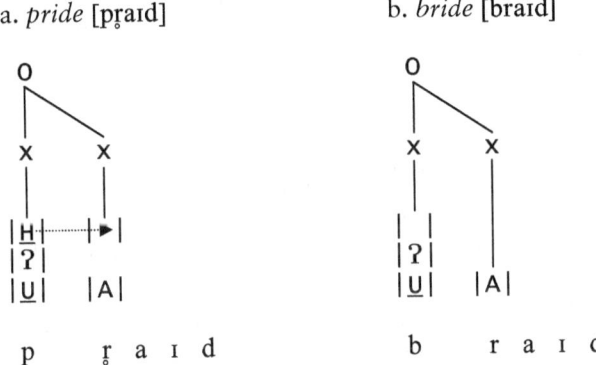

In (27a) headed |H| in *p* spreads voicelessness to *r*, producing a devoiced [r̥]. This is another example of voicing lag, in which a short period of voicelessness can be heard during the gap between stop release and the start of vocal fold vibration. Predictably, no sonorant devoicing occurs in (27b) because *b* has no |H| element and therefore displays no voicing lag. We also predict that this kind of devoicing will not occur in L languages, as these languages have no obstruents with |H|.

Assimilation is another process that confirms the presence of headed |H| in English. As (28a) shows, suffixes such as the noun plural marker -*s* and the past tense verb marker -*ed* assimilate in voicelessness to a stem-final consonant.

(28) a. sock[s] look[t]   b. flag[z] trie[d]
          lip[s]   laugh[t]   tail[z] save[d]
          fifth[s] reach[t]   eye[z]   boil[d]

The stems in (28a) end in consonants containing headed |H|. This |H| spreads to the suffix, causing the plural marker [z] to be reinterpreted as [s] and the past tense marker [d] to be realised as [t]. The assimilation process is illustrated in (29a). By contrast, the stems in (28b) end in a sonorant (*eye*, *tail*) or a neutral obstruent (*flag*, *save*), both of which are unspecified for laryngeal properties and therefore lack |H|. Because there is no |H| to assimilate, the suffixes appear in their original |H|-less forms [z] and [d], as shown in (29b).

(29) a. socks [sɒks]   b. flags [flægz]

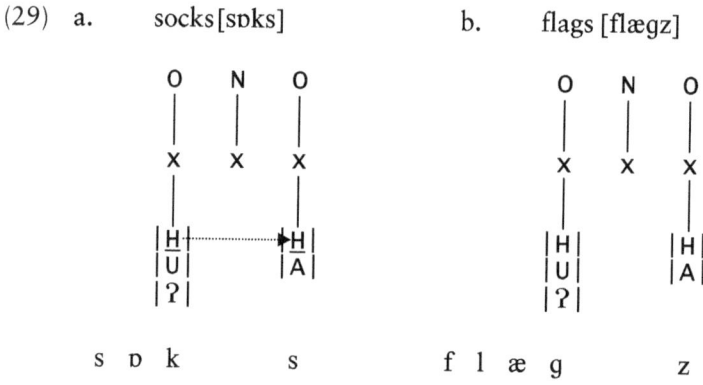

Note that in fast speech headed |H| can optionally assimilate between words too, e.g. *He ha*[s] *to* (cf. *He ha*[z] *done*), where [z] is again reinterpreted as [s] when it acquires headed |H| from the following *t*.

These examples confirm that English belongs to the group of H languages and that headed |H| is active in the phonology of English. And there are phonetic facts to support this analysis: for example, we have noted that the *p t k* series is cued by voicing lag (aspiration) while the *b d g* series is produced mostly without voicing. This is the sort of evidence needed to identify an H language, and if we were to analyse other H languages such as Swedish or Icelandic then we would find similar patterns. Let us now summarise what we have said about |H|. Note that some of the points in (30) will need to be revised later.

(30) a. |H| in fricatives

         non-headed: interpreted as frication (continuous noise)
         headed: defines the [f θ s ʃ] series in H languages
                      e.g. English *f* |U A H| vs. *v* |U A H|

b. |H| in stops

    non-headed: interpreted as audible release (transient noise)
    headed: defines the [pʰ tʰ kʰ] series in H languages
        e.g. English *p* |U ? H| vs. *b* |U ? H|

There are two comments to make regarding (30a). First, [f θ s ʃ] must have headed |H| in English because these fricatives pattern with the aspirated stops [pʰ tʰ kʰ], which have headed |H|; for example, they all trigger the sonorant devoicing process shown in (27a). By contrast, the neutral fricatives [v ð z ʒ], like the neutral stops, fail to trigger devoicing so they cannot contain headed |H|. However, neutral [v ð z ʒ] do have non-headed |H|, which is interpreted as regular frication. Second, fricatives in H languages are, like stops, not phonologically (contrastively) voiced. Of course we do find intervocalic fricatives produced with passive voicing, as in *cosy* ['kəʊzi]. But importantly, passive voicing carries no linguistic information – it is a predictable by-product of its vocalic context and is therefore not represented in the phonology. Interestingly, while [v ð z ʒ] with non-headed |H| can undergo passive voicing, [f θ s ʃ] with headed |H| cannot, hence *messy* ['mesi] (*['mezi]). The reason for this difference is that the voicelessness which cues headed |H| requires spread vocal folds while passive voicing requires vibrating vocal folds. The two are therefore physically incompatible – speakers cannot produce both at the same time. So in effect, |H| blocks passive voicing.

(30b) describes what we have said so far about the *p–b* contrast in English, but unfortunately it does not account for all aspects of laryngeal behaviour in the language. As we are about to see, there are actually three ways of realising stops in English, not just two, each one carrying different phonological information. These are given in (31).

(31)

	Category	Phonetic property	Contexts	Examples
pʰ	aspirated	long voicing lag	foot-initial	*repéat, impáired*
p	voiceless	short voicing lag	word-initial	*potáto, pásta*
			foot-internal	*háppy, cámper*
			word-final	*dróp, slópe*
			after *s*	*spám, respéct*
b̥ ~ b	neutral	no voicing lag	word-initial	*bát, behínd*
			word-internal	*rúby, robúst*

From a generative grammar viewpoint, (31) is unexpected because it treats aspirated stops as a separate series. Aspiration is known to be predictable in English, and should therefore be a matter for phonetic realisation rather than phonology. But remember that ET does not adhere strictly to the traditional division between phonetic and phonological facts. Instead, its aim is to represent linguistic information, whether this information relates to contrasts or to some other property of language. Now, although aspiration is not contrastive in English, it does provide listeners with valuable information of a different kind – namely, information about foot structure and, to a lesser degree, word structure. It does this by marking the left edge of a foot (e.g. *unim*[pʰ]*órtant*, [pʰ]*ícture*, *a*[pʰ]*árent*) or the left edge of a word (e.g. [pʰ]*otáto*, [pʰ]*oétic*). Psycholinguistic studies have shown that listeners rely on information about prosodic structure when they interpret spoken language; and specifically, knowing where foot and word domains begin can help them to divide the incoming speech signal into words and to process language more efficiently. In addition, prosodic structure is thought to play an important role in first language acquisition (see the references given at the end of this chapter). Aspiration is therefore rich in linguistic information, and for this reason, needs to be included in segmental representations alongside information about contrasts.

By using just the |H| element and its headedness properties it is possible to represent the three laryngeal categories in (31). An important acoustic cue for |H| is voicing lag, which is a property of p^h and p but not b. So let us assume that p^h and p have |H| whereas b does not. Next, to distinguish p^h from p we need to consider the extent of the voicing lag in each; and as (31) indicates, p^h has a longer voicing lag than p – that is, voicing lag is more prominent in p^h than in p. Since physical prominence translates into phonological headedness, this gives us the representations in (32), where we see the expected contrast between the aspirated series $p^h\ t^h\ k^h$ represented by headed |H̲| in (32a) and the neutral series $b\ d\ g$ without |H| in (32c).

(32)

		Category	Physical attribute		Structure
a.	p^h	aspirated	|H̲|	long voicing lag	[pʰ] = |U ? H̲|
b.	p	voiceless	|H|	short voicing lag	[p] = |U ? H|
c.	b	neutral			no voicing lag	[b̥] = |U ?|

So why do we also need to recognise the voiceless unaspirated series $p\ t\ k$ in (32b)? In certain contexts aspirated $p^h\ t^h\ k^h$ weaken to *p t k* by losing their aspiration; but when this happens, they remain distinct from the neutral stops *b d g*; that is, they retain |H| rather than suppressing |H| altogether and merging with *b d g*. In English, loss of aspiration (de-aspiration) occurs in all contexts except foot-initial and word-initial positions, which ties in with our earlier point that aspiration functions as a marker for foot and word domains. The de-aspiration process itself is another example of weakening via loss of headedness, as illustrated in (33b): in *stu*[pʰ]*idity* the labial stop has headed |H| because it is foot-initial, making it phonetically aspirated, but in *stu*[p]*id* the same stop is foot-internal, forcing headed |H| to weaken to non-headed |H|. The weakened structure is reinterpreted as a de-aspirated stop [p].

(33) a. *stu*[pʰ]*ídity* b. *stú*[p]*id* c. [b]*óok* d. *stá*[b] e. *ró*[b]*in*

x	x	x	x	x
|H|	|H|			
|ʔ|	|ʔ|	|ʔ|	|ʔ|	|ʔ|
|U|	|U|	|U|	|U|	|U|

The structures in (33c–e) demonstrate the behaviour of neutral *b*. Unlike aspirated *p*, which alternates between [pʰ] and [p] according to its context, neutral *b* is relatively stable: it has a fairly similar interpretation in all positions (although passive voicing is possible between sonorants, as noted earlier). This is exactly what we expect to find in phonologically neutral segments. Tables 4.8 and 4.9 present a revised summary of the laryngeal properties of English, and by extension, of H languages in general.

A final comment is in order regarding the representation of stops. (33) shows that in H languages neutral stops have no |H|, which suggests that they have no audible release burst – recall from (16) that suppressing |H| in stops results in non-release. Initially, this looks problematic; after all, speakers release neutral stops in much the same way that they release aspirated ones. But there is a difference: aspirated stops are released with an *audible* burst because this is an important cue which carries linguistic information; by contrast, the release burst in neutral stops is usually much weaker, often to the point of being *inaudible*. For instance, in terms of linguistic information it makes little difference whether a neutral stop is released or not, hence *stab* [stæb] ~ [stæb̚], which is consistent with the view that *b d g* have no laryngeal element. We may note here that some

Table 4.8 The |H| element in English stops

Category	Representation	Physical attribute	Contexts	Examples
|H̲|	aspirated *p* |U ? H̲|	aspirated	word-initial	*pat, perhaps*
				foot-initial	*pat, repeat*
|H|	voiceless *p* |U ? H|	unaspirated	word-final	*wrap, hope*
				intervocalic	*wrapper, hoping*
				after *s*__	*spy, respect*
				before a .C	*caption, upload*
			neutral *b* |U ?|	unaspirated	word-initial	*book, break*
				word-final	*grab, stub*
			passive voicing	intervocalic	*robin, cupboard*

Table 4.9 The |H| element in English fricatives

Category	Representation	Physical attribute	Contexts	Examples
|H̲|	aspirated (fortis) *f* |U A H̲|	voicing lag	all	*foot, effort, leaf*
|H|	neutral (lenis) *v* |U A H|	no voicing lag	word-initial	*vow, victorious*
				word-final	*nerve, save*
			passive voicing	intervocalic	*nervous, saving*

versions of ET take a different approach to laryngeal properties by employing a 'noise' element |h| in addition to |H|; in these models |h| represents frication and audible release while |H| represents voicelessness. There is no doubt that this increases the richness and expressive power of representations; however, a larger set of elements always brings with it the risk of overgeneration. So it is a costly option in generative terms, and it is not clear whether the advantages to be gained from recognising both |H| and |h| are sufficient to justify a set of seven elements rather than six. This approach becomes more questionable still when we consider that |h| and |H| have very similar phonological properties, which hints at the possibility that they are formally related. The version of ET described in this book expresses this relation by combining the properties of |h| and |H| into a single noise element |H|.

4.3.4 High Tone

We have seen how |H| plays a central role in consonant systems. But given the importance of consonant–vowel unity in ET, we can expect |H| to contribute to vowel systems too. In this section we look at how |H| functions as a vowel element in tone languages, where it represents high tone.

We know that |H| can function as a high tone element because we see a phonological link between high tone and voicelessness. When a language develops a tonal contrast in vowels, we often see high tone emerging after |H| consonants and low tone elsewhere. Then, once the tonal difference has established itself, the original contrast between |H| consonants and neutral consonants may be lost altogether. So in effect, the lexical contrast shifts from the consonant system to the vowel system. For example, Kammu originally had a contrast between |H| (voiceless) and Ø (neutral) in obstruents and sonorant consonants, but no lexical tone in vowels. It also had an aspirated stop series for pronouncing loanwords. The present-day Eastern dialect of Kammu shown in (34) preserves this system.

(34)
		Obstruents	Sonorants
voiceless	(|H|)	[p t c k]	[m̥ n̥ ɲ̊ ŋ̊ l̥ r̥ w̥ j̊]
neutral	(| |)	[b d ɟ g]	[m n ɲ ŋ l r w j]
aspirated	(|H|)	[pʰ tʰ cʰ kʰ]	

Now compare (34) with the laryngeal system of Northern Kammu. In this dialect there is still an aspirated series for pronouncing loanwords, but the voiceless and neutral series have merged into a single neutral series. The original contrast has not been lost, however; it is interpreted as a tonal contrast on the following vowel instead (v́ = high tone, v̀ = low tone).

(35)
Eastern Kammu	Northern Kammu	
taaŋ	táaŋ	'pack'
daaŋ	tàaŋ	'lizard'
raaŋ	ràaŋ	'flower'
r̥aaŋ	ráaŋ	'tooth'
tʰaaŋ	tʰáaŋ	'to clear'

A voiceless consonant in Eastern Kammu corresponds to a consonant followed by a high tone vowel in Northern Kammu, as in [r̥a]–[rá], while a neutral consonant in Eastern Kammu corresponds to a consonant followed by a low tone vowel in Northern Kammu, as in [ra]–[rà]. We have therefore a direct link between voicelessness/aspiration and high tone, suggesting that these are different interpretations of the same element |H|. (Note that, in this language, low tone is phonologically neutral or unspecified; it is interpreted by default when high tone is absent.) Two other findings also support the idea that voicelessness and high tone are phonologically equivalent. First, speakers of Eastern and Northern Kammu have no difficulty understanding one another, despite the fact that one dialect is a tonal system while the other is not. Second, perceptual experiments reveal that speakers of the two dialects are unaware of their phonological differences: Kammu speakers themselves claim that their dialects are distinguished by lexical differences rather than phonological differences.

The Songjiang dialect of Chinese provides another example of the link between voicelessness and high tone. This language has the contour tones shown in (36); there are five tone heights, numbered from 1 (the lowest) to 5 (the highest).

(36) ti 53 'low'   di 31 'lift'
      ti 44 'bottom'   di 22 'brother'
      ti 35 'emperor' di 31 'field'

Songjiang Chinese is an H language, and as (36) shows, words with a voiceless obstruent [t] have tones in the upper register (3–5) whereas words with neutral [d] have tones in the lower register (1–3). Tone distribution is therefore not entirely random but partially controlled by phonological context: if the onset consonant has |H| then the following vowel must have some kind of high tone. Now, the grammar can only express a link between voicelessness and high tone if the two have something in common phonologically. In ET the common property is |H|.

If two properties are represented by the same element, then we can expect to find phonetic similarities between them. In the case of voicelessness and high tone it is not immediately obvious what those similarities might be, though phonetic studies have revealed that laryngeal state (voiceless/voiced) and pitch (high/low) can both be described in terms of vocal fold tension. When the glottis is narrowly open, speakers control vocal fold vibration by adjusting the stiffness of the edges of the glottis. In obstruents vocal fold stiffness determines the presence or absence of vibration, which controls voicing, while in sonorants it determines the rate of vocal fold vibration, which controls pitch.

(37)
	Stiff vocal folds	Slack vocal folds
obstruents:	voicelessness	voicing
sonorants:	high pitch	low pitch

Of relevance here is the dual function of stiff vocal folds, which is responsible for voicelessness in obstruents and high pitch in vowels and other sonorants. (Slack vocal folds will be discussed in §4.4.) The phonetic studies mentioned above use the feature [+stiff vocal cords] to bring together voicelessness and high pitch as a natural class, while ET uses |H| for the same purpose (although ET also includes aspiration in the same class). We can now summarise the role of |H| as in (38).

(38)
	Context	Phonetic interpretation
headed |H|:	with |?|	aspiration in stops
	no |?|	frication in aspirated (fortis) fricatives
	in vowels	high tone
non-headed |H|:	with |?|	voicelessness in unaspirated stops (H languages)
	no |?|	frication in neutral fricatives

This completes our description of the |H| element. Next we turn to the remaining consonant element, |L|.

4.4 The |L| Element

4.4.1 Nasality

Whereas |H| is associated with high-frequency energy, |L| is associated with low-frequency energy. In particular, the |L| element is cued by an acoustic pattern called murmur, a broad band of low-frequency energy. The easiest way of producing murmur is to lower the velum, so for this reason we tend to associate murmur with nasals, hence the term 'nasal murmur'. And because |L| represents nasal murmur, the element itself is often called the nasal element. Some versions of ET even refer to this element as |N| (for nasality) rather than |L|. In this book we will use |L| in order to highlight the complementary relation between |L| (low-frequency energy) and |H| (high-frequency energy). The nasal murmur can be seen in the spectrograms in Figure 4.6.

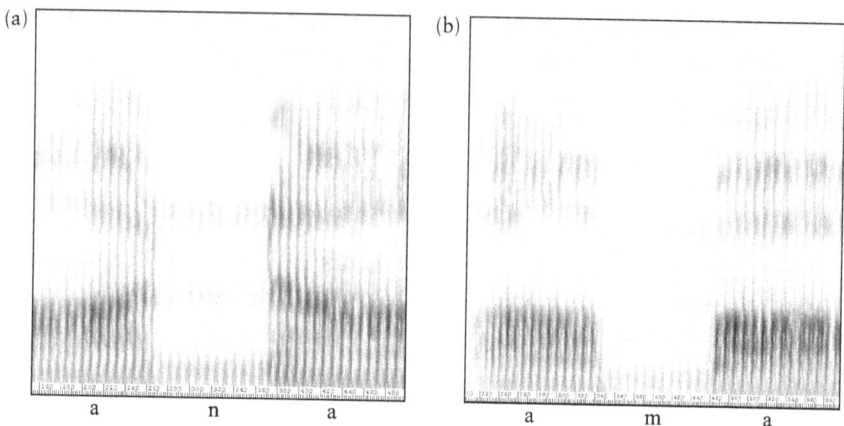

Figure 4.6 Energy patterns of nasal murmur. (a) Spectrogram of [ana]; (b) Spectrogram of [ama]

Note that, because nasals have a low amplitude, their upper formants are relatively weak compared to those in the surrounding vowels.

In structural terms, nasals such as [m n ɲ ŋ] are distinguished from oral stops by the presence of an additional |L| element. Compare the representation for neutral [p] with that of its corresponding nasal [m].

(39) [p] = |U ʔ|
 [m] = |U ʔ L| or |U L|

|L| functions in a similar way to the privative feature [nasal], in that expressions with |L| are interpreted as nasal while those without |L| are oral. Labial [m] therefore has the structure |U ʔ L|, which comprises labial resonance from |U|, a drop in energy from |ʔ| and nasal murmur from |L|. One minor complication concerning the representation of nasals has already been mentioned in §4.2.1. Recall that languages are divided over whether or not nasals contain |ʔ|. In some systems nasals appear to have |ʔ| since they pattern with oral stops, whereas in other systems they behave as continuant sounds which lack |ʔ|. For this reason (39) shows an alternative structure |U L| for [m]. Whether |ʔ| is present or absent has no bearing on the behaviour of |L|, which is interpreted consistently as nasality.

Several studies of nasality have been undertaken in ET, and although these differ in some respects they do all employ the |L|/|N| element. In this book we will follow the description of nasality found in Nasukawa (2005), though many of the examples we use below are taken from Botma (2004). As a segmental property, |L| defines the natural class of nasals. In most languages the nasal class is relatively small: Modern English has [m n ŋ], Old English [m n] and Oneida just [n], for example. At the other extreme there are some Australian languages with nasals across the full range of place contrasts. Recall from §3.7.3 that nasals in Yanyuwa are contrastive at seven different places of articulation. Their structures are shown in (40).

(40) [m]   [n̪]   [n]   [ɳ]   [nʲ]   [ɲ]   [ŋ]

```
       x     x     x     x     x     x     x
       |     |     |     |     |     |     |
      |L|   |L|   |L|   |L|   |L|   |L|   |L|
      |ʔ|   |ʔ|   |ʔ|   |ʔ|   |ʔ|   |ʔ|   |ʔ|
      |U|   |I|   |A|   |A|   |I|   |I|   |U|
                                |U|
```

|L| frequently behaves as an active property in assimilation processes. A well-known case is Korean, in which morpheme-final stops become nasals when another nasal consonant follows. For example, *kuk* + *mul* [kuŋ-mul] 'soup-broth' is represented as in (41).

(41) *kuk* + *mul* [kuŋ-mul] 'soup-broth'

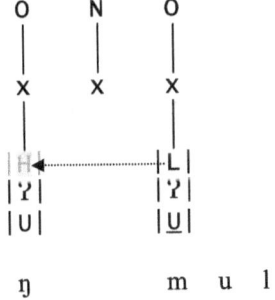

|L| extends from [m] to the preceding [k], which is reinterpreted as its nasal counterpart [ŋ]. Notice that when |L| spreads it overrides the |H| element already there. (This happens even when the target is an aspirated stop containing headed |H|, as in *supʰ* + *narim* [sum-narim] 'depending on forest'.) What this suggests is that |H| and |L| do not combine easily. Of course we cannot completely rule out combinations of |H| and |L|, and later we will see how some languages do tolerate |H| and |L| in the same expression. But Korean is not one of these. The problem with combining |H| and |L| is that their acoustic patterns conflict: |H| signals a raised F0 and |L| a lowered F0. So to avoid the possibility of one pattern masking the other, many grammars do not allow the two

elements to be interpreted simultaneously. This situation is reminiscent of what we have already seen with the antagonistic pair |I|–|U|.

Another form of nasal assimilation is vowel nasalisation, which can be understood in two ways: as a low-level phonetic effect it involves nasal co-articulation between adjacent segments, as illustrated by the English word [w̃ẽn] *when*, and as a phonological process it operates in languages that have a lexical contrast between oral and nasal vowels. Here we will focus on the latter. The |L| element is responsible for the nasality contrast in vowels; the example forms in (42) are from Yoruba (tone omitted).

(42) a. [da] 'to be rare' b. [dã] 'to polish'

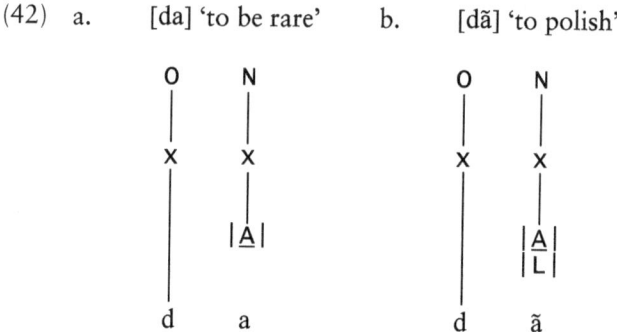

Nasal vowels have, in many cases, originated from sequences of an oral vowel followed by a nasal consonant. The path of development is typically $vN > \tilde{v}N > \tilde{v}$, where the vowel is first nasalised by a following nasal consonant; then the nasal consonant deletes, leaving a nasal vowel which can contrast with an oral vowel in the same context. To illustrate this, (43) shows the development of the French word *paysan* 'peasant (masc.)' at three stages in its history from pre-literature times to the present day.

(43) [peizan] → [peizãn] → [peizã]

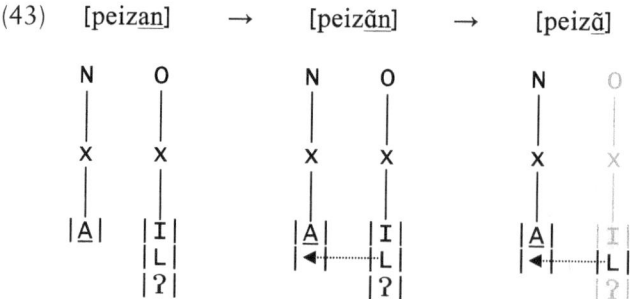

When a nasal consonant weakens in this way, it is usual for the |L| element to survive. In the French example [peizã] the surviving |L| gets interpreted in a neighbouring position instead, whereas in other languages nasal weakening can result in a nasalised glide, as shown in (44).

(44) Haitian Creole   [ɲ] > [j̃] |I L ʔ| > |I L ʔ|
      Shoshone   [m] > [w̃] |U L ʔ| > |U L ʔ|
      Yakut   [n] > [j̃] |I L ʔ| > |I L ʔ|
      Bishop Monachi   [m] > [w̃] |U L ʔ| > |U L ʔ|

Nasal weakening is also observed in the development of Hindi and Panjabi from Sanskrit; (45) shows how intervocalic [m] in Sanskrit is reinterpreted in the descendant languages.

(45) *Sanskrit* *Hindi* *Panjabi*
      kamala   kãval   (kaul >) kɔl   'lotus'
      graːma   gãːw   (grãːu >) grã   'village'

In Hindi [m] developed into [v] (most likely realised as an approximant [ʋ] or [β]) preceded by a nasalised vowel; in terms of element structure, |ʔ| was suppressed and |L| reinterpreted on the preceding nucleus. Vowel nasalisation took place in Panjabi too, although in this case |L| was also suppressed word-internally, hence [kɔl] (*[kɔ̃l]) 'lotus'. Additionally, [m] vocalised to [u], which then elided (to produce [grã]) or merged with a neighbouring vowel (to produce [kɔl]).

Nasals are mostly realised as sonorants. So, like other sonorants, they have inherent or spontaneous voicing – that is, they are phonetically voiced but their voicing is never phonologically active. And because voicing is not phonological in nasals, or in any other sonorants, it is not represented by an element. This leads us to the conclusion that 'sonorant' is not actually a grammatical category; it does not count as a natural class because sonorants (vowels, glides, liquids, nasals) have no phonological properties in common. In fact the only thing that characterises sonorants as a group is their lack of |H|, since |H| describes the non-sonorants (stops, fricatives). And as we know, the absence of a property cannot be expressed in the ET grammar because elements are inherently positive. A broader generalisation emerges from this too: we can say that all speech sounds (except for [ʔ]) are naturally voiced: in order for a segment to be voiceless it must have something in its structure, namely |H|, to override spontaneous voicing and give it the marked property of voicelessness. In this book we will continue to use 'sonorant' as an informal label, but we should remember that this does not describe a formal grammatical category.

In some languages sonorant nasals contrast with other nasal types such as voiceless nasals or laryngealised (creaky) nasals. For example, Burmese has a lexical distinction between sonorant and voiceless nasals, while Montana Salish distinguishes sonorant and creaky nasals. There is even a three-way nasal contrast in a small number of languages such as Jalapa Mazatec, as illustrated in (46).

(46) |L ʔ| sonorant nasal   [ma]   'be able'   [nà]   'women'
     |L ʔ H| voiceless nasal [m̥a]   'black'   [n̥ɛ]   'falls'
     |L ʔ̱| creaky nasal   [m̰e]   'dies, kills' [ṉà]   'shiny'

The presence of |L| unites all three nasal types as a natural class, but within this class we have a laryngeal distinction between sonorant (neutral), voiceless (|H|) and creaky (|ʔ̱|). Notice that we have already seen the exact same laryngeal distinctions in oral stops.

Finally, let us consider how |L| is interpreted as a single element. The first thing to say about the simplex expression |L| is that it is not very common. This is probably because it is perceptually weak and therefore not ideal as a means of conveying linguistic information. When a speaker produces nasal murmur without any accompanying resonance, noise or occlusion, the result is an almost imperceptible sound; acoustically it is very weak, and in articulatory terms it has few defining characteristics because the speech organs (other than the glottis) are not directly involved. An example segment with the structure |L| is the mora nasal of Japanese, also known as the syllabic nasal or placeless nasal. This segment, often written as N, has no resonance properties of its own, so when it precedes a consonant it copies the resonance properties of that consonant, as shown in (47a). Before a pause, however, there are no consonant resonance properties available and N must be interpreted as a placeless nasal (47b). The phonetic quality of the placeless nasal can vary within the range [ŋ] ~ [N] ~ [ũɰ̃]; in Botma (2004) it is described as a nasal glide.

(47) a. *saN+baN* [sam-baN] 'number three'   b. *saN* [saN] 'three'

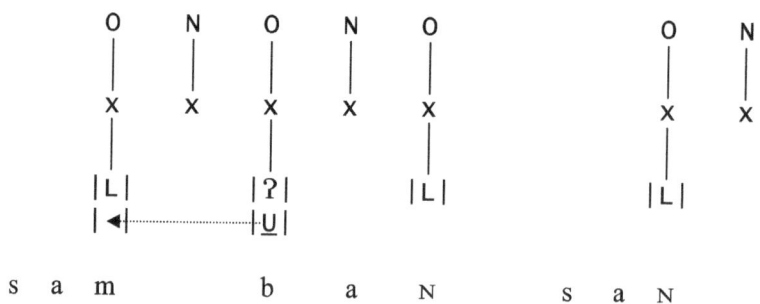

By acquiring headed |U| from a following *b* the placeless nasal N is reinterpreted as labial [m]. But without this additional resonance, N consists of just |L| and is produced as nasal murmur, as in (47b). The low perceptibility of N is demonstrated by the way [saN] in (47b) is almost indistinguishable from [sã] in terms of its segmental quality. (Note that they differ in terms of their prosodic structure, since [saN] is bimoraic in Japanese.)

In this section we have seen how non-headed |L| is interpreted as nasality in nasal stops and nasal vowels. Additionally, we have noted that simplex |L| can be produced as a nasal glide. Next we turn to the various interpretations of headed |L|.

4.4.2 Obstruent Voicing

In §4.3.3 we said that languages with a two-way laryngeal contrast divide into two types, H languages and L languages. We know that English is an H language because it has aspirated stops but no fully voiced stops; in addition, the |H| element representing voicelessness is phonologically active in this language. By contrast, languages such as French and Dutch are typical L languages since they have fully voiced stops but no aspirates. Moreover, we will see that |L| behaves as an active property in these systems. To be more precise, it is headed |L| that is phonologically active and present in fully voiced stops. It is therefore headed |L| that defines the set of L languages. We begin by looking at headed |L| as an active phonological property, and then consider why it should be headed |L|, rather than some other element, that represents obstruent voicing.

You will recall that L languages such as French make a distinction between neutral *p t k* and fully voiced *b d g*. This is shown in (48), where headed |L| provides obstruent voicing in [b].

(48) a. neutral   [p] |U ʔ| [pat]   *patte* 'paw'
     b. fully voiced [b] |U ʔ L| [bat]   *batte* 'bat'

Phonetically, headed |L| is cued by sustained voicing throughout the hold phase of the stop; voicing may even begin before the oral closure is formed, resulting in a pre-voiced stop. And because this kind of voicing is not a characteristic of H languages, it is sometimes possible to determine whether a language belongs to the H group or the L group just by hearing it. Ultimately, however, phonological evidence is needed in order to be certain how to classify individual languages. In the case of L languages, voicing assimilation provides the clearest indication that headed |L| is phonologically active. The forms in (49) confirm that Dutch is another example of an L language.

(49) *zakdoek* [zɑgduk] 'handkerchief'
      kasboek [kɑzbuk] 'cashbook'

As (49) shows, when a neutral obstruent such as [k] or [s] precedes a voiced obstruent, it becomes voiced by interpreting headed |L|. The process itself is shown in (50).

(50) *zakdoek* [zɑgduk] 'handkerchief'

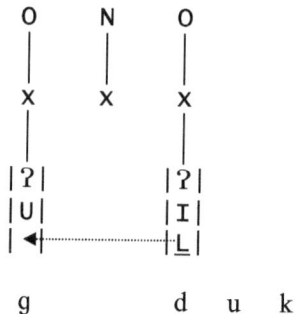

z   a   g   d   u   k

Note that voicing is phonologically active in obstruents but not in sonorants, hence *krui*[t]*nagel* (**krui[d]*nagel*) 'clove'. This is expected, because the element responsible for active voicing, headed |L|, is present in voiced obstruents but not in nasals or other sonorants. Predictably, voicing assimilation of the sort we find in Dutch is not a feature of H languages. And similarly, voicelessness assimilation as described in §4.3.3 (English *I ha*[v] vs. *I ha*[f] *to*) is not observed in L languages because it involves an active headed |H| element. Further examples of voicing assimilation can easily be found among the L languages.

Let us now turn to the question of why obstruent voicing is represented by headed |L| rather than by some other element. The elements we have described so far show that there is always a phonological connection between the headed and non-headed versions of an element. For example, aspirated stops in English (headed |H|) alternate with their unaspirated counterparts (non-headed |H|), while there are historical processes in which labials (headed |U|) interact with velars (non-headed |U|). Not surprisingly, the |L| element also follows this pattern – that is, a phonological link exists between obstruent voicing (headed |L|) and nasality (non-headed |L|). Different languages express this link in different ways: in some grammars there is an alternation between nasals and voiced obstruents, while in others we find prenasalisation on voiced stops or obstruent voicing triggered by nasals. The examples below are taken mostly from Botma (2004).

Tukuya is an L language in which nasality is active as a word-level property, dividing the lexicon into two sets of words, oral and nasal. As (51) shows, the voiced stops [b d g] and the nasals [m n ŋ] are in complementary distribution: voiced stops are restricted to oral words (51a) while nasals only appear in nasal words (51b). Tone has been omitted.

(51) a. bipi   'swollen'   b. m̃ip̃ĩ   'badger'
        diti   'to lose'   ñĩɾ̃ĩ   'coal'
        sɨge   'follow'   ɾ̃ĩŋõ   'Yapara rapids'
        pee   'to bend'   p̃ẽẽ   'to prepare soup'

What this pattern indicates is that voiced stops may be viewed as the oral equivalent of nasal stops – in other words, that voiced stops and nasals are similar except for their oral/nasal setting. In element terms, this similarity is captured by saying that the same |L| element is present in both, and that the difference between them refers to headedness: |L| is headed in [b d g] and non-headed in [m n ŋ]. If [m n ŋ] have non-headed |L| then they cannot also have headed |L|, because the same element cannot be both headed and non-headed at the same time. This prevents [b d g] in Tukuya from appearing in nasal words. Similarly, because [b d g] with headed |L| cannot also have non-headed |L| in their structure, they do not pattern with nasals. As a result, they are banned from nasal words. Notice that neutral stops such as [p] and [t] occur freely in oral and nasal words: because they contain no |L| element, they do not participate in any nasal–voice alternation.

Kpelle provides another example of the phonological connection between nasality and voicing. Again, nasals and voiced consonants are in complementary distribution, with nasals preceding nasal vowels (52a) and voiced consonants preceding oral vowels (52b). As (52c) shows, nasality is contrastive in Kpelle vowels.

(52) a. nĩã   'new'
         ŋʷãnã   'bitter'

     b. ɓɔɔ   'bag'
         ɣîla   'dog'

     c. k͡pãa   'species of tree'
         k͡paa   'cedar tree'

What interests us here is the behaviour of the definite marker. This prefix has only |L| in its lexical representation, but the way this |L| is interpreted varies according to the context. When the prefix attaches to a root beginning with one of the neutral obstruents [p t k k͡p f s], this obstruent incorporates the |L| and becomes voiced, as shown in (53a). But if it attaches to a root beginning with a nasal, the nasal gains a low tone (53b). And if the definite prefix attaches to a root beginning with any other consonant, |L| turns the consonant into a nasal with additional low tone (53c).

(53) *Indefinite* *Definite*
    a. sɛŋ   zɛŋ   'thing'
       k͡pala   g͡bala   'dry out'

    b. mɔ́lɔŋ   m̀ɔ́lɔŋ   'rice'
       ɲíliŋ   ɲ̀íliŋ   'termites'

    c. ɓɔ́ɔ   m̀ɔ́ɔi   'wax'
       lúu   ǹúui   'fog, mist'
       ɣîla   ŋ̀îlaĩ   'dog'
       já   ɲ̀ái   'water'

In this way, Kpelle displays three different interpretations of the same element |L|. In (53a) it is headed and interpreted as voicing, while in (53b) and (53c) it is interpreted as low tone; we will discuss the association between |L| and tone in §4.4.3. And in (53c) it appears in its non-headed form to produce a nasal consonant. It is worth noting that standard features cannot easily capture alternations such as this because the properties concerned – nasality, low tone and obstruent voicing – involve different articulations and therefore different features.

Postnasal voicing is another phonological effect that highlights the link between nasality and obstruent voicing. In languages with postnasal voicing, an obstruent must be voiced when it follows a nasal. For example, in the L language Japanese the past tense suffix *-ta* is pronounced [da] when the verb root ends in a nasal, as in *ʃin-ta* [ʃinda] 'died' (cf. *oshie-ta* [oʃieta] 'told'). Postnasal voicing is also a characteristic of Zoque (54a) and Wembawemba (54b).

(54) a. [tandan]   (*[tantan])   'mariposa'
         [min-ba]   (*[min-pa])   'viene'
         [saŋ-gowi] (*[saŋ-kowi]) 'muy sordo'

b. [milpʌ]   'to twist'
   [jandin]   (*[jantin])   'me'
   [panbar]   (*[panpar])   'shovel'

As (54b) shows, only nasals cause voicing; other sonorants such as [l] cannot trigger the process because they do not contain |L|, hence [milpʌ] 'to twist'. The process itself is one of |L| assimilation: when |L| extends from the nasal to the following consonant it is interpreted (in its headed form) as obstruent voicing.

The idea of a formal link between nasality and obstruent voicing is also supported by the existence of prenasalised stops such as [ᵐb ⁿd ᵑg]. In Fijian, for example, prenasalised stops occupy positions in the consonant inventory where we would expect to find fully voiced stops, as (55) shows.

(55) neutral   p   t   k
     prenasalised/voiced   ᵐb   ⁿd   ⁿdr   ᵑg
     nasal   m   n   ŋ

Furthermore, in word-initial position the prenasalised stops [ᵐb ⁿd ⁿdr ᵑg] and the voiced stops [b d dr g] are in free variation, suggesting that the two are likely to be different phonetic interpretations of the same phonological structure. A similar pattern is also found in other languages including Javanese and Reyesano. Meanwhile in Japanese, [b d g] in the standard Tokyo dialect correspond to [ᵐb ⁿd ᵑg] in dialects of the Northern Tohoku region.

(56) *Tokyo*   *Tohoku*
     kabu   kaᵐbu   'turnip'
     hada   haⁿda   'skin'
     kagi   kaᵑgi   'key'

Also, voiced stops in the Tohoku dialect are prenasalised in compounds: [tɕuːᵑgakkoː] 'middle school' (cf. [tɕuːgakkoː] in Tokyo Japanese), [oᵐbaːsaɴ] 'grandmother' (cf. [obaːsaɴ]).

In feature terms it is difficult to account for the presence of prenasalised stops in Tohoku Japanese because there is no obvious source for the nasality; some analysts simply propose an arbitrary rule of nasal insertion such as $\emptyset \rightarrow m/n/ŋ$. But this does not explain why the additional property should be nasality, or why only voiced stops can be prenasalised. In element terms, however, the interaction between [b d g] and [ᵐb ⁿd ᵑg] makes sense because both series contain |L|. Generally speaking, the properties of a non-headed element are inherent in those of its corresponding headed element: for example, noise (non-headed |H|) inheres in aspirates (headed |H̲|), occlusion (non-headed |ʔ|) inheres in ejectives (headed |ʔ̲|), and so on. And in the case of |L|, low-frequency murmur (non-headed |L|) inheres in voiced obstruents (headed |L̲|). Normally the acoustic cues for headed |L̲| and non-headed |L| are interpreted simultaneously to produce [b d g]. But in languages with [ᵐb ⁿd ⁿg] these cues are interpreted in sequence, allowing listeners to perceive nasality and voicing as separate acoustic events. Importantly, however, [b d g] and [ᵐb ⁿd ⁿg] are equivalent in phonological terms.

Finally, let us consider why voicing should be represented by headed |L̲| and nasality by non-headed |L|, and not vice versa. In fact language typology provides some helpful clues. Nasality is a near-universal property in natural languages, with only a handful of languages lacking nasal consonants. (And interestingly, those systems without nasals all have voiced obstruents which, historically, had nasal cognates.) By contrast, obstruent voicing is less widespread – by definition, only L languages can have this property. In other words, the presence of voiced obstruents implies the presence of nasals but not vice versa. And this asymmetry is reflected in the representations we have proposed: if a headed element is active in a language then its corresponding non-headed element will also be active, but the opposite is not necessarily true. For example, all languages with ejectives (headed |ʔ̲|) also have plain stops (non-headed |ʔ|), and languages with aspirated stops (headed |H̲|) also have released stops (non-headed |H|). And in the same way, all languages with fully voiced obstruents also have nasals. On this basis we will assume that headed |L̲| represents obstruent voicing and non-headed |L| represents nasality.

Phonological evidence to support this conclusion comes once again from Japanese. We have already noted that past tense verbs are formed by adding the suffix -*ta* ([ta] ~ [da]) to a verb root. So whenever the root ends in a consonant, a consonant sequence C.*ta* or C.*da* is created. Now, in many languages including Japanese, adjacent (hetero-syllabic) consonants form a head-dependency relation in which the right-hand consonant is the head. As a head, this consonant can contain more linguistic information and therefore more elements than its dependent. For example, in nasal–stop sequences the nasal cannot have a place element of its own, so it copies the place element belonging to its head: [baŋgo] (*[bango]) 'number', [sampo] (*[saŋpo]) 'stroll'. A similar asymmetry between head and dependent is also observed in stop–stop sequences, causing the past tense form *tob-ta* 'fly-PAST' to be interpreted as [ton-da] 'flew'. Its structure is shown in (57).

(57)   *tob-* 'fly' + *-ta* 'PAST'   →   [ton-da] 'flew'

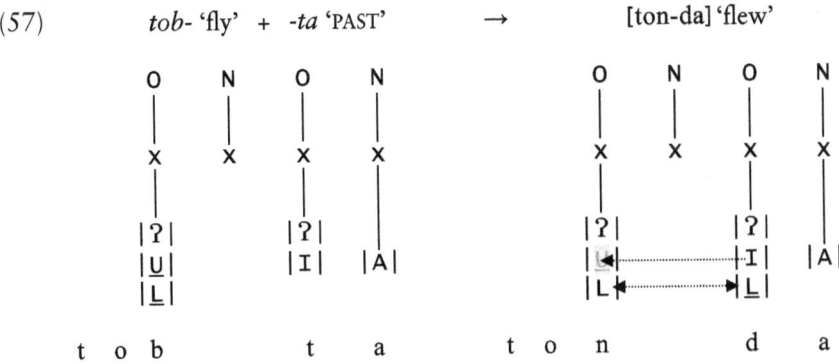

The morphology creates the sequence *bt*, but this is not a well-formed head-dependent pair because the dependent *b* carries more linguistic information and has a more complex element structure (three elements) than the head *t* (two elements). The grammar responds by weakening *b* in two ways: first, its |U| resonance is suppressed, forcing *b* to copy |I| resonance from its head *t* instead; and second, headed |L| is weakened to non-headed |L|, causing the voiced stop *b* to be reinterpreted as a nasal. This creates a nasal-stop sequence *nt*, which undergoes postnasal voicing to *nd* in the way we have described. Now, if the change from voicing to nasality takes place in a dependent position, then we can regard this as an instance of weakening. And as we have already seen, an effective way of weakening a structure is to demote a headed element to non-headed. Given that the output of weakening is nasality, we can assume that nasality is represented by non-headed |L|.

To summarise, when |L| is headed it is interpreted as obstruent voicing; as such, it is a property of voicing languages like French, Dutch and Japanese. And when |L| is non-headed it is realised as nasality. Typological and phonological evidence confirms that there is a strong link between nasality and obstruent voicing, which ET formalises by using the same element to represent both.

4.4.3 Low Tone

We have seen how the nasal element |L| can function contrastively in nuclei to distinguish between oral and nasal vowels. But in addition, |L| can have a quite different interpretation in nuclei, because in tone languages it is also used to represent low tone. Now, because nasality and tone can both be contrastive in the same vowel system, we need a way of separating them in the grammar. On the one hand, we could appeal to the idea that nasality and tone can operate at different levels of structure: one may be a property of individual segments while the other may be distributed across wider domains such as the prosodic word. On the other hand, we might appeal to headedness: for example, we could claim that nasal vowels have non-headed |L| while low tone vowels have headed |L|. It is likely that the grammar would have to employ both these strategies, though as yet there seems to be no consensus on this point. For the moment we will assume that non-headed |L| represents nasality in vowels, because nasal consonants have non-headed |L|, and that headed |L| represents low tone. (Recall that in (38) we represented high tone using headed |H|.)

It is reasonable to assume that low tone is represented by headed |L| because some languages display a phonological relation between low tone (headed |L| in vowels) and obstruent voicing (headed |L| in consonants). For instance, it is not uncommon to find voiced consonants producing a low tone on a neighbouring vowel. In Suma, imperfective verbs have an H tone (éé 'leave behind', kírí 'look for'), but if the verb has an initial voiced obstruent then the tone becomes LH (bǔsí 'be bland'). And in Siswati a voiced obstruent has the effect of repelling an H tone. In this language an H tone usually falls on the antepenultimate vowel (kulimí saana 'to cause to plough for each other'), but if there is a voiced obstruent such as z in the antepenultimate syllable then H is forced to shift rightwards to the penultimate (kucabuzeláana 'to kiss each other for'). However, if this penultimate syllable also contains a voiced obstruent then it too repels H, preventing H from docking. In such cases H remains in its original position, the antepenultimate syllable, which is realised with a rising LH tone on the vowel instead (lidǎdaana 'little duck').

In Suma and Siswati it is obstruent voicing that affects the tone of a following vowel. But there are also languages in which the process works in the opposite direction, that is, where low tone vowels cause a preceding consonant to become voiced. Jingpho has a morphological process of gemination (cát 'tight', cáttai 'it is tight'), but following a low tone vowel the geminating consonant is also voiced (yàk 'difficult', yàggai 'it is difficult'). These examples have a straightforward explanation if we assume that obstruent voicing and low tone share the same element, namely headed |L|. Thus we may view these effects as assimilation processes involving an active headed |L|. Notice how this link between voicing and low tone complements the link between voicelessness and high tone we described in §4.3.4, where we saw how languages such as Kammu developed high tone vowels after voiceless consonants containing |H|.

Finally, let us return to the phonetic reasons for recognising a link between tone and voicing properties. Recall that in §4.3.4 we noted how speakers can alter the stiffness of the vocal folds to signal the difference between voiceless and voiced and also the difference between high pitch and low pitch. We also noted that the shared feature [±stiff vocal folds] can be used to represent voicelessness and high pitch, where this feature roughly corresponds to the |H| element. But significantly, there is also a feature [±slack vocal folds], which can be used to represent voicing and low tone, as shown in (37). This feature broadly corresponds to |L|.

This completes our description of the |L| element. Its main phonological and phonetic properties are summarised in (58).

(58)
		Context	Phonetic interpretation
headed |L|:		with |H|	full voicing in fricatives
		with |? H|	full voicing in stops
		in vowels	low tone
non-headed |L|:		in consonants	nasal murmur in nasals
		in vowels	nasality

4.5 COMBINING THE MANNER ELEMENTS

So far we have only described languages with a two-way laryngeal contrast: H languages distinguish headed |H| versus neutral while L languages distinguish headed |L| versus neutral. But there are also languages with three-way and even four-way laryngeal distinctions. Some three-way systems such as Thai in (59) employ both headed |H| and headed |L| contrastively.

(59)
neutral	–	[pa:]	'forest'	[p]	= |U ?	
voiced	|L|	[ba:]	'shoulder'	[b]	= |U ? L|
aspirated	|H|	[pʰa:]	'cut, slit'	[pʰ]	= |U ? H|

We also find languages that contrast either headed |H| or |L| with headed |ʔ|; for instance, Kabardian has a three-way split between neutral [p], aspirated [pʰ] and ejective [p']. However, in order to account for the full range of laryngeal contrasts that we meet in natural languages, one additional category is needed, namely, voiced aspirates. The voiced aspirated segments [bʰ dʰ gʰ], also known as breathy-voiced or murmured stops, are represented by combining |H| and |L| in the same expression. We find series of voiced aspirates in a small number of four-way laryngeal systems such as Nepali. Examples of the relevant contrasts are given in (60).

(60) neutral   –   [pal]   'rear'   [p] = |U ? |
      voiced |L| [bal]   'burn'   [b] = |U ? L|
      aspirated |H| [pʰal]   'throw away'   [pʰ] = |U ? H|
      voiced aspirated |H L| [bʱal]   'forehead'   [bʱ] = |U ? H L|

The voiced aspirates [bʱdʱgʱ] combine the acoustic characteristics of voiced stops with those of aspirated stops. Their release phase displays the high-frequency aperiodic noise that we associate with headed |H|, but because they are produced with the vocal folds drawn together at one end, allowing them to vibrate, they are also voiced throughout. This indicates that they also have headed |L|, giving us the representation |H L| for the class of voiced aspirates. Now, some versions of ET object to the idea of having two headed elements in the same expression; and in §5.3 we will explore a way of controlling the number of headed elements that can coexist. At this point we will simply acknowledge those objections by suggesting a revised representation for breathy voicing which combines headed |L| with non-headed |H|, giving |H L|. The reason for demoting |H| to a non-headed element is that voiced aspirates are reportedly produced with only a 'moderately open glottis . . . about 50 percent of that used during aspiration' (Ladefoged and Maddieson 1996: 58). In other words, |H| seems to have a less prominent role in voiced aspirates than in voiceless ones, which we can formalise in terms of headedness.

It was noted earlier that the elements |H| and |L| do not combine easily because their acoustic patterns are in conflict: |H| is linked to high-frequency energy and |L| to low-frequency energy. But because |H| and |L| are independent categories representing distinct phonological properties, the possibility of combining them cannot be ruled out altogether. Not unexpectedly, however, there is a tendency for languages to avoid combinations of |H| and |L|, because when acoustic patterns oppose each other like this, they can easily lose their distinctiveness, and as a result, hinder the transfer of linguistic information. This goes some way towards explaining the marked status of voiced aspirates cross-linguistically. It also puts the combination |H|–|L| on a par with the other antagonistic pairings we have seen, namely |A|–|ʔ| and |I|–|U|. This topic will be discussed in §5.3.

In this chapter we have seen how it is possible to represent most manner and laryngeal contrasts using different combinations of |ʔ H L|. These are summarised in (61), which also includes some of the less common combinations that we have not yet described.

(61)

Category		Example segments	Example language
neutral stops	ʔ	p/b̥, t/d̥, t/ɖ̥	all
aspirated stops	ʔ <u>H</u>	kʰ, tʰ, pʰ	H languages
voiced/prenasalised stops	ʔ <u>L</u>	b, ⁿd, ɢ	L languages
ejectives	<u>ʔ</u> H	p', tʃ', q'	Montana Salish
implosives	<u>ʔ</u> L	ɓ, ɗ, ʄ	Kimatuumbi
breathy-voiced stops	ʔ H <u>L</u>	bʱ, dʱ, gʱ	Hindi
neutral fricatives	H	f/v̥, s/z̥, ʂ/ʐ̥	most
aspirated (fortis) fricatives	<u>H</u>	f, ʃ, x	H languages
voiced fricatives	H <u>L</u>	v, ð, z	L languages
nasals	L (ʔ)	m, n, ɳ	most
voiceless nasals	L H (ʔ)	m̥, n̥, ɲ̥	Jalapa Mazatec
breathy-voiced nasals	<u>L</u> H (ʔ)	m̤, n̤	Newar
laryngealised nasals	L <u>ʔ</u>	m̰, n̰	Kwakw'ala

Clearly, no single language can include all these combinations of |ʔ H L|, as this would result in an impossibly large consonant system. In reality, the majority of languages employ five or six categories at most. This does not necessarily mean that ET overgenerates, however, because it is still the case that each category in (61) is an observed natural class. The examples we have analysed in this chapter demonstrate how |ʔ H L| have sufficient expressive power to describe a wide range of segmental inventories. Even the largest consonant systems can be represented if headedness is employed as a contrastive property and if the antagonistic elements |H| and |L| are permitted to combine where necessary.

This completes our description of the six elements. The vowel elements |I U A| are responsible for vowel quality, but they also represent resonance properties in consonants. And the consonant elements |ʔ H L| provide manner and laryngeal properties in consonants, but they also represent secondary properties such as tone, nasality and creakiness in vowels. So, using these six elements it is possible to characterise most aspects of segmental structure. However, you may have noticed that there is one important category we have largely ignored until now, namely, the liquid consonants. In the next chapter we discuss the internal structure of laterals and rhotics in some detail.

We also address other remaining issues including the link between segmental and prosodic structure.

FURTHER READING

Element-based studies of nasality have been undertaken by Botma (2004), Nasukawa (2005) and Ploch (1999); Nasukawa (2005) also examines the headedness relation between nasals and voiced obstruents. Examples of nasal weakening can be found in Cohn (1993), while more general surveys of consonant weakening processes are provided in Kirchner (2001), Lavoie (2001) and Gurevich (2004). On the question of whether nasals and laterals pattern with continuants or non-continuants, see Botma (2004: 52), Hualde (1987: 77), Mielke (2005) and van de Weijer (1995: 47). An overview of Dependency Phonology can be found in Anderson and Ewen (1987). Harris (2006) discusses the problems arising from the use of sonority as an explanatory tool, while Halle and Stevens (1971) describe the phonetic link (in terms of vocal fold tension) between different laryngeal settings and pitch. For a discussion of the role of prosodic structure in language acquisition, see Cutler and Norris (1988), Harris and Urua (2001), Jusczyk, Cutler and Redanz (1993) and Marslen-Wilson and Tyler (1980).

The data presented in this chapter are from the following sources: Bao (1990), Chen (2000) and Yip (2002) for tonal contrasts in Songjiang Chinese; Elias-Ulloa (2009) for creaky vowels in Capanahua; Ewen and van der Hulst (2001: 71) for voicing assimilation in Dutch; Fallon (2002: 89) for ejectives in Maidu; Flemming, Ladefoged and Thomason (2008) for Montana Salish; González (2009) and Scheer (2003) for the weakening of stops in Spanish; Ladefoged and Maddieson (1996: 107) for nasal contrasts in Jalapa Mazatec; Mielke (2005) for Samish; Odden (2005: 55) for implosives in Kimatuumbi; Svantesson and House (2006) for laryngeal contrasts in Kammu; Yip (2002) for examples from Suma on the relation between obstruent voicing and low tone.

REFERENCES

Anderson, John M. and Colin J. Ewen (1987), *Principles of Dependency Phonology*, Cambridge: Cambridge University Press.
Bao, Zhiming (1990), 'On the nature of tone', PhD dissertation, MIT.
Botma, Bert (2004), *Phonological Aspects of Nasality: An Element-based Dependency Approach*, Utrecht, LOT Press.

Chen, Matthew (2000), *Tone Sandhi*, Cambridge: Cambridge University Press.
Clements, George N. and Elizabeth Hume (1995), 'The internal organization of speech sounds', in J. A. Goldsmith (ed.), *The Handbook of Phonological Theory*, Cambridge, MA and Oxford: Blackwell, pp. 245–306.
Cohn, Abigail (1993), 'The status of nasalised continuants', in M. Huffman and R. Krakow (eds), *Nasals, Nasality and the Velum*, San Diego: Academic Press, pp. 329–67.
Cutler, Anne and Dennis Norris (1988), 'The role of strong syllables in segmentation for lexical access', *Journal of Experimental Psychology: Human Perception and Performance* 14.1, 113–21.
Elias-Ulloa, José (2009), 'The distribution of laryngeal segments in Capanahua', *International Journal of American Linguistics* 75.2, 159–206.
Ewen, Colin J. and Harry van der Hulst (2001), *The Phonological Structure of Words: An Introduction*, Cambridge: Cambridge University Press.
Fallon, Paul D. (2002), *The Synchronic and Diachronic Phonology of Ejectives*, New York and London: Routledge.
Flemming, Edward, Peter Ladefoged and Sally Thomason (2008), 'Phonetic structures of Montana Salish', *Journal of Phonetics* 36, 465–91.
González, Carolina (2009), 'Continuancy and resonance in Spanish', in J. Collentine, M. García, B. Lafford and F. Marcos Marín (eds), *Selected Proceedings of the 11th Hispanic Linguistics Symposium*, Sommerville, MA: Cascadilla Press, pp. 196–206.
Gurevich, Naomi (2004), *Lenition and Contrast*, New York and London: Routledge.
Halle, Morris and Kenneth N. Stevens (1971), 'A note on laryngeal features', *MIT Quarterly Progress Report of the Research Laboratory of Electronics* 101, 198–213.
Harris, John (2006), 'The phonology of being understood: further arguments against sonority', *Lingua* 116, 1483–94.
Harris, John and Eno-Abasi Urua (2001), 'Lenition degrades information: consonant allophony in Ibibio', *Speech, Hearing and Language: Work in Progress* 13, 72–105.
Hualde, José, I. (1987), 'On Basque affricates', *West Coast Conference on Formal Linguistics* 6, 77–89.
Jusczyk, Peter, Anne Cutler and Nancy J. Redanz (1993), 'Infants' preference for the predominant stress patterns of English words', *Child Development* 64, 675–87.
Kirchner, Robert (2001), 'Phonological contrast and articulatory effort', in L. Lombardi (ed.), *Segmental Phonology in Optimality Theory*, Cambridge: Cambridge University Press, pp. 79–117.
Ladefoged, Peter and Ian Maddieson (1996), *The Sounds of the World's Languages*, Oxford: Blackwell.

Lavoie, Lisa (2001), *Consonant Strength: Phonological Patterns and Phonetic Manifestations*, New York and London: Garland.

Marslen-Wilson, William D. and Lorraine K. Tyler (1980), 'The temporal structure of spoken language understanding', *Cognition* 8, 1–71.

Mielke, Jeff (2005), 'Ambivalence and ambiguity in laterals and nasals', *Phonology* 22, 169–203.

Nasukawa, Kuniya (2005), *A Unified Approach to Nasality and Voicing*, Berlin and New York: Mouton de Gruyter.

Newman, Paul (1974), *The Kanakuru Language*, West African Languages Monograph Series 9, Leeds: The Scholar Press Ltd.

Odden, David (2005), *Introducing Phonology*, Cambridge: Cambridge University Press.

Ploch, Stefan (1999), 'Nasals on my mind: the phonetic and the cognitive approach to the phonology of nasality', PhD dissertation, School of Oriental and African Studies, University of London.

Scheer, Tobias (2003), 'On spirantisation and affricates', in S. Ploch (ed.), *Living on the Edge: 28 Papers in Honour of Jonathan Kaye*, Berlin and New York: Mouton de Gruyter, pp. 283–301.

Svantesson, Jan-Olof and David House (2006), 'Tone production, tone perception and Kammu tonogenesis', *Phonology* 23, 309–33.

Weijer, Jeroen van de (1995), 'Continuancy in liquids and in obstruents', *Lingua* 96, 45–61.

Yip, Moira (2002), *Tone*, Cambridge: Cambridge University Press.

Chapter 5

LIQUIDS, LICENSING AND ANTAGONISTIC ELEMENTS

5.1 LIQUIDS

5.1.1 Liquids as a Natural Class

A major consonant category we have not yet discussed is the class of liquids, which brings together rhotics (*r* sounds) and laterals (*l* sounds). These categories are traditionally classified in terms of their articulatory properties, so clearly, a different approach is needed here. In this section we will see that ET characterises liquids by their resonance properties instead. Liquids are |A| consonants: most rhotics are analysed as simplex |A| glides, while most laterals are analysed as complex glides containing |A| plus another element. Recall that glides are defined as consonant expressions containing only resonance elements.

(1) *r* sounds |A|
     l sounds |A I| or |A U|

Before looking at rhotics and laterals individually, we should be clear about the status of the class of liquids. The first question to ask is whether there is any reason to classify rhotics and laterals together at all. One view is that liquids do not form a phonological category because they do not have any specific properties in common; according to this view, 'liquid' is nothing more than a convenient label to describe sonorants that do not fall into any other category. Another view treats the liquids as an informal set without assigning this set any grammatical status. According to this second view, the class of liquids exists largely for historical reasons: in classical philology the liquids included rhotics, laterals and nasals (in Greek) or just rhotics and laterals (in Latin). It is this latter grouping which is still used widely today. There is also a third view which treats the liquids as a legitimate phonological class. This is the approach taken in ET, and in this section we review the evidence for a natural class of liquids.

The following observations are taken from two recent feature-based studies of liquids, Walsh Dickey (1997) and Proctor (2009).

Rhotics and laterals have a similar distribution, which suggests that they may be phonologically related. For example, some languages impose word-level restrictions on the appearance of liquids: Diyari disallows word-initial [l ɭ ʎ ʟ r ɻ], while Mongolian bans word-initial [l r] despite allowing other glides in this position. Conversely, liquids are sometimes the only consonants allowed to appear word-finally. This is the case in most varieties of French where word-final consonants, with the notable exception of the liquids [ʀ l], are left unpronounced (except in liaison contexts). Liquids show distributional patterns at the syllable level too. They are generally preferred as syllabic consonants, presumably because they have only vowel elements in their structure. In Czech, for instance, *l* and *r* are the only consonants to appear in the nucleus of a stressed syllable, as in ['br̩.no] *Brno*, ['vl̩.tava] *Vltava*. Additionally, the liquids frequently act as clustering consonants; that is, they make consonant clusters possible by occupying the syllable coda or the second slot of a branching onset. Based on these distributional facts, then, it seems that rhotics and laterals have something in common and form a distinct class that excludes other consonant types.

There is also evidence from phonological processes that rhotics and laterals pattern together as a natural class. In Hausa, for example, *n* assimilates in place to a following consonant, as in (2a). But if this consonant is a liquid, then the result is total assimilation, as in (2b).

(2) a. *sun bi*   [sumbi]   'they followed'
       gidansù   [gidansù]   'their house'
       hanyà   [haɲjà]   'road'

   b. *sôn râi*   [sârrâi]   'selfishness'
       Dan Lādì [ɗallādɪ]   a proper name

Latin displays a similar effect, resulting in place assimilation in words such as *i*[m]*perceptus* 'unknown' but complete assimilation in words such as *i*[l]*lectus* 'unread'. And as a result of borrowing, this pattern is also reflected in English *i*[l]*logical*, *i*[r]*relevant* (cf. *i*[m]*possible*, *i*[ŋ]*complete*). So in certain assimilation processes *l* and *r* behave as a natural class. But Latin is also well known for its process of lateral dissimilation, in which *l* in a suffix dissimilates to *r* if the adjoining stem contains a lateral, hence *vulg-aris* 'vulgar', *singul-aris* 'alone' (cf.

nav-alis 'naval'). Importantly, alternations arising from dissimilation usually involve segments from the same natural class – they are not random substitutions. It is unsurprising, then, that Latin *l* should dissimilate to *r*. Dissimilation in the opposite direction (*r* to *l*) is equally unremarkable. In Georgian, for example, *r* in a suffix dissimilates to *l* when there is a rhotic in the adjoining root, for instance *ungr-uli* 'Hungarian', *asur-uli* 'Assyrian' (cf. *dan-uri* 'Danish'). The examples we have just cited are all triggered by morphological changes, but dissimilation can also take the form of a sound change. For example, *rVr* sequences in Old Javanese became *lVr* in modern Javanese, as in *rereb* > *lereb* 'to rest', *roro* > *loro* 'two'. A similar change took place in the development of Spanish from Latin, giving *arbor* (Lat.) > *àrbol* (Sp.) 'tree', *rebur* (Lat.) > *roble* (Sp.) 'oak'.

Historically, rhotics and laterals show a tendency to become involved in metathesis, with vowel–liquid metathesis having taken place in a range of unrelated languages including Breton, Eastern Eskimo and some Slavic languages. This is illustrated in (3).

(3) | Proto-Slavic | Bulgarian | Polish | |
|---|---|---|---|
| *orbota | rábota | robota | 'work' |
| *melko | mléko | mleko | 'milk' |

The relatedness of *r* and *l* comes across even more clearly in cases where metathesis involves two liquids exchanging places. This is observed in the history of several languages including Spanish (*miraglo* > *milagro* 'miracle'), Telugu (**ural* > *rôlu* 'mortar') and Gayo (**telur* > *terul* 'egg'). Elsewhere the relatedness of rhotics and laterals has caused the two to neutralise instead. For instance, during the development of Campidanian Sardinian the contrast between *l* and *r* in Latin neutralised to *r* in onset clusters. This left the descendant language Sardinian with just one liquid, for example *plus* (Lat.) > ['prus] 'more', *frater* (Lat.) > ['fradi] 'brother'.

Another characteristic of liquids is their tendency to delete after a vowel, often causing the preceding vowel to lengthen. Again, the fact that *l* and *r* display parallel behaviour suggests that the two classes are related. In some varieties of English, for example, compensatory lengthening has been triggered by *l* deletion (*half* ['hɑːf], *almond* ['ɑːmənd]) and *r* deletion (*varnish* ['vɑːnɪʃ], *far* ['fɑː]). Interestingly, the deletion of liquids usually takes place after a low or back vowel – that is, after a vowel containing |A| – which is presumably related to the idea that *r* and *l* are represented as |A| glides. The English pattern is found elsewhere too, among languages as diverse as Komi (Uralic),

Onondaga (Iroquoian) and Turkish (Altaic). In Salar (Turkic), for instance, we get realisations such as *varyar* [va(ː)ʁɑ(ː)] '(s)he will go', *gelmiʃ* [kɛːmiʃ] '(s)he reportedly came'. If further evidence were needed for a phonological relation between rhotics and laterals, then we could appeal to those languages in which a single liquid has *r* and *l* realisations, alternating either freely or systematically. For example, some Papuan languages have just a single liquid which can be interpreted variously as a tap, a trill or a lateral. Jita is another language with only one liquid, which is produced as a lateral in morpheme-initial position and as a rhotic elsewhere. Variation is even possible in systems which have a contrast between two liquids. For example, Kikongo Kituba has a contrast between *r* and *l*, but in some contexts these two sounds neutralise and occur in free variation, as in *bilo* [biro] ~ [bilo].

Observations like these make it clear that rhotics and laterals function together as a natural class. In ET terms, this means that they have an element in common. And as we examine the behaviour of rhotics and laterals in the following sections, it will emerge that this common element is |A|.

5.1.2 Rhotics

The term 'rhotic' is notoriously vague, as is the generic symbol *r* used for signifying rhotic consonants. The class of rhotics takes in a wide range of segment types including several manner categories (trills, taps, approximants, fricatives) and place categories (alveolar, retroflex, uvular). Yet despite this phonetic variation, rhotics show a remarkable unity in their phonological behaviour, especially when it comes to their distribution. On this basis we will assume that most *r* sounds are phonologically identical, and represent them as |A|.

There are two points to note here. First, the coronal tap [ɾ] cannot always be included in the class of rhotics. Although [ɾ] sometimes functions as an *r* sound, in which case it is represented as |A|, there are also languages in which it behaves more like an |I| segment – recall from §4.3.2 that in tapping dialects of English, [ɾ] is represented as a non-headed |I| glide. Second, some languages have a contrast between two or more rhotics. If the contrast is between [ɹ]/[r] and [ɾ] then it can be expressed simply as |A| versus |I|. But if the contrast is between [ɹ] and, say, a trilled [r] or a retroflex [ɻ], then clearly the single representation |A| is inadequate. One solution would be to make a distinction based on headedness; for instance, [ɹ] as |A| could contrast with

[r] as |A|. In fact, headedness may even be an appropriate way of capturing the fairly common alternation between trilled [r] and tapped [ɾ]. For example, in §3.6.2 we noted that [r] and [ɾ] are in complementary distribution in Munster Irish, [r] appearing word-initially and [ɾ] in word-final and intervocalic positions. This suggests that [r] is the stronger of the two and is represented by headed |A|, whereas the weaker [ɾ] has the non-headed structure |A|. A similar analysis may work in European Spanish and Portuguese too, where [r] and [ɾ] are in contrast word-internally but in word-initial position only [r] is permitted. If we assume that [r] is headed whereas [ɾ] is not, then this is the kind of distributional pattern we expect, where a strong (headed) segmental expression is associated with a strong (word-initial) prosodic position. In the majority of languages, however, the question of a contrast between different rhotics does not arise. This leaves us free to employ the symbol *r* and the representation |A| for most *r* sounds including the trill [r], the approximant [ɹ], the retroflex [ɽ] and even the uvulars [ʀ ʁ].

To understand why it is |A| that represents *r*, we must consider again the glide formation process described in Chapter 3. In §3.2.3 we saw how |I| and |U| are interpreted as glides in English, lexically ([j]*ellow*, [w]*ater*) and in liaison contexts (*high*[j]*est*, *go*[w]*ing*). But if |I| and |U| can form glides, then we expect the remaining vowel element |A| to do the same. English provides the evidence we need, where the simplex expression |A| is interpreted as an *r* glide in non-nuclear positions. The set of vowel–glide pairs in English can now be given as in (4).

(4) [i]   [j]   [u]   [w]   [ə]   [ɹ]

     N   O   N   O   N   O
     | | | | | |
     x   x   x   x   x   x
     | | | | | |
    |I| |I| |U| |U| |A| |A|

Alongside the established vowel–glide pairs [i]–[j] and [u]–[w] we now have [ə]–[ɹ]. Clearly, [ə]–[ɹ] is not an obvious vowel–glide pairing in the same way that [i]–[j] and [u]–[w] are. This is because the phonetic similarity between [ə] and [ɹ] is less apparent than it is between [i] and [j], and [u] and [w]. As we saw in §2.8.4, English [ə] is a weak vowel represented by non-headed |A|. Its formants are fairly evenly spaced, as the left half of Figure 5.1 shows. Nevertheless

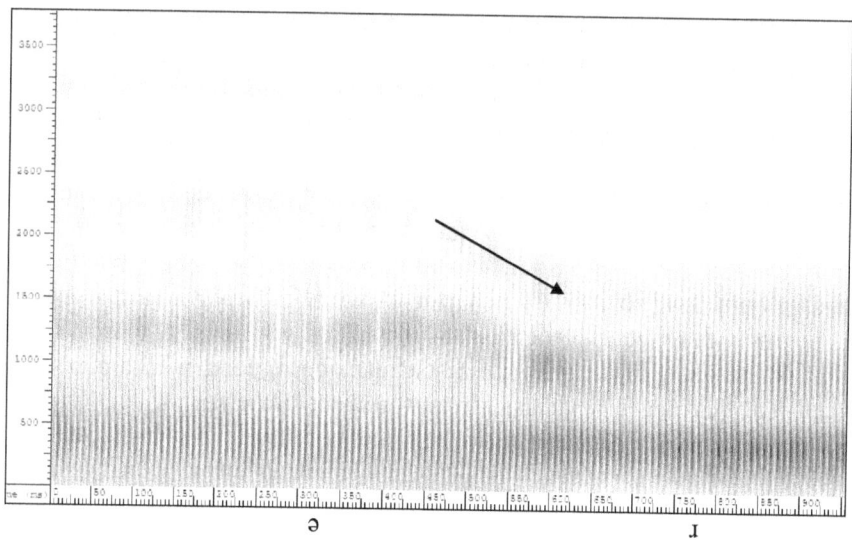

Figure 5.1 Spectrogram of [əɹ]

it is still possible to detect a weak *mAss* pattern in [ə], which produces a concentration of energy in the lower central region of the spectrum. The *mAss* pattern signals the presence of |A|, but because |A| is non-headed in [ə] its acoustic cues are relatively weak.

Now compare the formant pattern of [ə] with that of [ɹ] in the right half of Figure 5.1. The pattern for [ɹ] is very similar, except that it has a lowered F3, as indicated by the arrow. This lowered F3 is caused by lip rounding, which is a feature of English [ɹ] but not of [ə]. (If you make a continuous schwa sound and then add lip rounding, the sound becomes [ɹ] – in other words, [ɹ] is a rounded schwa in a non-nuclear position.) Now, if a segment is phonetically rounded, then we can expect it to have the |U| element in its representation. But in the case of [ɹ] there is no indication that this consonant patterns with other |U| segments such as labials or velars – which implies that rounding is not actually a linguistic property of English [ɹ]. So how do we explain its rounded quality? Rounding in [ɹ] appears to function as an enhancement, that is, as an additional acoustic cue which helps listeners to perceive weak phonological contrasts. The role of an enhancement is to make a segment perceptually stronger by increasing the acoustic distance between it and other segments. To illustrate this, consider the distinction between [s] and [ʃ] in English. Because both sounds are voiceless strident fricatives with similar phonetic properties, it is easy for listeners to confuse them in certain phonological contexts. So in order to make the distinction easier to perceive, speakers round the lips for [ʃ] but not for [s], thereby enhancing or exaggerating the acoustic distinction between them. Enhancements such as this typically involve redundant or non-contrastive properties; for instance, the contrast between [s] and [ʃ] need not refer to rounding at all. In other words, enhancements have mainly a perceptual role rather than a lexical role.

Like rounding in [ʃ], rounding in [ɹ] is an enhancement; its effect is to lower all formants but particularly F3. Without a lowered F3, [ɹ] would be a fairly nondescript, almost imperceptible consonant that could easily merge with neighbouring vowels and be missed altogether by listeners. To avoid this, rounding enhances the overall perceptibility of [ɹ], and in particular, strengthens the otherwise weak contrast in English between *r* and *l*. Because of the acoustic similarity between *r* and *l*, listeners can have problems distinguishing them. However, these problems are reduced by enhancing *r* through lip rounding. This lowers F3 in *r*, which is particularly effective because *l* has, by contrast, an unusually high F3. The outcome is therefore an enhanced acoustic difference between *r* with a very low F3 and *l* with a very high F3. This ensures that *r* and *l* are kept distinct, which in turn reinforces the phonological contrast between them. Further evidence that English *r* is enhanced by rounding comes from child language, in which *r* is regularly interpreted as a labial glide in words such as *hurry* [hʌwi], *train* [tweɪn]. We can suppose that, during the earliest stages of acquisition, infants build lexical representations mainly on the basis of acoustic input; and because they hear a *rUmp* pattern in *r* they naturally assign it the representation |U|. This is what produces forms such as *hurry* [hʌwi]. But as their phonological awareness increases, they discover that *r* actually functions as an |A| segment rather than as an |U| segment, and that |U| is an acoustic enhancement rather than a lexical property. This causes them to revise their representation for *r*, and once it is reassigned as |A| it can be phonetically interpreted as coronal [ɹ], the adult form.

Returning to the representation of *r*, we can now assume that the *rUmp* pattern in *r* is an enhancement rather than a lexical property, which means that *r* does not have any |U| element in its structure. But we still need positive evidence that *r* contains |A|. One piece of evidence comes from the history of German, in which *r* was reinterpreted as the schwa-like vowel [ɐ]. This is confirmed by modern spellings, which have post-vocalic <r> in those contexts where we now get [ɐ], for example *vier* [fiːɐ] 'four', *Pferd* [pfeːɐt] 'horse'. And moreover, a similar pattern is observed in non-rhotic English, where we find a phonological relation between English *r* and the vowel [ə]. This is described in the next section.

5.1.3 Linking and Intrusive *r* in English

Linking *r* is a feature of non-rhotic varieties of English including Australian English and some dialects of British English. In these systems *r* is pronounced only before a vowel. *r* appears lexically in single-morpheme words (*red, carry*) but it can also be produced phonologically between two vowels; this happens at morpheme boundaries (*pouring, car engine*) where there is no pause. When *r* is produced in this way it is known as a linking *r* because it creates a link between two vowels that would otherwise be in hiatus.

(5) | *Silent r* | *Linking r* |
|---|---|
| fea(r)less | fea[ɹ]ing |
| wate(r) | wate[ɹ]y |
| ca(r) keys | ca[ɹ] engine |
| Pete(r) | Pete[ɹ] is here |

There are several element-based analyses of the phonology of *r* including Broadbent (1991), who views linking *r* as |A| glide formation. This parallels the processes of |I| glide formation (linking |I|) and |U| glide formation (linking |U|) that we described in §3.2.3. As (6) shows, the three processes are in complementary distribution. The preceding vowel provides the context that determines which of the three glides appears.

(6)
	Linking |I|	*Linking* |U|	*Linking* |A|
preceding vowel	{iː ɪ eɪ aɪ ɔɪ}	{uː ʊ əʊ aʊ}	{ɜː ɑː ɔː ə ɪə eə ʊə}
resulting glide	[j]	[w]	[ɹ]
example	*fly* [j]*away*	*go* [w]*away*	*far* [ɹ]*away*

The contexts for linking |I| and linking |U| should already be familiar: linking |I| follows a vowel containing the |I| element and linking |U| is produced by a vowel containing |U|. Let us now generalise this to include linking |A|, which follows a vowel from the set {ɜː ɑː ɔː ə ɪə eə ʊə}. Predictably, each of these vowels contains |A| in its structure.

The process of linking *r* is illustrated in (7). For non-rhotic speakers, *water* ['wɔːtə] has no lexical *r* – its structure ends in a vowel, as shown in (7a). There is no need to specify a lexical *r* in the word *watery* ['wɔːtəɹi] either: when the adjectival suffix -*y* is added,

|A| extends from the preceding nucleus to produce the glide [ɹ], as in (7b).

(7)   a. *water* [ˈwɔːtə]   b. *watery* [ˈwɔːtəɹi]

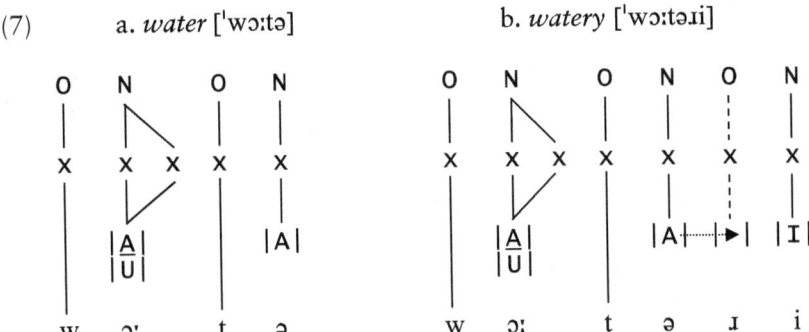

In fact it is only in single-morpheme words such as *real* and *berry* that [ɹ] must be specified lexically as an |A| glide. Elsewhere [ɹ] is the product of |A| linking, which breaks up vowel sequences across morpheme boundaries, both internal (*water-y, fear-ing*) and external (*her own, far away*). Note that, in contrast to the situation we have just described for non-rhotic systems, *r* in rhotic dialects has a wider distribution and is specified lexically as a glide in all contexts.

The examples of linking *r* we have seen so far involve historical *r*, where <r> in the spelling shows that [ɹ] was once pronounced but has since been lost (except before a vowel). For many non-rhotic speakers, however, linking *r* also occurs in contexts where *r* was never present, and hence, where there is no <r> in the spelling. Again, this happens word-internally (*draw*[ɹ]*ing*) and within a phrase (*media*[ɹ]*empire, Pizza*[ɹ]*Express, I saw*[ɹ]*it*). Note that these instances of linking *r* are structurally identical to the historically motivated example shown in (7b). We therefore see the same glide formation process operating in (8a) and (8b), the first illustrating historical linking *r* and the second non-historical linking *r*.

(8)   a.   *Peter* [ɹ] *is*   b.   *Lisa* [ɹ] *is*

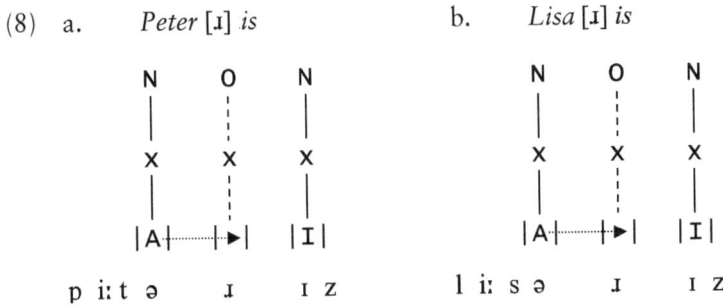

Yet traditionally, (8a) and (8b) are analysed differently and even go by different names: (8a) is viewed as a true case of linking *r* since it takes place in a historical *r* context, whereas (8b) is known as intrusive *r* because [ɹ] 'intrudes' in a position where it is historically unmotivated. One reason why traditionalists make a distinction between linking *r* and intrusive *r* has to do with the distribution of these sounds in different dialects of English: they argue that some dialects have both linking *r* and intrusive *r* whereas others have only linking *r*. This implies that linking *r* and intrusive *r* exist as independent processes, which is unlikely in view of the fact that they occur in the same contexts and have the same outcome [ɹ]. Furthermore, linking and intrusive *r* are both absent from rhotic dialects, which we have to regard as a coincidence unless they are actually two different forms of the same process. On balance, it seems we are justified in breaking with tradition here and assuming that linking *r* and intrusive *r* are phonologically identical: both are glide formation processes involving active |A|.

So can we simply disregard the claim that some dialects have intrusive *r* while others do not? Perhaps we can, since this 'observation' seems to be less accurate than we might suppose. It appears that most non-rhotic speakers of English now produce both linking *r* and intrusive *r* to varying degrees. Of course there is still a clear sociolinguistic difference between the two: linking *r* is grammatical in almost all sociolinguistic contexts whereas intrusive *r* is generally less acceptable from a stylistic point of view. But having said that, it is no longer the case that intrusive *r* is stigmatised to the extent that it once was; for instance, we now hear RP speakers using intrusive *r* in formal settings and on radio and television. Evidently, the difference between historical and non-historical *r* is, strictly speaking, not a phonological matter. If a dialect appears to lack intrusive *r*, this may simply be a successful attempt by its speakers to avoid |A| glide formation in non-historical contexts. Although these speakers may be more attentive to sociolinguistic conventions and spelling pronunciations than other non-rhotic speakers, this does not mean that they have a different grammar.

We have now seen how the vowel elements |I U A| are interpreted as the glides [j w ɹ] in non-nuclear positions, with non-rhotic English illustrating how |A| is present in [ɹ]. It is worth noting, however, that |A| glide formation is cross-linguistically less common than either |I| glide formation or |U| glide formation, which suggests that |A| may not make an ideal consonant element in the way that |I| and |U| do.

In fact we have already remarked on an asymmetry among the vowel elements: earlier we said that |A| is naturally more vocalic than |I| or |U|, making it better suited to appearing in nuclear than non-nuclear expressions. This makes English relatively unusual in employing |A| glide formation as a hiatus breaker.

5.1.4 Laterals

Most feature theories employ the manner feature [±lateral] to distinguish [+lateral] sounds such as [l ɬ ɭ ʎ] from the [–lateral] sounds (which include rhotics). But if lateral is really a manner property in the way that, say, nasal is a manner property, then why do we not find laterals at all the major places of articulation? We would expect languages to have contrasts between labial laterals, velar laterals and coronal laterals, for example, just as we do with nasals. In reality, laterals are overwhelmingly coronal: according to one survey, 99.2% of laterals are coronal (which includes dental, alveolar, retroflex and palatal) while the remaining 0.8% are velar. It is not difficult to capture the link between lateral and coronal in the grammar. For example, some models of feature geometry take [lateral] to be a dependent of the coronal place node. But unfortunately, this amounts to nothing more than an observation; although it expresses the idea that lateral entails coronal, it does not explain why a manner feature like lateral should be associated with a particular place property such as coronal.

If lateral implies coronal place, then it is reasonable that we should view lateral as some form of coronal resonance. In other words, it makes sense to treat lateral as a place property rather than as a manner property. We have already said that rhotics and laterals form a natural class of |A| glides (§5.1.1), so if rhotics are represented by |A| then laterals must have |A| plus another resonance element: the additional element may be either |I| or |U|, depending on the language and the phonological context. That is, laterals are complex glides with the structure |A I| or |A U|. Before discussing these structures in detail, let us be clear about why laterals should be treated as glides. In ET, glides are consonants that have only vowel elements in their structure. And in the case of laterals, there is nothing in their behaviour to suggest that they contain anything but |A I U|. It is true that in some languages laterals do pattern with stops (§4.2.1), in which case they presumably contain an additional |ʔ|. But on the other hand, we never find them displaying the acoustic cues associated with

|H| or |L|, such as nasality, active voicing, frication or voicelessness (voiceless laterals and lateral fricatives will be discussed below). The idea that laterals should be classified as glides is confirmed by their distribution, which is typical of glides: like [j w ɹ], laterals are mostly favoured in weak contexts such as pre-consonantal position (*belt, silver*) and the second position in a branching onset (*clue, employ*).

The main difference between rhotics and laterals has to do with complexity: rhotics have a simplex structure |A| while laterals have a complex structure |A I| or |A U|. This affects natural class membership, and below we will see how laterals pattern with other |I| or |U| segments in a way that rhotics do not. But complexity also relates to phonological strength, with complex segments being preferred over simplex segments in strong positions. As we saw in §2.8.4, for example, stressed syllables in English can support vowels of any complexity whereas weak syllables are associated with the simplex vowels [ɪ ʊ ə]. And we find a similar asymmetry between rhotics and laterals. In Andalusian Spanish, *l* is pronounced as a lateral in the onset of a CV syllable but it reduces to a tap [ɾ] before a consonant. The forms in (9) show how Andalusian Spanish compares with Castilian Spanish, where *l* has a wider distribution.

(9) *Andalusian Spanish*　*Castilian Spanish*
　　[e.lo.so]　　　　　　[e.lo.so]　　　　'the bear'
　　[eɾ.θo]　　　　　　　[el.θo]　　　　　'the zoo'
　　[puɾ.po]　　　　　　[pul.po]　　　　'octopus'

Since [ɾ] is represented as non-headed |I| (§4.3.2), this amounts to a straightforward weakening process in which the lateral |A I| reduces to |A I| by suppressing |A| in a weak context. The same weakening process takes place in Florentine Italian, where [l] and [ɾ] are contrastive in onsets but only simplex [ɾ] may appear in the syllable coda. This is exemplified in (10).

(10) *Florentine Italian*　*Standard Italian*
　　 [doɾ.tʃe]　　　　　　[dol.tʃe]　　　　'sweet, dessert'
　　 [sɔɾ.di]　　　　　　　[sol.di]　　　　 'money'
　　 [paɾ.ko.ʃɛ.ni.ko]　　[pal.ko.ʃɛ.ni.ko]　'stage'

Some Australian languages also ban laterals from the coda, though the process has a slightly different outcome. In Linngithigh and Alngith [l] is reinterpreted as the palatal glide [j], represented as |I|. Again [l] loses its complexity by suppressing |A|, but this time the surviving |I| element is headed and pronounced as [j].

As we have noted, *l* sounds that pattern with stops have an additional |ʔ| element, giving them the representation |A I ʔ|. This makes them similar in structure to the coronal stops *t d*, which are |I ʔ| or |A ʔ| depending on whether the language in question has |I| coronals or |A| coronals. And this similarity between *l* and *t d* provides a reason for why we sometimes find laterals interacting with coronal stops. For example, *d* and *l* alternate in Setswana, with *d* appearing before high vowels (11a) and *l* before non-high vowels (11b).

(11) a. dumɛla   'greetings'   b. loleme   'tongue'
        mosadi   'woman'   xoɲala   'to marry'
        badisa   'the herd'   selɛpɛ   'axe'

These two contexts are distinguished by the presence or absence of |A|: *l* precedes vowels with |A| while *d* precedes vowels without |A|. In other words, *d* is reinterpreted as *l* when it acquires |A| from a following vowel. The process is shown in (12), where it is assumed that Setswana has |I| coronals.

(12) [xoɲala] (*[xoɲada]) 'to marry'

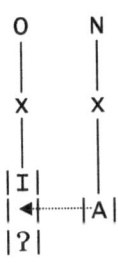

x   o   ɲ   a   l   a

Whether a lateral is represented as |A I| or |A U| will depend on its phonological properties, which may or may not be reflected in its phonetic quality. Sometimes the difference between |A I| and |A U| is heard as a difference between clear [l] and dark [ɫ]. Clear *l* is purely coronal and therefore has the representation |A I|, a combination of the two coronal elements |A| and |I|. As shown in (9) and (10), *l* is clear in Spanish and Italian. On the other hand, dark or velarised *l* has both coronal and velar characteristics; this suggests the structure |A U|, which combines the coronality of |A| with the velarity of |U|. When it comes to English, *l* is variable. Some dialects such as Tyneside English have clear *l* in all environments, so the structure is always |A I|. Other dialects such as Glasgow English have dark *l* everywhere, represented as |A U|. But in many varieties we find an alternation between the two. The traditional account of English *l* distribution is well known: clear [l] precedes a vowel while dark [ɫ] appears elsewhere. However, this is not entirely accurate. A better generalisation would be to say that [l] precedes the |I| vowels [ɪ e æ iː eɪ ɪə] and [j] (*limb, let, land, lean, late, leer, value*) while [ɫ] appears in all other positions. Contrary to the standard description, then, we get dark *l* in *luck, lock, look, alarm, law, lose, learn, film* and *fall*, subject to dialect variation. In other words, the choice between |A I| and |A U| seems to be conditioned by the surrounding segments: English *l* is represented as |A U| but is coloured by |I| from a following |I| vowel; and when this happens, |U| is displaced by the incoming |I| element because |U| and |I| do not easily combine. This process is illustrated in (13a).

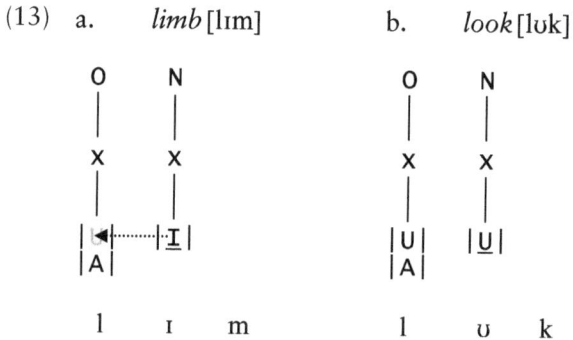

Looking beyond English, it is not always possible to determine whether *l* has the structure |A I| or |A U| just by hearing it. As always, acoustic evidence is never conclusive – it is the phonological behaviour of a segment that reveals its element structure. In the case of *l* we have identified two types, a coronal *l* containing |A I| and a velarised *l* containing |A U|, which means that we can expect to see two patterns of behaviour among laterals: in some cases laterals should pattern with coronals and in other cases they should behave like velars. The first type has been more widely documented than the second. In Diola Fogny, for instance, laterals behave phonologically as coronals. In this language the consonants in a cluster must be homorganic, hence *famb* 'annoy', *bunt* 'lie', *kaŋg* 'be furthest away', *jensu* 'undershirt', *salte* 'be dirty'. And as the form *salte* shows, *l* must be phonologically coronal in order for it to cluster with *t*. Finnish is another example. In this system coronals are the only consonants to appear word-finally: *talot* 'house (nom.pl.)', *vieras* 'guest', *talon*

'house (gen.sg.)', *sammal* 'moss'. And as the noun *sammal* confirms, the class of coronals includes *l*.

In comparison, much less attention has been paid to the fact that laterals can also have a velar component. In feature theories, velars and laterals have little in common: velars are marked [−ant −cor] and laterals [+ant +cor]; velars are also [+high +back] whereas laterals are (redundantly) [−high −back]. However, there is now a growing awareness that laterals have two place specifications, coronal and velar. Some phonetic descriptions have noted that the tongue dorsum is always involved in the production of English *l*, while some phonological studies have argued that laterals are specified for multiple (coronal and dorsal) place. Moreover, some dialects of English provide evidence that laterals and velars are related. In Jamaican English, for example, dark *l* is preceded by velars rather than coronals in words such as *little* [lıkɫ], *handle* [hæŋgɫ]. And if [ɫ] is represented as |A U|, then this can be viewed as a straightforward place agreement in which the velar element |U| extends from [ɫ] to the preceding consonant to become a property of the whole cluster. In Pittsburgh English too we see evidence that velars and laterals form a class, with [ɫ] and [g] causing a preceding vowel to shorten, as in *meal* [mıɫ], *mail* [meɫ], *pool* [pʊɫ], *league* [lɪg], *frugal* [ˈfrʊgəɫ].

Another indication that laterals have |U| comes from their tendency to vocalise in weak positions, typically to [o u w]. This happened in the Belear dialect of Catalan, where *l* in the standard dialect was reinterpreted as *u*, hence [auba] 'sunrise' (cf. [alba] in Standard Catalan). In Mehri, on the other hand, *l* vocalisation is a synchronic process which is responsible for the alternation [l]~[w]: in forms constructed from the root *ɫlθ* 'third' we get [l] in the onset of a full CV syllable ([ɫoːləθ] 'third, masc.') and [w] elsewhere ([ɫəwθeːt] 'third, fem.'). In both these languages, weak positions are unable to support *l* because of its complex structure |A U|. The phonology responds to this by suppressing |A| to leave just |U|, which is interpreted as *u* or *w*. The process of *l* vocalisation takes place in many other languages besides Catalan and Mehri, including Slovenian, Serbo-Croatian and Brazilian Portuguese. It is also a well-known feature of some dialects of English. For example, in London English we get alternations such as *fee*[l]*ing~fee*[ʊ], and in Liberian English vocalisation produces forms such as [pipo] *people*, [lito] *little*, [kio] *kill*.

If laterals are represented as |A I| or |A U|, then we can include them in the set of glides. Strictly speaking, glides do not form a natural class since there is no common element that unites them.

But informally we can still treat them as a set because they stand apart from other consonants in having only resonance elements in their representation. As a member of this set, *l* ought to show certain glide-like properties; in particular, we expect it to function as a hiatus-breaker in glide formation processes, like the other glides *j w r* do. And indeed there are dialects of English with intrusive *l*, that is, a glide formation process involving complex |A I| or |A U|. The best known of these are the dialects of Pennsylvania in the USA and Bristol in the UK. Intrusive *l* is only found in systems that have undergone *l* vocalisation or *l* loss and then developed linking *l*; in this sense it parallels intrusive *r*, which is restricted to non-rhotic dialects where *r* suffered a similar fate. As (14) illustrates, some north-eastern dialects of the USA have developed linking *l* following the loss of *l* morpheme-finally.

(14) Context   Loss of *l*   Linking *l*
       ɔː   [drɔː] *drawl*   [drɔːlɪŋ] *drawling*
       ə   [kruːwə] *cruel*   [kruːwəl ækt] *cruel act*
       ɑː   [dɑː] *Dahl*   [dɑːl ɪz] *Dahl is*

And those same dialects now display intrusive *l* too, for example ['drɔːlɪŋ] *drawing*, [ðə 'lɔːl ɪz] *the law is*. Predictably, intrusive *l* only appears after [ɔː] |A U|, the vowel with the same structure as *l*. Thus the process of intrusive *l* can be expressed as in (15).

(15) *drawing* [drɔːlɪŋ] (Pennsylvania English)

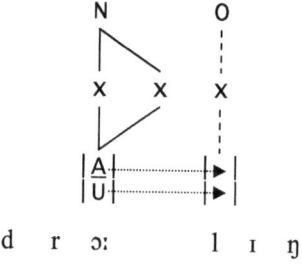

Note that glide formation ought to result in a dark *l* |A U| because it derives from [ɔː], which has the structure |A̲ U|. But the *l* in (15) may also be interpreted as a clear *l* |A I| because it precedes [ɪ] in the suffix and is therefore a target for the |I| spreading process described in (13).

The English 'nationality' suffix *-ese* ['iːz] provides further evidence that *l* has complex resonance. When *-ese* attaches to a proper noun ending in a consonant, no phonological adjustment is needed except for a shift in stress: *Taiwan-ese, Nepal-ese, Siam-ese*. But when *-ese* is added to a noun ending in a vowel, the result is a VV sequence – something that most languages like to avoid. In this case the strategy is to drop the first of the two vowels: *Malt(a)-ese, Burm(a)-ese, Chin(a)-ese*. Exceptionally, however, if the first of these vowels has the spelling <o>, then we get *l* insertion instead, as in *Congo-*[l]*ese, Togo-*[l]*ese*. In one respect, this appears to be just an alternative way of avoiding a vowel sequence, but significantly, it applies only after <o>, which is pronounced [əʊ] or [oː] in the basic noun. It appears, then, that [əʊ]/[oː] acts as the trigger for *l* insertion, which suggests a phonological relation between the two. Specifically, if [əʊ] and [oː] are compounds of |A| and |U|, then presumably *l* is too. (We can be fairly certain that *l* is not present historically in *-ese* because the suffix derives from French *-ais(e)* and ultimately from Latin *-ensis*, neither of which contains *l*.)

Earlier we said that laterals are overwhelmingly coronal. Yet this still allows for place distinctions among laterals because the term 'coronal' is broad enough to cover a range of place categories (§3.4.2). A good number of languages have two lateral consonants, and we can assume that in most cases they will have the structures we have already proposed, |A I| and |A U|. Phonetic descriptions suggest that this is the case in Albanian: compared with the alveolar *l* in *pala* [pala] 'pair', the dental *l* in *halla* [haḷa] 'aunt' requires an articulation in which 'the back of the tongue is retracted . . . so that a narrowed pharynx results' (Ladefoged and Maddieson 1996: 186). Without phonological evidence to indicate otherwise, we can take this as evidence that the retracted *l* has the structure |A U| and the non-retracted *l* has |A I|. A similar contrast between |A I| and |A U| may also operate in the Argol dialect of Breton where there is a contrast between post-alveolar *l* and alveolar *l*: the first appears only after *i* or historical *i*, suggesting the structure |A I|, whereas the second presumably has |A U| since it is not phonologically related to |I| segments. Palatal laterals are also possible in some languages, as are velar and retroflex laterals. Because they are members of the lateral class, we can assume that they have complex resonance consisting of |A| plus another resonance element. In the case of palatal [ʎ], |A| combines with headed |I̲| for palatal resonance, giving the structure |A I̲|. This expression is contrastive in the São Paulo dialect of Brazilian Portuguese, as demonstrated by the forms in (16a). Moreover, [ʎ] displays the predictable set of alternations shown in (16b), where [ʎ] → [j] involves the loss of |A| while [ʎ] → [l] involves the loss of headedness on |I|. These alternations are controlled by factors such as register and speech rate.

(16) a.   [maʎa]   *malha* 'sweater'   [ʎ] = |A I̲|
         [mala]   *mala* 'suitcase'   [l] = |A I|
   b.
         [muʎer] ⎫   [ʎ] = |A I̲|
         [mujer] ⎬ *mulher* 'woman'   [j] = |A̲ I̲|
         [muler] ⎭   [l] = |A I|

It is likely that the much rarer velar lateral [L] can be represented by the expression |A U|. Note that this is also the structure for velarised [ɫ], so we predict that no language has a lexical contrast between [L] and [ɫ]. The retroflex lateral [ɭ] is common among Australian languages. Since retroflex resonance is represented by headed |A| (§3.6.3), we can assign it the structure |A̲ I|.

In phonetic terms most laterals are approximants because they contain only resonance elements. And as we have seen, this gives them a vowel-like quality that allows us to classify them as glides. But because laterals appear in consonant positions, it should be possible to add consonant elements to their structure too. In fact any of the consonant elements |ʔ H L| can be added to a basic *l* expression, producing a range of effects. Adding |ʔ| makes no difference to the phonetic shape of laterals, because laterals are already characterised by low acoustic energy when compared to surrounding vowels. It does make a difference phonologically, however, as it links *l* to the class of stops.

Adding the |L| element to a lateral changes it into a nasal – recall from §4.4.1 that nasals consist of resonance plus the nasal element, non-headed |L|. This makes nasals and laterals fairly close in representational terms, which helps to explain why the two sometimes interact or pattern together in phonological processes. Adding |H| to a lateral also brings about a change of category: |H| introduces voicelessness (§4.3.3), creating voiceless laterals that can be contrastive in some languages. For example, Burmese distinguishes between a plain lateral [l] and a voiceless lateral [l̥].

(17)   plain *l*:   [l] |A I| [la] 'moon'
      voiceless *l*:   [l̥] |A I H| [l̥a] 'beautiful'

But |H| can also be interpreted as frication (§4.3.1), which means that it should be possible to pronounce the structure |A I H| in (17) as a fricative. Voiceless lateral fricatives do exist, and they are transcribed using the symbol [ɬ]. But interestingly, the terms 'voiceless lateral' and 'lateral fricative' tend to be used interchangeably, since 'it is difficult to decide whether a voiceless lateral should be described as an approximant or a fricative' (Ladefoged and Maddieson 1996: 199). Certainly there are no languages with a contrast between [l̥] and [ɬ], which supports the idea that both are represented by the same expression |A I H|. In Chapter 4 we noted that |H| is informally equivalent to the feature [–son] because it identifies the class of obstruents by bringing together stops and fricatives. On this basis, [l̥]/[ɬ] should be counted as an obstruent too, since it contains |H|. And indeed there is general agreement on this point; for example, Walsh Dickey (1997) proposes a class of liquids comprising rhotics and sonorant laterals but excluding obstruent laterals. And if [l̥]/[ɬ] is an obstruent, then we can expect it to participate in voicing contrasts in the same way that other obstruents do. This happens in languages such as Zulu, which distinguishes between voiceless [ɬ] and voiced [ɮ]. Recall from §4.4.2 that obstruent voicing is represented by headed |L̲|.

(18) sonorant *l*:   [l] |A I| [lálà]   'lie down'
      voiceless fricative *l*: [ɬ] |A I H| [ɬàɫá]   'cut off'
      voiced fricative *l*:   [ɮ] |A I H L̲| [ɮálà]   'play'

5.1.5 Summary

In this section we have described a natural class of liquids represented by |A|. This class includes rhotics with the simplex structure |A| and laterals with the complex structure |A I| or |A U|. Liquids are classified as glides because they are consonants with only vowel elements in their representation.

Many languages have very simple liquid systems with just a single liquid or with just one rhotic and one lateral. But there are also languages with two or more contrastive rhotics. How these contrasts are represented will partly depend on the liquid system of the language concerned. In general, [ɹ ɽ r] will have |A| whereas the coronal tap [ɾ] will be represented as coronal |I| (§4.3.2). Strictly speaking, this places the coronal tap outside the class of liquids. We also find languages with contrasts among laterals. Again, the representations are to some extent language-specific, but laterals displaying coronal behaviour will generally have the structure |A I| whereas back or velar(ised) laterals are likely to be |A U|. Further variations in place

Table 5.1 Representations for glides

	|I|	|U|	|A|	|A I|	|A U|	|I U|
headed	j	w	r,ɾ	ʎ,l̨		
non-headed	ɻ	ɰ	ɹ	l	ɫ,L	ɥ

and laryngeal setting are also possible: for example, |A I̲| denotes palatal [ʎ] and |A I H| represents fricative [ɬ]. Glide representations can now be summarised as in Table 5.1.

5.2 ELEMENTS AND PROSODIC STRUCTURE

5.2.1 Introduction

One of the goals of phonology is to describe the internal structure of segments, and clearly that is the focus of ET. But phonology must also account for the way segments are organised within prosodic domains such as syllables, feet and words. And as we are about to see, the two are connected. In this section we look at the relationship between elements and the units of prosodic structure.

Sometimes, individual elements are subject to distributional restrictions. For example, in §3.5.2 we saw that labials and velars in Lardil cannot appear in word-final position. This is effectively a restriction on |U|, since |U| is the element common to labials and velars. Other elements can be banned from particular contexts too, usually weak contexts such as word-final, intervocalic or coda position. But to make generalisations about the link between segments and positional strength, we sometimes have to look beyond individual elements and focus instead on other aspects of element structure such as complexity and headedness. Both of these things are tied to the notion of segmental strength: complex expressions are generally stronger than simplex ones, and headed expressions are generally stronger than non-headed ones. And in turn, segmental strength relates to prosodic strength: strong segments are attracted to strong positions while weak segments are preferred in weak positions. A segment's distribution can therefore be affected by any of the following factors: (1) which elements it contains, (2) the number of elements it contains, or (3) the presence or absence of a headed element.

We have already seen examples of the link between segmental structure and prosodic strength. For instance, in the previous section we noted that complex *l* in Florentine Italian reduces to simplex *r* in codas, and in Chapter 2 we saw that full vowels in English usually occupy strong nuclei whereas the reduced vowels [ɪ ʊ ə] belong in weak nuclei. The fact that [ɪ ʊ ə] are represented by simplex non-headed |I|, |U| and |A| is not an accident – their minimal structure reflects the weakness of the positions where they occur. Overall, then, we find an asymmetry in the way segmental information is distributed: strong positions are rich in segmental information, as confirmed by their ability to support a broader range of contrasts than is possible in weak positions. But what is it that determines whether a position is strong or weak in the first place? In this section we will see that one factor concerns the ability of a position to act as a marker for prosodic domains.

Strong positions provide listeners with information about prosodic structure. They do this by marking the edge, invariably the left edge, of prosodic domains like the syllable and the word. For example, onsets are stronger than codas as a result of being located at the left edge of a syllable. Similarly, word-initial position is stronger than word-final position because it serves as a marker for the beginning of a new prosodic word. Psycholinguistic studies have shown that knowing the location of prosodic domains, and in particular the left edge of domains, helps listeners to break up the speech stream into words and, more generally, to process incoming speech more efficiently. It may also be an advantage during the early stages of acquisition. It is for these reasons that listeners instinctively focus on strong positions during communication. But to gain access to this information about prosodic domains, listeners must first be able to identify where the strong positions are, and this is where segmental phonology comes in: certain elements or element combinations – and therefore, certain acoustic cues – are favoured in strong positions but are noticeably absent from weak positions. In this sense, segmental weakening processes act as a mechanism to ensure that the cues associated with strong positions are suppressed in positions that are considered to be weak because they have no prosodic marking function to perform.

5.2.2 The Syllable Domain

Examples of segmental weakening were described in §4.3.2, so let us focus here on the contexts where these processes occur. Weakening processes usually operate within one of three prosodic domains, namely, the syllable, the foot or the word; and in each case the beginning of the domain is marked by a strong position. By contrast, other positions in the domain are relatively weak, and as a result, are susceptible to weakening. We begin at the syllable level, where there is an asymmetry between a strong onset and a weak coda. The clearest indication of this comes from the fact that some languages such as Hawaiian lack codas altogether, whereas there are no languages which lack onsets. In some cases onsets are even obligatory. In Tamil, for example, the phonology includes a process of glide formation which creates an onset consonant in syllables that begin lexically with a vowel: *ellaam* [yɛllãã] 'all', *uusii* [wuusii] 'needle', *aasay* [ʔaasɛ] 'desire'. Onsets are important because they mark the left edge of the syllable domain; and to draw attention to their special status the grammar favours perceptually prominent segments in onset position. In Guayabero, for example, *p t k* are aspirated syllable-initially but unaspirated elsewhere: *pá-mal* ['pʰamʌl] 'her husband', *táka* ['tʰakʰʌ] 'a shoulder', *sát* ['sat] 'earth'.

Aspiration is one way of enhancing a consonant's perceptibility, but perceptual prominence can also come from other consonantal properties too, such as those which refer to manner or laryngeal setting. So in many languages, |ʔ| and |H| are present in onsets but absent from codas. The absence of |H| rules out obstruents as coda consonants – recall that |H| provides frication in fricatives and audible release in stops. And a ban on obstruents also means a ban on active voicing or voicelessness, because laryngeal contrasts such as these are only found in obstruents. In addition, codas are usually unspecified for place – that is, they do not have any resonance elements of their own; this explains why they often assimilate in place to a following onset. So for a sizeable number of languages, nasals and glides (including laterals and rhotics) are the only consonants permitted in the coda. By banning certain consonant properties from the syllable coda, the grammar makes it easy for listeners to distinguish between coda and onset consonants. Importantly, this helps them to locate syllable boundaries, which in turn allows them to exploit information about syllable structure during language processing.

5.2.3 The Foot Domain

Strength differences found at the syllable level are replicated at the foot level. In a metrical foot with the shape $C_1V_1.C_2V_2$, for example, the onsets containing C_1 and C_2 are not equal in strength: in general, strong syllables have strong onsets while weak syllables have weaker onsets. In English we rely on stress for locating strong syllables, so in the word *pétty* the first syllable, including its onset, is prosodically strong while the second syllable is weak. Now, in Chapter 4 we saw how segments in weak positions are targeted by various weakening processes whereas strong positions resist weakening. This correctly predicts that *pétty* ['pʰeti] may also be pronounced ['pʰeʔi] (London English) or ['pʰeɾi] (Australian English), where *t* in the weak syllable weakens to [ʔ] or [ɾ] by losing some of its element structure (§4.3.2). By contrast, *p* in the strong syllable never weakens; it always remains a stop. The reason for this asymmetry between *p* and *t* again comes down to prosodic domains. As (19) shows, both consonants mark the left edge of a syllable (N") domain, but only *p* has the additional function of marking the left edge of a foot (Ft) domain. The two syllables in *pétty* form a left-headed foot with *p* at its left boundary.

(19)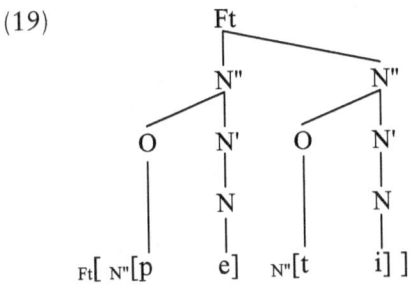

There is evidence that the foot domain plays an important role in speech perception and language processing. And certainly, the foot appears to be an important unit in the phonology of English. This is clear from the fact that in English there are multiple acoustic cues to help listeners locate foot domain boundaries. Not only is there a stressed syllable at the beginning of a foot, but the onset of this syllable always contains a full (unreduced) consonant. Furthermore, if this consonant is from the *p t k* series then it is aspirated, which is also a reliable boundary marker. Importantly, none of these properties is found elsewhere in the foot. For example, the *t* in *pétty* is unaspirated and susceptible to weakening since it occupies an intervocalic position, which is widely regarded as being weak. Harris (1997) accounts for the inherent weakness of intervocalic position by recasting it as a foot-internal position: foot-internal onsets are weak because they are not located at the left edge of the foot domain. Because it does not act as a boundary marker at the foot level, foot-internal position is a relatively low-information context; and the grammar expresses this by limiting the amount of segmental structure it can support, just as it does in the case of codas. For example, in the *t* of *pétty* headed |H| reduces to non-headed |H| to produce an unaspirated stop and, as we have already mentioned, individual elements may be suppressed to produce tapping or glottalisation. We may note here that, just as aspiration is tied to foot-initial position in English, so too is [h] (*vé(h)icle*, *ve*[h]*ícular*). They have the same distribution because they share the same headed |H| element: the *p t k* class is captured by |ʔ H| while [h] has single |H|. Evidently, headed |H| operates as a foot-level property in English.

The asymmetry between foot-initial and foot-internal onsets also shows up in other languages besides English. Predictably, foot-initial onsets retain their segmental properties because they mark the left edge of the foot domain, whereas foot-internal onsets are targeted by weakening processes, resulting in a loss of element structure. Spirantisation involving the suppression of |ʔ| is very common (§4.3.2): foot-internal [p] reduces to [f] in Amele, for instance, while in Panamint the entire [p t k kʷ] series spirantises to [β ð ɣ ɣʷ] respectively. Vocalisation processes are also widespread, in which consonant expressions are reduced to bare resonance: in West Tarangan [g dʒ] are realised foot-internally as [w j], while in Somali [b d ḍ g] are reinterpreted as [β ð ɾ ɣ] in the same context. As the [ḍ] → [ɾ] effect in Somali shows, tapping may be viewed as a form of vocalisation since the outcome is a bare resonance element, in this case |I|. Other forms of foot-internal weakening include debuccalisation to [h] (Tubatulabal) and to [ʔ] (London English). Finally, when a weakening process targets a consonant with just one element in its structure, the expected outcome is deletion; this is illustrated by Hawaiian ([h] → Ø), Navajo ([ɣ] → Ø) and Gbeya ([ʔ] → Ø). The examples given here are all taken from a survey of strength-related processes described in Lavoie (2001). Further references are given at the end of this chapter.

5.2.4 The Word Domain

Like syllable and foot domains, word domains have their left boundary marked by a strong position. And again the result is an asymmetry between the left edge of the domain, where consonants contrast freely, and other positions, where weakening and neutralisation are the norm. Languages usually display a complete set of contrasts in word-initial position; indeed, this is sometimes the only position where all contrasts are realised. For example, Doyayo has a contrast between implosives and plain stops, but only in root-initial position; elsewhere implosives cannot appear. Meanwhile, Shilluk allows consonants to be palatalised or labialised, and this is also restricted to the initial onset. With many other examples besides, it is clear that domain-initial onsets have a privileged status in terms of their contrastive ability.

But word-initial onsets are also unique in being able to acquire additional properties, often non-contrastive properties such as aspiration, which are associated with perceptual prominence. English is a good example of this. Earlier we said that aspiration in English marks the beginning of a foot; but optionally it can also mark the start of a word domain. Many speakers therefore aspirate the first consonant of a word even if it is not foot-initial, as in [pʰ]o*étic*, [tʰ]*errífic*, [kʰ]*orréct*. Of course, listeners cannot entirely rely on aspiration as a way of identifying a word boundary. For one thing, there is the possibility of confusing word-level aspiration with foot-level aspiration; and there is also the fact that aspiration is only possible when the initial consonant happens to be a stop from the *p t k* series. Nevertheless, when aspiration does occur it can provide listeners with useful information about prosodic structure. Interestingly, the properties we have associated with word-initial position are all represented by headed elements: implosives (Doyayo) have headed |ʔ|, palatalised consonants (Shilluk) have headed |I|, labialised consonants (Shilluk) have headed |U| and aspirated stops (English) have headed |H|. This is consistent with the point made in §5.2.1 that there is an inherent link between the strength of domain-initial positions and the strength of certain segmental expressions.

Further evidence for a link between headed expressions and prosodic structure comes from the distributional restrictions that are sometimes imposed on aspirates (|H|), ejectives (|ʔ| with |H|) and implosives (|ʔ| with |L|). These restrictions typically operate within the foot or word domain, and control the co-occurrence of strong segments. One such pattern disallows two stops in the same root from having an identical head; so for example, a root cannot contain two ejectives (20a) or two aspirates (20b).

(20) a. *Shuswap*   [s-kʼlep]   'coyote'   *[s-kʼlepʼ]
     b. *Souletin Basque* [tʰipil]   'nude'   *[tʰipʰil]

In another pattern, two stops must have the same headed element. As a result, we find roots with two ejectives (21a), two aspirates (21b) or two implosives (21c).

(21) a. Chaha   [ji-t'ək'ir]   'he hides'   *[ji-t'əkir]
     b. Zulu   [ukú-kʰetʰa]   'to choose'   *[ukú-kʰeta]
     c. Kalabari Ijo [ɗábá]   'lake'   *[ɗábá]

And in a third pattern, stops with the same resonance property must have the same head, whereas stops that differ in resonance cannot have the same head. So for instance, two labial stops may both be aspirates (22a) and two velars may both be ejectives (22b), but a velar and a labial (or, say, a palatal and a labial) must have non-identical laryngeal settings (22c).

(22) a. Peruvian Aymara [pʰuspʰu]   'boiled beans' *[pʰuspu]
     b. Chol   [k'ok']   'health'   *[k'ok]
     c. Peruvian Aymara [kʰapi]   'strong'   *[kʰapʰi]
        Chol   [tʃ'ip]   'to open'   *[tʃ'ip']

The generalisation that emerges here is that a headed |H| or headed |ʔ| can only be specified once in a root domain; in other words, these headed elements function as root-level properties in the languages concerned. In (20) they are interpreted in only one segment in the domain, while in (21) they are specified in one segment but shared with other stops within the domain. (22) is similar except for the fact that the shared |H| or |ʔ| is accompanied by shared resonance. To complete the picture we will include headed |L| in this generalisation too, because its distribution can also be controlled by higher prosodic domains. For example, a condition in Japanese known as Lyman's Law prevents native words from containing more than one voiced obstruent, hence *geta* 'clogs' but **geda*. And because Japanese is a voicing language, obstruent voicing must be represented by headed |L|.

We said earlier that word-initial onsets may take on additional properties in order to give them greater prominence. And we noted how this happens in English, where word-initial *p t k* can be aspirated as a way of drawing listeners' attention to the word-initial position itself. But other languages also have their own strategies for giving prominence to word-initial consonants. These strategies are sometimes described as strengthening (fortition) processes because they produce a stronger, more consonant-like segment than there would otherwise have been. In the most common form of strengthening, a fricative or glide becomes a stop by acquiring an additional |ʔ|; this happens in Creole French ([v] → [b]) and Pawnee ([w] → [p]), for example. Notice, however, that this process actually has two effects.

It achieves the intended effect of producing a strong consonant in a strong position, but in doing so it also causes the contrast between stops and fricatives/glides to neutralise, since stops can no longer contrast with continuants word-initially. This goes against what we have been stressing throughout this section, which is that contrasts should be maximised in domain-initial positions, not neutralised. Evidently, grammars like Creole French and Pawnee, which sacrifice contrastive ability for the sake of perceptual prominence, are motivated by some overall gain in terms of language processing. On the one hand, the loss of certain contrasts in word-initial position is detrimental to a language's expressive power; but on the other hand, having low-sonority stops to mark important domain boundaries must be a significant advantage to listeners whose task it is to break up continuous speech into separate words. So whether a language gives priority to segmental (contrastive) information or prosodic (domain boundary) information, the end result is always a compromise.

Having focused on word-initial position, which is prosodically strong, we now turn to word-final position, which is widely recognised as a weak context. This is confirmed by the many cases of weakening and neutralisation that affect word-final consonants. In Chapter 3 we saw several examples of this. In Skikun (§3.5.2) labials with headed |U| are in the process of merging with non-headed velars word-finally, while in Guugu Yimidhirr (§3.4.2) and other Australian languages the contrast between palatal [ɲ] with headed |I| and coronal [n] with non-headed |I| has neutralised to coronal. Notice how once again it is the weaker non-headed member of the original contrast that is favoured in the weak position. A more widespread form of final neutralisation is one which affects laryngeal properties such as voicing, aspiration and glottalisation. In some languages these properties are contrastive except in domain-final position, where they are suppressed altogether. For example, Thai has a three-way laryngeal distinction in initial stops (§4.5) which neutralises to a plain unreleased stop word-finally. This applies to the entire stop series, and is illustrated in (23) by labials.

(23) domain-initial: voiceless |H| [p]aa 'forest'
 voiced |L| [b]aa 'shoulder'
 aspirated |H| [pʰ]aa 'cut, slit'
 domain-final: neutral – si[p̚] 'ten' (*si[p], *si[b], *si[pʰ])

Not only are voicing (headed |L|) and aspiration (headed |H|) suppressed word-finally, but so is voicelessness (non-headed |H|). The outcome is a bare stop with no marked laryngeal properties. The *p* in [sip̚] 'ten' is therefore represented as |U ʔ|; and because |H| is suppressed, the stop has no audible release. Laryngeal neutralisation also takes place in Sanskrit and Bengali. Like the Nepali system described in §4.5, Bengali has a four-way laryngeal distinction in strong positions. The Bengali facts are illustrated in (24) using the labial series.

(24) voiceless |H| [p]*andita*   'wise'
      voiced |L| [b]*arga*   'tribe, species'
      aspirated |H| [pʰ]*arasā*   'fair, clear'
      breathy |H L| [bʱ]*asma*   'ashes'

Again these contrasts are neutralised to a plain stop in domain-final position, as shown by the compounds in (25). Notice how the right member of each compound begins with a strong domain-initial consonant [k tʰ d dʱ. . .] which may bear any laryngeal property, while the left member ends in a weakened stop which is either neutral ([lap-kɔra] 'profit making') or voiced as a result of regressive voicing assimilation ([šad-bʱali] 'seven brothers').

(25)   [lap-kɔra]   [labʱ] 'profit' + [kɔra] 'making'
      [lop-tʰaka]   [lobʱ] 'greed' + [tʰaka] 'remaining'
      [mɔt-kʰaoa]   [mɔd] 'alcohol' + [kʰaoa] 'drinking'
      [pɔd-dækʰa]   [pɔtʰ] 'road' + [dækʰa] 'seeing'
      [maǰ-dʱɔra]   [mač] 'fish' + [dʱɔra] 'catching'
      [pãǰ-gun]   [pãč] 'five' + [gun] 'times'
      [šad-bʱali]   [šat] 'seven' + [bʱali] 'brothers'

As in Thai, neutralisation in Bengali involves the suppression of all laryngeal properties from the weak domain-final position to leave just a bare oral stop such as [p] (= |U ʔ|).

Domain-final neutralisation is also a feature in languages with a two-way laryngeal distinction, where the process is often described as 'final devoicing'. In Chapter 4 we said that languages are divided into two types, H languages and L languages, according to how they represent their laryngeal contrast. But when it comes to neutralisation they can be analysed in parallel because in all cases laryngeal neutralisation involves a segmental change in the direction of the unmarked setting. So in H languages it is voicelessness that is suppressed in weak positions, whereas in L languages it is active voicing that is lost. In both types the outcome is a neutral segment, as we saw in Thai and Bengali. Let us illustrate this with an example of each type. In Russian, final neutralisation produces the alternations in (26).

(26) gro[b]u   'coffin (dat.)' |U L H ʔ| (voiced)
    gro[p] (*gro[b]) 'coffin (nom.)' |U L H ʔ| (neutral)

Because Russian is an L language, [b] is fully voiced and contains headed |L|. But in word-final position headed |L| is lost and the remaining structure is interpreted as a neutral obstruent; for example, [p] has the structure |U ʔ|. In Russian, then, final devoicing is an accurate description of the process since active voicing is lost in the weak context.

But in the case of H languages, final devoicing is not so easily accounted for. In German, devoicing is phonetically similar to devoicing in Russian; but phonologically it turns out to be quite different.

(27) gel[b]e   'yellow (attrib.)' |U ʔ| (neutral with passive
                                                  voicing)
    gel[p] (*gel[b]) 'yellow (predict.)' |U ʔ| (neutral, no passive
                                                  voicing)

Lexically, the *b* in *gel[b]e* is a neutral stop containing neither |H| nor |L| – recall that in H languages the contrast is between voiceless/aspirated and neutral. But because of its intervocalic position neutral *b* has passive voicing, making it phonetically similar to the [b] in the Russian form *gro[b]u*. However, passive voicing is not a phonological property since it carries no linguistic information, and is therefore not represented in a segment's structure (§4.3.3). Rather, it is a phonetic effect that comes as a result of being in a resonant environment. Neutral *b* therefore has the structure |U ʔ|. With no laryngeal elements to lose, it cannot be a target for neutralisation; and as a result, it has the same representation in *gel[b]e* and *gel[p]*. The only difference between these two forms is the context where *b* appears. In *gel[b]e* it is intervocalic and therefore passively voiced, whereas in *gel[p]* it is domain-final and has no passive voicing. In *gel[p]*, then, *b* is phonologically neutral and phonetically voiceless. This is exactly as we would expect in an H language such as German. So in H languages the term 'final devoicing' refers to the loss of passive voicing, not phonological voicing.

5.2.5 Summary

In this section we have seen evidence of a link between strength at the prosodic level and strength at the segmental level. A position is prosodically strong if it conveys information about prosodic structure by marking the beginning of a prosodic domain. But in order to be an effective marker it must contain a strong, perceptually prominent segment such as a stop. Listeners therefore associate strong consonants with strong positions, and conversely, weak consonants with weak positions. The classic weakening contexts of word-final, intervocalic (foot-internal) and pre-consonantal position are weak because they do not act as markers for important domains. And to reflect this, segments weaken in these contexts by losing parts of their structure – individual elements, or headedness, or both.

5.3 Relations between Elements

5.3.1 Antagonistic Pairs

Several times we have noted that certain combinations of elements are more marked than others. Specifically, we described the element pairs |A|–|ʔ|, |L|–|H| and |U|–|I| as antagonistic because the members of each pair are reluctant to combine; generally speaking, one member of the pair tends to repel the other. The phonetic explanation for this is that the elements in each pair have conflicting acoustic properties, making it difficult for speakers to produce, and for listeners to perceive, their acoustic cues simultaneously. In the case of |L|–|H|, for example, |L| lowers fundamental frequency whereas |H| raises it; and murmur, the principal cue for |L|, corresponds to low-frequency energy whereas noise, the principal cue for |H|, corresponds to high-frequency energy. These phonetic conflicts have an impact on phonology because in some languages they prevent certain element combinations – and therefore, certain classes of segments – from appearing. For instance, breathy-voiced stops (with |L̲ H|), front rounded vowels (with |I̲ U|) and pharyngeal stops (with |A̲ ʔ|) are cross-linguistically quite rare.

Notice, however, that antagonistic pairs in ET work differently from 'illogical' feature combinations such as *[+high +low]. Feature theories assume that pairs such as *[+high +low] are universally ungrammatical because they contain a phonetic contradiction – a vowel cannot be both high and low at the same time. Yet if [+high] and [+low] really are abstract grammatical categories in the way that some feature theorists tell us, and not just phonetic labels, then in principle they should not be prevented from combining – being phonetically incompatible should not necessarily result in being ungrammatical. By contrast, antagonistic element pairs such as |L|–|H| also involve a phonetic contradiction, but this does not make them ill-formed – there are languages in which the combinations |A|–|ʔ|, |L|–|H| and |U|–|I| do appear. These are possible because elements function as linguistic units rather than as phonetic descriptions; so when a phonetic conflict arises, it is an issue for communication rather than for the grammar. For the sake of efficiency in communication, some languages may prefer to avoid antagonistic pairs because the linguistic information they contain is difficult to perceive; but this does not mean that it is impossible for the grammar to generate such expressions.

Let us think of the element set as comprising three antagonistic element pairs, rather than six autonomous elements. In doing so, we reveal three variables that are even more basic than the acoustic patterns associated with the elements themselves. These are described in (28).

(28)

Variable	Relevant values	Elements Dark	Light
resonance	resonant vs. non-resonant	|A|	|ʔ|
frequency	low frequency vs. high frequency	|L|	|H|
colour	dark vs. bright	|U|	|I|

Each antagonistic pair refers to a basic sound variable, and the two elements in each pair mark the opposing values of that variable. For example, the |A|–|ʔ| pair refers to resonance, and the elements |A| and |ʔ| each have cues which represent one of the significant values for resonance: |A| marks high resonance while |ʔ| marks very low resonance. We can think of the perceptual variables in (28) as the fundamental properties of spoken language – properties which humans instinctively pay attention to during communication. That is, language users pick out linguistic information by focusing on cues that relate specifically to resonance, frequency and colour. Now, because contrast is based on acoustic differences, it makes sense for languages to exploit cues that are maximally different, since these are the easiest to distinguish. The cues that are relevant to phonology are therefore the cues that identify the most extreme values of the three variables. In other words, the elements in each pair are opposites. Later we will discuss what is meant in (28) by dark and light elements, but first let us look at each of the three variables in turn.

5.3.2 Resonance: |A| versus |ʔ|

As (28) shows, |A| and |ʔ| have cues that refer to (opposing values for) resonance. But what exactly is resonance? Speakers create resonance by allowing air in the vocal tract to resonate, or vibrate naturally, at certain frequencies. All sonorant sounds can produce resonance, but vowels containing |A| (the mid and low vowels) have a particularly high resonant frequency. This comes as a result of allowing the air behind the tongue to resonate freely in these sounds. This resonance is associated with a high F1, which signals the presence of |A| (§2.3). Listeners perceive |A| vowels as having a deep, warm, sonorous quality. By contrast, oral stops have very low resonance, which renders them maximally distant from |A| vowels in acoustic terms. The hold phase of stops is characterised by a sharp reduction in acoustic energy as airflow is interrupted. If no air passes through the glottis, the vocal folds naturally stop vibrating; and by eliminating vocal fold vibration, the sound source itself is eliminated and the possibility of producing resonance is greatly reduced. Stops are therefore marked by a period of low resonance. In language, this drop in resonance functions as a positive acoustic cue because it carries linguistic information to distinguish stops from other segments; and as such, it is represented by an element in the grammar, namely |ʔ|. So, |A| and |ʔ| represent opposing values for resonance, in that vowels with |A| allow air to resonate freely in the vocal tract whereas stops with |ʔ| mostly lack resonance. Furthermore, the polarity of |A| and |ʔ| is reflected in the way these elements are syllabified. The |A| element is typically a vowel property and belongs in the syllable nucleus, the most resonant part of the syllable. By contrast, the |ʔ| element is overwhelmingly a consonantal property and for this reason belongs in a less resonant onset or coda.

Although |A| and |ʔ| have conflicting acoustic properties, they are still able to combine. In languages with |A| coronals, for example, both elements are present in coronal stops such as [t], represented as |A ʔ H|. Interestingly, however, headedness has an effect on their ability to combine. If either |A| or |ʔ| is headed, then they can still combine in some languages but the resulting expression is relatively marked; for instance, retroflex [ṭ] and ejective [t'] in (29b) are both marked when compared to the plain dental or alveolar [t].

(29)   a. non-headed   b. single-headed   c. double-headed
      [t] |A ʔ H| [ṭ] |A̲ ʔ H| [t'] |A̲ ʔ̲ H|
                   [t'] |A ʔ̲ H| [ɗ] |A̲ ʔ̲ L|

And if |A| and |ʔ| are both headed, the outcome is one of the very rare segments shown in (29c): Yawelmani is reported to have a retroflex ejective stop [ṭ'] while, according to some sources, Sindhi employs a retroflex implosive [ɖ]. These are isolated cases, however, and we can say that in general headed |A̲| and headed |ʔ̲| do not combine, hence *|A̲ ʔ̲|. This seems reasonable, given that |A| and |ʔ| both relate to the same perceptual variable, resonance. After all, we can make the resonance variable more prominent by making one of its values headed, producing a segment with exaggerated high resonance (headed |A̲|) or exaggerated low resonance (headed |ʔ̲|). But there is nothing to be gained from making both elements prominent because their acoustic cues are in conflict – a strong cue for high resonance (headed |A̲|) will be masked by an equally strong cue for low resonance (headed |ʔ̲|), and vice versa. As a result, the resonance variable will not display the intended level of prominence.

5.3.3 Frequency: |L| versus |H|

Besides paying attention to resonance, listeners also focus on the way acoustic energy is distributed across the spectrum; in particular, they distinguish between low-frequency and high-frequency energy. Some segments, such as nasals and voiced stops, display a murmur pattern represented by |L|; in these sounds, energy is concentrated at the lower end of the spectrum. Other segments, such as fricatives and voiceless stops, are characterised by a noise pattern represented by |H|; and in these sounds, energy is mostly concentrated in the upper frequencies. So clearly, the frequency variable in (28) is linguistically significant, as it refers to cues that help listeners identify broad categories such as obstruents and nasals.

The low frequency of |L| and the high frequency of |H| are in conflict: in fact they are maximally distant in terms of frequency, just as |A| and |ʔ| are maximally distant in terms of resonance. In other words, |L| and |H| form another antagonistic pair. And as with |A|–|ʔ|, the acoustic difference between |L| and |H| prevents these elements from combining freely. Furthermore, in those languages where they are allowed to combine, the result is always a relatively marked expression. Some examples are given in (30). Unlike |A|–|ʔ| combinations, |L|–|H| combinations do not appear to show a strong link between headedness and markedness.

(30) fully voiced fricatives [z] |A H L̲| voicing languages
 breathy-voiced stops [dʱ] |A H L̲ ʔ| Nepali, Marathi
 voiceless nasals [n̥] |A H̲ L (ʔ)| Burmese, Jalapa Mazatec
 aspirated nasals [nʰ] |A H̲ L (ʔ)| Hindi, Tsonga

Although fully voiced fricatives such as [z ð ʒ] are widespread among L languages, they are still relatively marked compared with neutral fricatives. Meanwhile the other categories in (30) are intrinsically marked, and for this reason are restricted to a small number of languages with multiple nasal or laryngeal contrasts; for example, Nepali has a four-way stop system including breathy-voiced stops (§4.5) while Jalapa Mazatec has a three-way nasal system including voiceless nasals (§4.4.1). Finally, it should be noted that the representations given in (30) for voiceless and aspirated nasals are tentative, being based only on phonetic descriptions of how these sounds are pronounced: voiceless nasals in Burmese are produced almost entirely with an open glottis (hence, headed |H̲|) whereas aspirated nasals in Hindi begin with modal voicing followed by a period of glottal opening towards the end of the closure (hence, the weaker non-headed |H|). Clearly, phonological evidence would be needed in order to confirm these representations. However, we can be fairly certain that |L| and |H| never appear together when they are both headed; indeed, it is not obvious what kind of category this would create. In other words, the frequency variable, like the resonance variable, can be headed by one of its values but not by both.

5.3.4 Colour: |U| versus |I|

The final variable in (28) is not easy to describe. Here we will use the term colour, but labels such as tonality and timbre may also be appropriate. To understand what colour refers to in this context, it is helpful to bear in mind that its two values are |I| and |U|. On one level, |I| and |U| function simply as units of lexical contrast in the same way that other elements do. But in a broader sense they also create quite distinct sound qualities, giving |I| segments and |U| segments their individual character. For example, the quality of the front |I| vowels [i e æ] is altogether different from the quality of the round |U| vowels [u ɔ ɒ]; likewise, clear *l* |A I| differs notably in character from dark *l* |A U|. More generally, the |I| consonants (palatals, coronals) are thin, bright sounds, which is consistent with their tendency to be produced as sibilants. By contrast, the |U| consonants (labials, velars) are generally produced as non-sibilants, and this matches their fuller, richer sound quality – compare the strident |I| sounds [s ts ʃ] with the more mellow |U| sounds [ɸ kχ x], for example. Like resonance and frequency, colour is a variable property that helps language users to differentiate between speech sounds. Segments that are similar in resonance and frequency can still be distinguished by their colour if they differ in terms of |I| or |U| sound quality.

Some languages use colour to organise segments into broad classes that cut across the usual segment categories. In Russian, for example, consonants have two distinct phonetic forms, hard [p m z. . .] and soft [pʲ mʲ zʲ. . .]. We can describe the difference between them in terms of colour, since the soft (palatalised) consonants have |I| colouring whereas the hard consonants are plain. A similar situation holds in Irish (§3.6.2), where slender (palatalised) consonants have a secondary |I| element and contrast with their broad (velarised, or sometimes labialised) equivalents, which have secondary |U|; for example, compare slender [kʲuːʃ] *ciumhais* 'edge' with broad [kuːʃ] *cúis* 'reason'. This way of splitting the consonant system into a set of |I| segments and a set of |U| segments highlights the polarity between |I| and |U|. Like other antagonistic elements they represent opposite values of the same variable, and we expect them to show complementary behaviour – the presence of one usually excludes the presence of the other, as we have noted several times already. For example, when palatalisation targets velars in Italian (§3.7.4), velar |U| is lost in order to avoid combining with the active |I| element, hence *medici* [meditʃi] (*[medici]) 'doctors' (cf. *medico* [mediko] 'doctor'). And in §2.6 we noted that front rounded vowels such as [y ø œ] are also universally marked because they contain |I| and |U|. The reason why languages avoid combinations of |I| and |U| is that, once again, these elements have conflicting acoustic cues: |I| causes F2 to rise whereas |U| causes F2 (and other formants) to lower.

Of course, |I| and |U| do combine in a minority of languages; and as we have already seen, this produces marked categories such as front rounded vowels [y ø œ] and palatovelar consonants [c ɟ ç ʝ]. However, like the other antagonistic pairs, |I| and |U| do not combine if both elements are headed; language users give prominence to the colour variable either by making |I| headed or by making |U| headed, but not both. Hence, *|U̲ I̲| is ill-formed. This leaves |U̲ I| and |U I̲| as possible combinations, both of which are contrastive in Norwegian.

(31) do [du] 'outhouse' |U|
 dy [dy] 'forbear!' |U I̲|
 du [dʉ] 'you (sing.)' |U̲ I|

The Norwegian vowel system is very unusual in having a contrast between the three high rounded vowels shown in (31). [y] and [ʉ] are both non-back, so we can assume that they have |I| in addition to |U|.

But importantly, they differ in their degree of rounding: [ʉ] is produced with an inward rounding of the lips and [y] with an outward protrusion of the lips. On this basis, [y] appears to be similar in character to the vowel [y] described in §2.6 – a rounded version of the front vowel *i*, which we represented as |I̲ U|. This leaves |I U̲| as the representation for [ʉ], which may be described as a fronted version of the round vowel *u*. Phonological evidence would be needed to confirm these structures, of course, but the point here is that there is no vowel, in Norwegian or elsewhere, which corresponds to the double-headed expression *|I̲ U̲|. Let us therefore propose a general ban on double headedness across all three antagonistic pairs, hence *|A̲ ʔ̲|, *|L̲ H̲| and *|I̲ U̲|. Note that this does not rule out double headedness altogether; it is grammatical in expressions such as [p'] |U̲ H ʔ̲| and [ʃ] |I̲ H̲|, where the heads belong to different variables. But what the grammar does not tolerate is an expression with two headed elements from the same antagonistic pair.

5.3.5 Dark versus Light

We have seen how the six elements form three opposing pairs, where the elements in each pair represent different values of the same variable. The question now is this: by allowing a single property to have two values, have we inadvertently introduced bivalency into the element system? Apparently not, or at least, not in a way that contradicts the arguments we made against bivalency in Chapter 1. Recall from §1.4 that bivalent features such as [±lateral] are problematic because (1) they allow the grammar to refer to properties that are absent, and (2) they result in the marked and unmarked values of a feature being given equal status. But in the case of the antagonistic pairs we have just described, the elements in each pair are both positive. That is, every element represents a marked, positive property that can be phonologically active and can behave independently of the other member of its pair. So although the elements in each pair have opposite values, it is not the case that one has a positive value and the other a negative value.

Elements represent phonological categories and function as grammatical units. By contrast, the three variables that we are calling resonance, frequency and colour are not formal units of grammar. In fact they are nothing more than descriptive terms to help us understand how elements are related to one another. So, although they describe aspects of spoken language and give us an insight into the nature of contrasts, they are themselves non-linguistic. There is a parallel to this in prosodic structure. Many languages distinguish between two values for vowel length, long and short; and the difference between long and short is of course a grammatical difference, whereas its physical correlate, the variable that we may call duration, is external to the grammar. So, unlike elements, the three general properties in (28) should not be viewed as linguistic units; instead, they describe three variables of spoken language that carry segmental information. Notice that a segment need not refer to all three variables. For example, glides such as [j w ɹ l] refer only to resonance and colour – frequency is irrelevant because glides do not contain |L| or |H|. Similarly, resonance is irrelevant to some fricatives including [ʃ ç] because their representations do not have |A| or |ʔ|. But nevertheless, resonance, frequency and colour may still be viewed as the basic properties of spoken language that language users rely on for accessing information about segmental structure.

You may have noticed that the elements in (28), besides being arranged horizontally into pairs, are also arranged vertically into two sets labelled dark and light. Like the three variables we have just discussed, dark and light are not linguistic terms – they describe aspects of spoken language that are too vague to belong in any formal linguistic theory. In essence, they are impressionistic labels that capture the overall sound quality of segments. And by grouping elements into dark and light sets, we can begin to understand certain aspects of element behaviour. Generally speaking, it is the light elements |ʔ H I| that languages use to mark the left edge of a prosodic domain (§5.2), and for this reason they are favoured in syllable onsets. For example, there are languages that require domain-initial positions to contain stops (with |ʔ|) or aspirates (with headed |H|); and there are other languages in which light segments such as ejectives (with headed |ʔ|) are restricted to initial onsets. And because |ʔ H I| are associated with strong positions, they are often targeted by weakening processes and suppressed in weak positions. (32) lists some of the processes we discussed in §4.3.2.

(32) | *Process* | *Suppressed* | *Example* | |
|---|---|---|---|
| spirantisation of stops | ʔ | d → ð | Tiberian Hebrew |
| non-release of stops | H | p → p̚ | Korean |
| glottalisation | I | t' → ʔ | Arbore |

By contrast, the dark elements |A L U| do not usually function as prosodic markers, and this is consistent with the fact that they tend to prefer nuclear or coda position. For instance, some languages allow only nasals (with |L|) in the coda, while others allow nasals (with |L|) and liquids (with |A|). Even in languages like English, where coda position is less restricted, we see a tendency for dark segments to appear in the coda and light segments in the onset. For example, a coda *k* or *p* (with |U|) may be followed by an onset *t* or *tʃ* (with |I|), but not vice versa: a[k.t]*ive* (cf. *a[t.k]*ive*), o[p.t]*imal* (cf. *o[t.p]*imal*), le[k.tʃ]*ure* (cf. *le[tʃ.k]*ure*). Meanwhile the dark elements, unlike the light elements, are fairly stable in weak contexts. For instance, the nasality element |L| usually resists weakening so that nasals remain nasal, while liquids usually stay as liquids by retaining their |A| element. (Liquids which do lose their |A| element tend to drop altogether because they have simple structures to begin with.) The apparent exceptions to this are velars (with |U|) and |A| coronals (with |A|), which have dark resonance but can still lose their velar or coronal resonance in a weak position. However, this may have more to do with being non-headed than with being dark, since their headed equivalents are almost always stable in lenition contexts: labials (with headed |U̲|) and pharyngeals (with headed |A̲|) retain their resonance properties under most conditions.

Segments containing a light element tend to have a bright or thin sound quality, and there are several ways of achieving this effect – by lowering overall resonance (using |ʔ|), by concentrating acoustic energy in the upper frequencies (using |H|), or by raising F2 (using |I|). Moreover, the effect will be stronger if there is more than one light element in the same segment – which may help us to understand the nature of enhancements. Specifically, it may provide a reason for why languages typically enhance a light segment by adding another light property. In Navajo, for instance, the |I| glide [j] can be interpreted as a fricative [j̞] by adding noise, thereby enhancing the light quality of the segment as a whole. This reinforces the contrast in Navajo between a light glide [j] ~ [j̞] and a dark glide [ɰ]. Note that enhancements such as this do not necessarily add an element to the original representation; they should be viewed primarily as phonetic effects rather than as phonological changes.

As for dark segments, these tend to have a rich or sonorous sound quality. And again this can be achieved in several ways – by raising F1 (using |A|), by concentrating acoustic energy in the lower frequencies (using |L| and |U|), or by lowering all formants (using |U|). And just as light segments are enhanced by gaining another light property, dark segments can be enhanced by adding another dark property. For example, the English approximant *r* has the representation |A|, but is typically produced with rounding. As we noted in §5.1.2, rounding on *r* is a phonetic enhancement which does not alter the structure of the original segment. However, it does add a dark acoustic cue (the cue which is normally associated with |U|) to an already dark segment. Another example of acoustic enhancement is provided by nasal vowels, which are generally perceived as being lower than their non-nasal equivalents. The difference between nasal and oral vowels can be difficult to perceive, so in order to exaggerate this distinction speakers enhance nasality by adding another cue. And because nasality/|L| is dark, the enhancement is also dark – in this case it is the cue associated with |A|, which creates the impression of vowel lowering.

It is clear from these examples that dark and light are not formal linguistic categories. We should instead view them as descriptive labels that capture the overall acoustic quality of segments. A simple summary is given in (33).

(33) *Dark properties*   *Light properties*
      |A|: resonant |ʔ|: non-resonant
           open vocal tract   obstructed vocal tract
           vowel-like   consonant-like
      |L|: low-frequency |H|: high-frequency
           voiced   voiceless
           nasal   oral
      |U|: rich colour |I|: bright colour
           back and round   front and non-round
           mellow   strident

Although these lists are not exhaustive, they do capture some of the differences between dark and light, offering a flavour of what it means to be a dark or light segment. And although dark and light are not linguistic concepts themselves, they do have an effect on phonological behaviour by influencing the distribution of segments and shaping phonotactic patterns; they also help us to understand phonetic enhancements and patterns of consonant weakening.

Further Reading

Typological surveys of liquids are presented in Walsh Dickey (1997) and Proctor (2009). In addition, the idea that laterals are specified for multiple (coronal and velar) place is argued by Walsh Dickey

(1997) on phonological grounds and by Sproat and Fujimura (1993) on phonetic grounds. Giegerich (1999) describes the distribution of linking and intrusive *r* in dialects of English, while Scheer (1999: 221) examines the vocalisation of *r* in the history of German. Gick (2002) and Bermúdez-Otero (2005) focus on intrusive *l*. On the relation between prosodic strength and segmental strength, see Barnes (2006), Beckman (1999), Harris (1997) and Smith (2002). Summaries of the distributional restrictions on aspirates, implosives and ejectives can be found in MacEachern (1999) and Gallagher (2008). The role of prosodic domains in language processing is discussed in Beckman (1999: 50), Cutler and Norris (1988), Echols *et al.* (1997) and Jusczyk, Cutler and Redanz (1993), while Harris (2009) analyses laryngeal neutralisation as a change in the direction of unmarked phonological structures. The enhancement of consonants is discussed in Stevens and Keyser (1989).

The data presented in this chapter are from the following sources: Blevins and Garrett (1998) for metathesis in Slavic languages; Hancock (1974) for *l* vocalisation in Liberian English; Johanson and Csató (1998) for the deletion of liquids and compensatory lengthening in Salar; Keels (1985) for aspiration in Guayabero; Kenstowicz (1994) for Bengali; Mufwene (2001) for the neutralisation of *l* and *r* in Kikongo Kituba; Odden (2005: 50) for *l* ~ stop alternations in Setswana and rounding contrasts in Norwegian vowels; Smith (1996) for Alngith and Linngithigh; Steriade (1997) for laryngeal neutralisation in Sanskrit; Walsh Dickey (1997: 12) for *l* ~ *r* effects in Andalusian Spanish and Florentine Italian.

REFERENCES

Barnes, Jonathan (2006), *Strength and Weakness at the Interface: Positional Neutralization in Phonetics and Phonology*, Berlin and New York: Mouton de Gruyter.

Beckman, Jill (1999), *Positional Faithfulness: An Optimality Theoretic Treatment of Phonological Asymmetries*, New York and London: Garland.

Bermúdez-Otero, Ricardo (2005), 'The history of English intrusive liquids: using the present to ascertain the past', handout of paper presented to the Department of Linguistics and English Language, University of Manchester, 24 May 2005. Available at www.bermudez-otero.com/intrusion.pdf.

Blevins, Juliette and Andrew Garrett (1998), 'The origins of consonant-vowel metathesis', *Language* 74(3), 508–56.

Broadbent, Judith (1991), 'Linking and intrusive *r* in English', *UCL Working Papers in Linguistics* 3, 281–302.
Cutler, Anne and Dennis Norris (1988), 'The role of strong syllables in segmentation for lexical access', *Journal of Experimental Psychology: Human Perception and Performance* 14.1, 113–21.
Echols, Catherine H., Megan J. Crowhurst and Jane B. Childers (1997), 'The perception of rhythmic units in speech by infants and adults', *Journal of Memory and Language* 36, 202–25.
Gallagher, Gillian (2008), 'The role of contrast in laryngeal cooccurrence restrictions', in N. Abner and J. Bishop (eds), *Proceedings of the 27th West Coast Conference on Formal Linguistics*, Somerville, MA: Cascadilla Proceedings Project, pp. 177–84.
Gick, Bryan (2002), 'The American intrusive *l*', *American Speech* 77.2, 167–83.
Giegerich, Heinz (1999), *Lexical Strata in English: Morphological Causes, Phonological Effects*, Cambridge: Cambridge University Press.
Hancock, Ian (1974), 'English in Liberia', *American Speech* 49.3/4, 224–9.
Harris, John (1997), 'Licensing inheritance: an integrated theory of neutralisation', *Phonology* 14, 315–70.
Harris, John (2009), 'Why final obstruent devoicing is weakening', in K. Nasukawa and P. Backley (eds), *Strength Relations in Phonology*, Berlin and New York: Mouton de Gruyter, pp. 9–45.
Johanson, Lars and Éva Csató (1998), *The Turkic Languages*, London and New York: Routledge.
Jusczyk, Peter, Anne Cutler and Nancy J. Redanz (1993), 'Infants' preference for the predominant stress patterns of English words', *Child Development* 64, 675–87.
Keels, Jack (1985), 'Guayabero: phonology and morphophonemics', in R. M. Brend (ed.), *From Phonology to Discourse: Studies in Six Columbian Languages*, Dallas: Summer Institute of Linguistics, pp. 57–87.
Kenstowicz, Michael (1994), *Phonology in Generative Grammar*, Oxford: Blackwell.
Ladefoged, Peter and Ian Maddieson (1996), *The Sounds of the World's Languages*, Oxford: Blackwell.
Lavoie, Lisa (2001), *Consonant Strength: Phonological Patterns and Phonetic Manifestations*, New York and London: Garland.
MacEachern, Margaret (1999), *Laryngeal Co-occurrence Restrictions*, New York: Garland.
Mufwene, Salikoko (2001), 'Kikongo Kituba', in J. Garry and C. Rubino (eds), *Facts about the World's Languages: An Encyclopedia of the World's Major Languages, Past and Present*, New York: H. W. Wilson.
Odden, David (2005), *Introducing Phonology*, Cambridge: Cambridge University Press.
Proctor, Michael (2009), 'Gestural characterization of a phonological class: the liquids', PhD dissertation, Yale University.

Scheer, Tobias (1999), 'A theory of consonantal interaction', *Folia Linguistica* 32, 201–37.
Smith, Jennifer (2002), 'Phonological augmentation in prominent positions', PhD dissertation, University of Massachusetts, Amherst.
Smith, Norval (1996), 'Shrinking and hopping vowels in Northern Cape York: minimally different systems', Ms., HIL, University of Amsterdam.
Sproat, Richard and Osamu Fujimura (1993), 'Allophonic variation in English /l/ and its implications for phonetic implementation', *Journal of Phonetics* 21, 291–311.
Steriade, Donca (1997), 'Phonetics in phonology: the case of laryngeal neutralization', Ms., UCLA.
Stevens, Kenneth N. and Samuel J. Keyser (1989), 'Primary features and their enhancement in consonants', *Language* 65, 81–106.
Walsh Dickey, Laura (1997), 'The phonology of liquids', PhD dissertation, University of Massachusetts, Amherst.

LANGUAGE INDEX

Albanian, 181
Alngith, 176
Amele, 188
Amuesha, 19
Arabic, 19, 85–6, 89
Aranda, 91
Arapaho, 81
Arbore, 129, 201
Assamese, 128
Axininca Campa, 130, 132

Bari, 31
Basque, 116, 189
Bengali, 192
Bishop Monachi, 149
Brazilian Portuguese, 72, 106, 181–2
Breton (Argol), 181
Bulgarian, 91, 167
　vowel reduction, 34–5
Burmese, 150, 182, 197–8
Bzhedukh, 103

Cantonese, 78
Capanahua, 123–4
Catalan, 98, 179
Chaha, 190
Cham, 95
Chol, 190
Chukchi, 31, 82
Corsican (Northern), 128
Czech, 166

Diola Fogny, 178
Diyari, 166
Doyayo, 189
Dutch, 136, 151, 152

English
　aspiration, 41, 134–6, 140–1, 188, 189
　coronal realisation, 90
　debuccalisation, 133
　diphthongisation, 28
　empty nuclei, 37–8, 50, 52–3
　glide formation, 68–9, 172–4
　glottaling, 129, 132, 133
　H language properties, 137–42
　intrusive l, 180–1
　laryngeal distinction, 134–6
　linking and intrusive r, 172–4

Middle English, 27–8, 46, 49, 55, 57, 80
monophthongisation, 27–9, 54
Old English, 46, 79, 147
rhoticisation, 132, 133
tapping, 130, 132, 133, 168
vowel representations, 43–59

Fe?fe?-Bamileke, 72–3
Fijian, 155
Finnish, 178–9
French, 89, 90, 166
　fortition (Creole French), 190–1
　nasal vowels, 148–9
　place assimilation (Midi French), 82–3
　voicing contrast, 134–6, 151
　vowel-glide alternation, 68
Frisian, 117

Gadsup, 19
Garifuna, 78, 98
Gayo, 167
Gbeya, 188
Georgian, 167
German
　final devoicing (H languages), 193
　final empty nucleus, 37
　palatovelars, 103
　r vocalisation, 171
　tapping (Low German), 130
Greenlandic, 19
Guayabero, 186
Guugu Yimidhirr, 76, 191

Haitian Creole, 149
Hausa, 166
Hawaiian, 186, 188
Hindi
　aspirated nasals, 197–8
　nasal weakening, 149
　voiced aspirated stops, 161

Icelandic, 132, 133
Irish, 88, 169, 199
Italian, 37, 106, 176, 199

Jalapa Mazatec, 122, 150, 161, 197–8
Japanese
　consonant weakening, 156–7

Japanese (*cont.*)
    Lyman's Law, 190
    monophthongisation, 29
    placeless nasal, 150
    postnasal voicing, 154, 157
    prenasalised stops, 155–6
    vowel adaptation, 44–5
Javanese, 155, 167
Jingpho, 158
Jita, 168

Kabardian, 159
Kalabari Ijo, 190
Kammu, 143–4
Kanakuru, 130
Kikongo Kituba, 168
Kimatuumbi, 120, 161
Korean, 101, 116, 147
    |l| dissimilation, 73
    stops, 119–20, 128, 201
    |U| assimilation, 79–80
Kpelle, 153–4

Lahu, 73–5, 97
Laotian, 129
Lardil, 80, 92, 97
Latin, 80–1, 166–7
Lhasa Tibetan, 74
Linngithigh, 176

Maga Rukai, 29–30
Maidu, 119
Malay, 129
Mapila Malayalam, 63, 77–8
Marathi, 197
Margi, 104
Mehri, 179
Miami-Illinois, 129
Mon, 76
Mongolian, 166
    pharyngeal harmony, 100
    vowel harmony, 39–40
Montana Salish, 86, 118–19, 150

Navajo, 188, 202
Nepali, 160, 197, 198
Nez Perce, 128
Ngiyambaa, 71–2, 90–1, 97
Nootka, 100–1
Norwegian, 95, 199–200

Páes, 129
Panamint, 188
Pawnee, 190–1
Peruvian Aymara, 190
Pitta-Pitta, 91
Polish
    metathesis, 167
    palatalisation, 106–8

Quechua, 19, 99, 127, 128

Romanian, 80–1
Russian
    final devoicing (L languages), 1, 192–3
    hard versus soft consonants, 199
    vowel reduction, 35

Salar, 168
Samish, 117
Sanskrit, 67–8, 101, 149, 192
Sardinian, 167
Setswana, 177
Shuswap, 189
Sindhi, 196–7
Slovak, 72
Somali, 188
Songjiang Chinese, 144
Spanish, 19, 84, 169
    consonant weakening, 126–7, 131
    debuccalisation, 129, 131, 132
    liquid dissimilation, 167
    liquids, 176, 177
    metathesis, 167
    vowel-glide alternation, 68
Suma, 158
Swahili, 120
Swedish, 89, 95

Tagalog, 130
Taiwanese, 130
Tamazight, 19, 87
Tamil, 91, 186
Telugu, 167
Thai, 159, 191–2
Thompson, 86
Tiberian Hebrew, 85, 127, 201
Toba Batak, 129
Toda, 93
Tsonga, 197
Tubatulabal, 188
Tukuya, 153
Tunica, 41, 42
Turkish, 31, 35–6, 108, 168

Wambaya, 93–4, 96
Wapishana, 31
Warao, 8–9
Warndarang, 130, 132
Watjarri, 95
Welsh, 37
Wembawemba, 154–5
West Tarangan, 188
Wolof, 31, 47

Yakut, 149
Yanyuwa, 102, 147
Yawelmani, 196
Yoruba, 148

Zina Kotoko, 120
Zoque, 108–9, 154–5
Zulu, 19, 183, 190

SUBJECT INDEX

acquisition, 3–4, 6, 46, 140, 171, 185
affricates, 101–2, 108–10, 116, 119
  plosive–affricate complementarity, 109
aspiration, 41, 134–7, 139–42, 143, 144, 145, 147, 155–6, 159–60, 161, 186–7, 188, 189–90, 191–2, 201
assimilation, 46, 48, 63, 70, 71, 77–8, 79–80, 82, 83, 86, 99, 100, 104, 117, 137–8, 147, 148, 151–2, 155, 158, 166, 177, 186, 192

breathy-voiced (voiced aspirated) stops, 159–60, 161, 192, 194, 197, 198

colour variable, 195, 198–200, 201
consonant lenition (weakening), 76, 79, 83, 84, 119–20, 126–33, 140–1, 148–9, 157, 176, 185–8, 191–3, 201, 202
consonant–vowel unity, 62–5, 69–70, 92, 105, 143
coronal resonance, 72–7, 79, 87–91, 102, 107–8, 125, 133, 165

de-aspiration, 141
debuccalisation, 129–30, 131, 132, 133, 188
Dependency Phonology, 41, 42, 114
diphthongisation, 28, 55
Direct Realist Theory, 3
Dispersion Theory, 20, 22
dissimilation, 73, 78, 166–7

ejectives, 118–20, 121, 156, 159, 161, 189–90, 196, 201
elements
  acoustic properties, 22–6, 38–9, 41–2, 44, 66, 75, 81, 115–16, 122, 124–5, 145–6, 195
  headedness, 41–3, 44, 49, 50, 75–6, 81–4, 87, 88, 93, 100–1, 118–19, 120, 139, 141, 152, 156–7, 158, 189–90, 196–7, 198, 199, 200
  and linguistic information, 5–7, 13, 14, 32, 39, 51, 115, 118, 126, 140, 150, 157, 160
  marked combinations, 38–40, 101, 106, 147–8, 160, 194–203
  phonetic variation, 19–20, 24, 47, 55, 56, 57, 96, 105, 108, 119, 127, 155, 168

and prosodic structure, 48, 93–4, 95, 119, 120, 123–4, 139–40, 141, 184–93
reinterpretation, 28, 29, 45, 55, 56, 58, 80–1, 94, 98, 117, 119, 120, 149, 154, 176, 179
and the speech signal, 3–7
empty nuclei
  and baseline resonance, 33, 34, 35, 36, 37, 52–3, 63, 77
  phonetic evidence, 31–3
  phonological evidence, 34–8
enhancement, 170–1, 202–3

features, 1–2
  articulatory, 2, 7, 18, 62–3, 79, 92
  bivalent, 7–10
  overgeneration, 9, 10, 18, 142, 161
  versus elements, 17–18, 21–2, 53, 70, 89–90, 92, 114, 120, 121, 134, 175, 194–5
final devoicing, 108, 192–3
fortition (strengthening), 94, 190–1
frequency variable, 195, 197–8, 201

glottal, 115–16, 124, 131
glottalisation, 129, 132, 133, 188, 191, 201

H (aspiration) languages, 136, 137, 138, 139, 141, 144, 193

implosives, 120–1, 161, 189, 197

labial resonance, 70, 77–8
labiodental resonance, 71, 96, 98, 109
laryngealised (creaky) vowels, 122–4
laryngeal neutralisation, 191–2
liquids, 49–50, 165–8
l sounds, 175–83
  clear versus dark *l*, 177–8
  intrusive *l*, 180–1
  lateral fricatives, 182–3
  place contrasts, 181–2
  presence of |ʔ|, 116–17, 175, 177
  vocalisation, 179, 180
L (voicing) languages, 136, 137, 151–2, 153, 154, 156, 192–3, 198

metathesis, 167
monophthongisation, 27–8, 29, 54, 58–9
monovalency (privativeness), 7–11, 12, 18, 92
Motor Theory of Speech Perception, 3

nasality, 145–51, 161
　nasal harmony, 8, 153
　nasal vowels, 8, 148, 153, 158, 203
　place contrasts among nasals, 102, 147
　placeless nasal, 150–1
　prenasalised stops, 155, 161
　presence of |ʔ|, 116–17, 146
　typological distribution, 156
　velar nasal, 82–3, 150
　voiceless nasals, 149–50, 161
non-release, 126, 128–9, 141, 191, 201

palatalisation, 70, 71–2, 88, 103, 105–8, 189, 199
palatal resonance, 41, 64, 70, 71–2, 75, 91, 101, 105–8, 181–2, 198
palatovelar resonance, 101–4, 199
pharyngeal resonance, 84–6, 87, 95–6, 97, 99, 100–1, 194, 202
prosodic domains, 36, 40–1, 54, 140, 158, 184–9
　and element headedness, 169, 188, 189–90
　strong versus weak positions, 83, 93, 94, 119, 120, 184–9, 191–3, 201

Quantal Theory, 20, 24, 25

resonance variable, 195–7, 201
retroflex resonance, 6, 91–6, 196
rhoticisation, 132, 133
r sounds, 49, 88–9, 91, 166, 167, 168–74
　acoustic properties, 169–70
　and headedness, 88, 168–9
　intrusive r, 174
　linking r, 172–4
　phonetic variation, 168

sonorant devoicing, 137, 139
sonority, 114–15, 191
spirantisation, 126–8, 188, 201

tapping, 130, 132, 133, 188
tone, 120, 143–5, 154, 157–9
　tonogenesis, 143

Underspecification Theory, 10, 11
uvular resonance, 84, 86, 97, 98–101, 169

velar resonance, 79–84, 97, 98–9, 100, 101, 103–4, 106, 107, 127, 133, 178–9
vocalisation, 130, 131–2, 149, 179, 180, 188
voicing, 114, 121, 134–7, 145, 149, 183, 191, 192
　assimilation, 151–2, 192
　in obstruents, 151–7, 158, 159–60, 161, 190
　passive (non-contrastive), 139, 141, 142, 149, 193
　postnasal, 109, 154–5, 157
voicing lag, 135, 137, 138, 139, 140
voicing lead, 135, 151
vowel-glide alternation, 66–8, 86
vowel harmony, 35–6, 39–40
vowel processes
　fronting, 73–4, 104
　lowering, 85–6, 88–9, 99, 100
　merger, 30, 54, 149
　reduction (weakening), 34–5, 49, 50–4, 55–6, 57, 84
　rounding, 46, 63–4, 77–8, 79–80

EU representative:
Easy Access System Europe
Mustamäe tee 50, 10621 Tallinn, Estonia
Gpsr.requests@easproject.com

www.ingramcontent.com/pod-product-compliance
Lightning Source LLC
Chambersburg PA
CBHW052040300426
44117CB00012B/1902